Play and Literacy

Play and Literacy

Play & Culture Studies

Volume 16

Edited by
Myae Han
James E. Johnson

Hamilton Books

Lanham • Boulder • New York • Toronto • London

Published by Hamilton Books
An imprint of The Rowman & Littlefield Publishing Group, Inc.
4501 Forbes Boulevard, Suite 200, Lanham, Maryland 20706
Hamilton Books Acquisitions Department (301) 459-3366

6 Tinworth Street, London SE11 5AL, United Kingdom

British Library Cataloguing in Publication Information Available

Library of Congress Control Number: 2020949160

ISBN 978-0-7618-7231-3 (pbk.)
ISBN 978-0-7618-7232-0 (electronic)

Dedicated to

Jim Christie, my forever mentor
Kern and Minjie, loving family
From Myae Han

Jim Christie, my forever friend
Karen McChesney Johnson, loving wife
From Jim Johnson

Contents

Part III: Classroom Dynamics

Part IV: Teacher and Adult Education

List of Figures

List of Tables

List of Tables

Preface

As noted in the preface to the previous volume in this Play & Culture Studies series, both Play and Curriculum (volume 15) and Play and Literacy (volume 16) are dedicated to the memory of James F. Christie, Past President of The Association for the Study of Play and outstanding scholar known for his research in play and curriculum and in play and literacy. I first met Jim at a TASP meeting in 1980 in Ann Arbor, MI. However, it was three years later in Baton Rouge, LA, at the 1983 annual TASP conference that we became friends. I remember how on a special bus tour of the area sponsored by TASP how we sat together and conversed the whole time about our mutual interests, even outlining a book idea that did come to fruition a few years later. We saw the need to bring together research and practice on play in early childhood education. At the time it seemed that although there were publications dealing with play that were either theory- or research-based, or were practical, how-to books, there was not a single book that did both functions.

Jim also told me on this bus trip about another dichotomy—this one from his brief kindergarten teaching career. His room was split physically, according to the expected practices at the time—one side equipped for play with blocks, dolls, and so forth, and the other side with materials for academic instruction. And never the two shall meet! A half a century has past and we have seen otherwise. Jim has had no small role in this transition. The pages of this book are testimony to this.

All of the contributors show in different ways how much play and literacy go together. Research is reported and discussed in some of the chapters about how play and literacy can catalyze each at different points, from preschool to higher education. The first two chapters are research reviews and commentary that explicitly bring to the forefront the enormous influence Jim Christie has had on the field of play and literacy.

I have had the pleasure of knowing and working with Jim over the years since we met way back when. So much has happened. He was a great guy, wonderful collaborator, very special friend. There is really no way with words to sum up what he has meant to us personally and professionally. Hopefully reading this book becomes a good sharing time and provides useful knowledge, opening new vistas. Jim would like this. I think he saw his scholarly mission as primarily a social practice.

James E. Johnson
Play & Culture Studies Series editor

Acknowledgments

We would like to thank the following people, who reviewed chapters for this edited collection and a graduate student who assisted with this book. They have shared their expertise with us and provided valuable comments for the chapters. This volume couldn't be completed without their support.

Doris Bergen, PhD, Miami University, Ohio
Gail Boldt, PhD, Penn State University, University Park
Thomas Hendricks, PhD, Elon University
Alison Hooper, PhD, University of Alabama
Michael Patte, PhD, Bloomsburg University of Pennsylvania
Jeffrey Trawick-Smith, PhD, Eastern Connecticut State University
Sandra Waite-Stupiansky, PhD, Edinboro University of Pennsylvania
John Sutterby, PhD, University of Texas, San Antonio
Annette Pic, Doctoral student, University of Delaware

Introduction

Myae Han, James E. Johnson

In 2018 when we solicited a call for papers for Play & Cultures Studies Volume 15, a special topic on *"Play and Curriculum,"* we received an overwhelming number of proposals. This was unexpected for us and it was as if people were waiting for the call on this topic. We expected this topic would attract educational researchers, especially early childhood educators, but we had no idea how many submissions we would receive. After we reviewed the proposals we learned that about half of the proposals were related to play and literacy. This allowed us to plan for a separate volume on play and literacy and that would be published after the Volume 15. Thankfully, all authors in this volume welcomed the idea of having a separate volume on *Play and Literacy* and have been patient with the delay of Volume 16. We would like to express special thanks to the contributors of Volume 16 for their patience and collaboration. We would also like to thank all authors who submitted their proposals for *Play and Curriculum*. They are the ones keeping play in the current play -deficit educational environment.

The Play & Culture Studies Volume 16, *Play and Literacy*, has a special meaning in the history of play and literacy research. It has been approximately 30 years since the first edited book on Play and Literacy was published (Christie, 1991). For the past 30 years, play and literacy research has been a critical part of maintaining play in the curriculum and school environment especially during the political shift toward standard driven education. Play advocates have been defending play for a long time; but it seems that this battle has never ended in the field of education. The evidence of the necessity of play in childhood and over our lives can be witnessed in every previous volume in the Play & Culture Studies series.

But here again we are presenting evidence to show why play is a better way to learn cognitive skills such as literacy. Someday perhaps the academic world will not need to defend play anymore. Defending play should not be necessary. As Stuart Brown and Christopher Vaughan wrote (2009), "*I sometimes compare play to oxygen- it's all around us, yet goes mostly unnoticed or unappreciated until it is missing*" (p. 6).

Before we introduce each chapter we like to clarify one important notion about play and literacy research. Most strategies linking play and literacy are not meant to replace self-initiated free play. Sometimes adults mistakenly think that using strategies linking literacy and play leading to playful learning can replace free play time in the school. *The linking of literacy with play or playful learning strategies that are teacher-guided or teacher-directed forms of play are good alternatives to direct instruction or other traditional methods that are often developmentally inappropriate instruction. But they are never meant to replace independent or unstructured free play time for children or adolescents or adults because free play provides opportunity for more comprehensive development or learning during childhood and indeed the entire lifespan of the individual.*

Keeping this notion in mind, this volume introduces a collection of chapters showing the link between play and literacy that works synergistically to foster a variety of positive outcomes that support school readiness skills as well as learning at other points along the life course. These chapters provide research reviews and historical background as well as evidence and commentary from the contributors' own empirical studies about why and how play is a better way to learn and to teach language and literacy skills for both children and adults. This volume is organized into four sections: Part I, Foundation of Play and Literacy; Part II, Play and Books; Part III, Classroom Dynamics; and Part IV, Teacher and Adult Education.

FOUNDATIONS OF PLAY AND LITERACY

The first chapter by Myae Han, "The History of Play and Literacy Research: Contribution of Dr. James F. Christie," provides a history of play and literacy research accomplished by Jim Christie and his colleagues from 1980 to 2015. While the 1980s saw the genesis of research that brought play into literacy studies, subsequent decades were when Jim and others who worked with him did a variety of studies that advanced the new field. There were empirical articles that probed more deeply the nature of literacy outcomes from play activities during the early years. Seminal reviews and edited books by Jim in the early 1990s and the new millennium ushered in new waves of investigations on the play-literacy nexus. In productive partnership with Kathy Roskos, the field was enriched considerably as a result of their important methodological and theoretical reviews and contributions to understanding the processes involved in the relation of play with literacy.

Chapter 2, "The Book-Play Paradigm in Early Literacy Pedagogy" written by Kathleen A. Roskos, provides the history of book-play paradigm tracing back to Smilansky's and Saltz's work on sociodramatic and thematic-fantasy play as forerunners of the current book-play model. Roskos discusses early effective and evidence-based strategies linking play and literacy and provides a set of recommendations for the book-play paradigm as a promising evidence-based practice for all early educators. She discusses the future of the paradigm in a digital learning environment and suggests future researchers to explore links between digital books and play.

PLAY AND BOOKS

The chapters in this section show the link between the books and play. The books can be used as a means to play or as an outcome of play.

Chapter 3, "'I Wrote a Mona Lisa!' Preschoolers' Play During Traditional and Digital Writing" written by Renée Casbergue and Julie Parrish, presents the examples of how play can be manifested in e-book writing. As our society becomes more digital, the need to study the impact of digital materials during childhood is crucial. Based on play motivation theory, digital materials-novelty of new objects, can serve as a motivation to do more object play. Authors of this chapter show that apps like Book Creator on Ipad can encourage children to do writing on their own with their choices and intentions and actions different from traditional book making activity. This chapter reports the cases of how children's play inside their heads (mind play, imagination) can be expressed in the digital form of e-book. Children play everywhere even in the virtual world. Casbergue and Parrish provide positive ways to use digital media to encourage children's play and creativity.

Chapter 4, "Children's Literature as a Means to Provide Time for Playful Learning While Meeting Academic Standards" written by M. Angel Bestwick, introduces many examples of high quality children's literature depicting various play activities. Bestwick identified and discussed eight types of play presented in these books and provided a plethora of cross-curricular applications for playful learning. She claims that literature is storytelling, and thus imaginative play. This chapter is a great resource for teachers' wanting to encourage children play while they are reading. While providing ideas for using books to promote play, the chapter also addresses standards in multiple subjects such as social studies, science, reading/writing, art, and math.

Chapter 5, "Responsive Play: Exploring Language and Literacy Through Play as Reader Response" by Tori K. Flint, introduces a study conducted in a first-grade classroom in which young children's play is taken as a form of reader response. Children bring play spontaneously to each book reading experience often also with a touch of humor, imagination, or singing. Vignettes of children's dialogue in this chapter are well worth reading. The chapter's author coins the term *responsive play as* children's play as a form of reader response. Children transform the written text into different media of expression such as storytelling, dramatic play, pantomime, puppetry and gesture. In the case of children, much of these creations cannot be separated from play. These types of explicit negotiations, or *metaplay* that is "out-of-play" talk in which children propose new ideas or suggest modifications of their play—allow children to clarify story structure and story comprehension.

CLASSROOM DYNAMICS

Chapter 6, "Play and Emerging Literacy: A Comparative Analysis of Kindergarten and Mixed-Age (K–2) Children's Scaffolding During Symbolic Play Transformations" written by Sandra J. Stone and Brian A. Stone, discusses a mixed-methods research study comparing classrooms (same age or cross age peers) with respect to scaffolding symbolic play transformations. Observations focused on the 'home center' dramatic play area in both the age- homogeneous and the age -heterogeneous classrooms. Age admixtures in the social context of play emerged as a favorable attribute in providing increased opportunities for peer scaffolding and engagement in collaborative pretense.

In chapter 7, "Preschool Teachers' Responsive Interactions With Children in Dramatic Play and the Children's Vocabulary Outcomes" by Sohyun Meacham and Myae Han, reports and discusses the results of their mixed-methods study of 11 Head Start classrooms that focused on the teacher responsiveness to children's pretend play and children's verbal productivity during play and subsequently assessed vocabulary outcomes. Based on Vygotskian and Bakhtinian theoretical perspectives, and a review of recent relevant research in this area, this chapter provides a careful and useful discussion and study of the teacher's roles in play, with special attention to teacher responsiveness levels when interacting with young children at play. Teacher sensitivity to children's interests and being flexible and spontaneous are valuable qualities to bring to interactions, as opposed to directiveness, when the goal is to advance oral language in preschoolers.

TEACHER AND ADULT EDUCATION

Chapter 8, "Re-Learning to Play: Mediating Pre-Service Teachers' Exploration of Drama-Based Instruction" written by Timothy M. Vetere and Matthew E. Poehner, draws attention to the importance of play and playfulness in older learners, in this case teacher candidates who partook in a drama based workshop prior to a field experience devoted to second language learning. As part of a longitudinal project informed by Vygotskian and neo-Vygotskian theoretical lenses, one student teacher in this study one was chosen to be highlighted in this chapter. The chapter describes the use of play-based pedagogy in a second language learning in an elementary classroom. The benefits and challenges and struggles involved in employing theoretically informed play pedagogy are discussed.

Chapter 9, "The Element of Play and Dynamics of Interaction in an Adult L2 Classroom With the Communicative Language Teaching Approach" by Marine Pepanyan and Sohyun Meacham, investigates the value of play pedagogy in adult second language learning. The exploratory case study presented in this chapter was done from within the Communicative Language Teaching paradigm that stresses authentic, meaningful communication and used three robotics activities to achieve a playful and safe learning situation. The study's methods and procedures using Beebots in three activities made it possible to explore the value of the play component in teaching and learning for low to intermediate English Second Language Learners. The study yielded data supporting the value of play-based education for adult learners of English for positive affect, attitudes of self-confidence, and vocabulary retention and retrieval.

These chapters demonstrate a certain depth and breadth of scholarship and research on the play-literacy nexus across a variety of topics and age groups—but they represent only the tip of the iceberg. Since research began in this field many years ago, coinciding with the beginning of Jim Christie's academic career, we have learned a great many things about the ways play and literacy interconnect, and now also something about how these two incredibly important processes influence each other.

There are, to change the metaphor, many islands to this archipelago that inter-relate and form the play and literacy entity, islands of research with many wonderful beaches with "empirical pebbles" of so many published and unpublished studies, theses and dissertations, and conference proceedings. Areas of this beach now also show new signs of recent integrative and theoretical work. We see Jim walking along these beaches, because he has had such an influence, and also because we want to honor him for what he accomplished and how he related to us while doing his scholarship and research on play and literacy—as a social practice. Let us embrace and celebrate a long sunset with him, as these beaches shift and transform our study of play and literacy and how to use the results of our study in applied settings to enrich communities, families, schools, and lives.

REFERENCES

Christie, J. (Ed.). (1991). *Play and early literacy development.* Albany, NY: State University of New York Press.

Brown, S., & Vaughan, C. (2009). *Play: How it shapes the brain, opens the imagination, and invigorates the soul.* New York: Penguin Group.

Part I

Foundation of Play and Literacy

Chapter One

History of Play and Literacy Research: Contribution of Dr. James F. Christie

Myae Han

Play and literacy have been the subjects of intensive research for the past several decades although these two fields of research have been conducted in isolation from one another for a long time. These two subject areas are commonly conceived as having a critical difference: play is a natural activity of children while literacy is something that needs to be taught. However, the links between play and literacy were soon recognized by researchers like James Christie, a professor at the Arizona State University who passed away in 2015 at 68 years.

He authored/co-authored or edited/co-edited 16 books and published scores of peer-reviewed articles; and he mentored many students during his lifetime. Professor Christie had an outstanding academic career and was a terrific person who cared about his colleagues and students. I was fortunate to be one of his doctoral students in the late 90s.

Perhaps, the best way to understand the history of academic research on play and literacy is to trace the work of this most well-known scholar in the field. Jim Christie was a living history of play and literacy research along with other colleagues with whom he worked. His first article on play was published in 1980 and the last article in play and literacy appeared in 2015, the year he passed away. This chapter provides only a snapshot of his published works. Since Jim has published numerous articles and book chapters. it is impossible to include all of them in this chapter, or to discuss any of them at length. Thus, I will only focus on his major publications in play and literacy here. I hope to provide adequate coverage of the ones selected. As a pioneer and leader of play and literacy research in the US and abroad, Jim

Christie's work has influenced many scholars, inspiring them to continue this line of work today, including myself.

In order to prepare for this chapter, first I traced his scholarly works between 1980s to 2015; and then I examined the others who have cited his work in their play and literacy publications to select significant publications of his works. I also examined references Jim frequently cited in his writing. The ERIC [ProQuest] database helped make this approach possible.

I had a lively scholarly moment while I was working on this chapter and I truly felt, "History is a conversation between the past and present."

1980S. CLAIMING PLAY AND BIRTH OF PLAY AND LITERACY

In the 1970s, Jim studied syntax and syntactic structure of texts in relation to reading comprehension (Christie, 1978, 1980a) and then he shifted the research to children's play. I wondered why and how? It is my hypothesis since he focused on children's oral reading errors during the study, and he might have realized that there is a bigger factor in children's construction of learning.

In 1980, his first article on play appeared in The Journal of Education titled 'The cognitive significance of children's play: a review of selected research (Christie, 1980b). It was surprising to find out that even in the 1960s, the role of play in early education began to be seriously challenged as a result of the compensatory education movement. The same concern has stayed with us even today. In an effort to keep play from being completely forced out of the curriculum, play proponents began publishing articles expounding the values of play in the 80s and Jim was one of those scholars. He wanted to provide the review of empirical research evidence to support the cognitive significance of play beyond theoretical arguments and inferences in this article. He reviewed three major types of research at that time: correlational studies, experimental studies, and play-training studies. I recommend future scholars to read this review and his future review articles. Aside from the conclusion of the study, I think Jim was best at writing an exemplary review article. From the review of these studies, he summarized: (1) Playfulness is a trait which is related to divergent, creative thinking. (2) Allowing young children to play with objects can lead to increased performance on problem-solving and divergent thinking tasks involving the same or similar objects. (3) Play training leads to short-term gains in young children's cognitive performance. He included critiques of each research review without diminishing the value of each study and without using harshly critical language. This is the strength of Jim's scholarly attitude which I learned from him as a former student and which made him a well-respected colleague among other scholars. Extensive studies were reviewed in this article including research studies by Lieberman (1965, 1977), Hutt (1971), Sylva, Bruner, & Genova (1976), Dansky & Silverman (1973), Smilansky (1968), Rosen(1974), Lovinger(1974), Saltz, Dixon, and Johnson (1977), Fink (1976), Golomb & Cornelius (1977), etc.

The same year an article entitled 'Play for cognitive growth' appeared in The Elementary School Journal (Christie, 1980c) where Jim focused on symbolic play and play training. This brief but strongly messaged article showed a direction for his future studies impacting the curriculum and practice. At the conclusion of the article, he wrote "Play training will require that more time be devoted to symbolic play activities and less to structured academic activities. The result will be a more balanced curriculum that will offer children the benefits of both types of activity (p.118)." Jim Christie, a developmental psychologist, was building another line of research in his career, practice-based research, and was opening the door to impact early childhood practitioners.

His next article on sociodramatic play training appeared in Young Children, a journal for early childhood practitioners (Christie, 1982). He realized that most information on play training was only accessible in psychology journals, and that few teachers had easy access to these publications. This lack of access has undoubtedly prevented many early childhood educators from using play training techniques. Thus, he wrote this article to share a play observation system and sociodramatic play training procedures which teachers could use to enhance the quality of children's play.

In 1983, Jim and his colleague E. P. Johnsen published an extensive review on the role of play in social-intellectual development in the Review of Educational Research. This article has widely been cited even today globally. This is another exemplary review article. They reviewed the studies in terms of the correlates or dependent variables: creativity, problem solving, language development, logical skills (IQ, conservation), and social knowledge. The designs of the studies were critically examined and problems of internal and external validity were noted. They reported that unstructured activity with objects could lead to gains in divergent thinking and problem-solving ability; and training in dramatic play was also shown at times to result in gains in divergent thinking, IQ scores, measures of logical development, and in social knowledge. However, they warned the reader about the limitations of these studies as well noting other concerns including the challenges of distinguishing play from other types of behavior, the limitation of dependent variable measures, the lack of random selection and the lack of long term effects. The influence of this article can be seen in later review articles such as Russ'(2003) review on play and creativity and Lillard et al's(2012) review of the impact of pretend play. In addition to the studies previously mentioned in Jim's 1980 review, this review article included additional studies such as Sutton-Smith (1968), Zammarellie & Bolton (1977), Iannotti (1978), Smith

& Syddall (1978), Collier (1979), Guthrie & Hudson (1979), Dansky (1980), Yawkey (1980), Vandenberg (1981), etc.

Along with an extensive review article, he also published his experimental study on play tutoring in the same year. This experimental study investigated which factor—play or adult contact—is responsible for gains in verbal intelligence and creativity from play tutoring. He reported that adult contact was found to be the chief reason for cognitive gains (Christie, 1983) which ignited many researchers to examine the role of adults in children's play later.

In the 80s, Jim and his colleague, James Johnson and Thomas Yawkey published the first edition of the popular book, *Play and early childhood development*, a comprehensive textbook for play (1987). Later, the second edition was published in 1999. These co-authors became well known globally with this book as this book had been translated into multiple languages around the world. I studied with this book as an undergraduate student in Korea in the early 90s and I used the latest edition of this book in my current Play and human development course.

In the late 80s, Jim's work focused more in depth on literacy outcomes related to play, which is evidenced in the article titled, Play and story comprehension: a critique of recent training research (Christie, 1987). Using his expertise in reading research, he was establishing a new field and his scholarly identity as a play and literacy researcher. This article critically investigated the relationship between dramatic play and story comprehension. The field of play and literacy was being established around this time and recognized as an important field even by the reading researchers.

I like to present another research study Jim published during the 80s but lesser known and less cited compared to other works. During professional development workshops I give, I often receive the question from early childhood teachers and child care providers regarding how much play time is needed for children in the classroom. I use this particular research to respond to their questions. In 1988, Jim and his colleagues Johnsen and Peckover published a study entitled, "The effects of play period duration on children's play patterns" in the *Journal of Research in Childhood Education*. (Christie, Johnsen, & Peckover, 1988). This was a rare study, to examine the variable play duration. He reported that children exhibited a higher percentage of behavior coded as falling into mature play categories during longer play periods than they displayed during shorter play periods. Children engaged in a significantly higher percentage of group play, constructive play, and group-dramatic play in longer periods. This study provided important evidence for designating enough free play time in early childhood classrooms and curriculum. Later Jim and Wardle (1992) wrote a practitioner version of this article sharing the findings along with recommending guidelines for early childhood programs. This article appeared in the Young Children and was entitled "How much time is needed for play?"

Generally, the 1980s became the time to defend and claim the importance of play in cognitive development; and the field of Play and Literacy was emerging as a stand-alone area. Jim's scholarship during this time had been cited widely by many developmental psychologists and it also gained more visibility in the field of education; this co-occurence allowed him to focus more on play and literacy later. Prior to the 80s, the majority of play research was published in psychology-related journals but Jim published his play related work in educational journals as well which influenced others educators to join in studying play and literacy later. He found his role not only as a researcher but also as an educator.

1990S. HEYDAY OF PLAY AND LITERACY RESEARCH

The 1990s is marked with a new wave of research on play and literacy. Jim's pioneering book *Play and early literacy development* was published in the beginning of 90s ushering in play and literacy as a self-contained significant field of research (Christie, 1991). In this edited book, Jim, in collaboration with multiple researchers who were on the cutting edge of play and literacy research, introduced readers to their studies investigating play's contributions to early reading and writing development; and their chapters also provided applied research on how teachers can promote literacy learning through play.

In this book three foundation of the relationship between play and literacy was discussed by Nigel Hall: (1) play as a fundamental cognitive activity is preparation for more complex cognitive activities such as literacy; (2) symbolic behavior in play is related to the understanding of a representation system like written language; and (3) language behavior in play is related to literate language. Jim provided psychological research on play highlighting indirect and direct connections with early literacy in this book. He introduced two of these research areas-play settings and play training – that form the foundation for much of the later applied research. This book also included a longitudinal study on play and literacy (metalinguistic verbs, emergent literacy) by Pellegrini and Galda, and a study of thematic-fantasy play and story comprehension by Williamson and Silvern.

This important book also brought to attention a number of studies with educational applications for teachers: (1) classroom environment to promote literacy during play by Morrow and Rand; (2) the influence of literacy-enriched play center on preschoolers' conceptions of the functions of print by Neuman and Roskos; (3) promoting literacy during play with materials and modeling by Vukelich. Many of these authors subsequently became his collaborators and over time and they disseminated play and literacy research actively during the 90s. Of particular note, Jim and Kathy Roskos began to work together and their collaboration lasted for Jim's lifetime, benefitting us with their many outstanding publications in the field of play and literacy.

In 1992, Jim and Billie Enz published an experimental study on the effects of literacy play interventions on preschoolers' play patterns and literacy development in the journal Early Education and Development. They experimented with two types of interventions: (1) materials only condition where literacy materials were available in play areas; (2) materials plus adult involvement condition, in which the teachers used suggestions and modeling to encourage children to incorporate the literacy materials into their dramatic play. The result revealed that the materials plus adult involvement condition was more effective in encouraging literacy-related play. In another study (Enz & Christie, 1997) they reported that teachers assumed a variety of roles when interacting with children during play. Some roles, such as stage manager and co-player, were often successful in enriching children's play episodes and encouraging play-related literacy activities.

Jim continued his play and literacy study in a multi-age classroom with his colleague, Sandra Stone (Christie & Stone, 1999, Stone & Christie, 1996). They reported that children in the multi-age group engaged in a larger amount and in a broader range of collaborative literacy activities than did the children in the same-age kindergarten during the sociodramatic play. Interestingly, complex forms of collaborative behavior that were found was reported as challenging the theory of the zone of proximal development in the multi-age classroom. Their collaborative interactions were multi-directional in nature, with the "expert" and "novice" roles not firmly set.

During the 90s significant play and literacy research was conducted with promising outcomes of play and literacy connection. Neuman and Roskos (1992) examined the effects of literacy-enriched play settings on preschoolers' literacy behaviors by adding literacy objects to all play centers in free play and reported significant differences for the intervention group in the frequency, duration, and complexity of literacy demonstrations in play. Other studies investigated the effects of teacher scaffolding of literacy during play (Morrow, 1990; Vukelich, 1994). Results of these studies indicated that scaffolding did increase the amount of literacy activity during play. Rowe's (1998) ethnographic study of toddlers' book-related play showed connections between play and literacy at an earlier age. Rowe investigated how two-year-old children use play to remember and make sense of books. Some of the children's book-related play appeared to have a key role in comprehension, helping the children combine ideas, feelings, and images from books with their own prior knowledge to create meaning.

Likewise, the 1990s was a fortunate era with abundant empirical studies published by play and literacy researchers. These studies have been cited frequently in the 2000s until today. Jim introduced and conducted key studies on play as a process and a context for early literacy development. Jim was instrumental in gathering other researchers in the field of play and literacy. He invited many respected early literacy scholars to be part of the world of play. He was one of few researchers regularly attending and presenting at both play associations such as The Association for the Study of Play (TASP) and at literacy associations such as International Literacy Association (ILA) and Literacy Research Association (LRA). He was an active member of TASP during this time, including serving as a president. He contributed a great deal to the visibility of TASP, reaching the world of literacy scholars. This personal connection was important to bringing the two fields closer together and solidifying the play and literacy intersect.

2000–2015: UPS AND DOWNS OF PLAY/LITERACY RESEARCH

The 2000s marked ups and downs of Jim's personal life and also the field of play and literacy. He was diagnosed with a rare blood cell cancer, Waldenstrom macroglobulinemia in the beginning of 2000 and battled with the cancer for the rest of his life. At the same time, his reputation was at high point and he and his colleagues published several landmark books on play and literacy and reading textbooks. Additionally, he and his colleague, Karen Burstein, received large federally funded grants, Early Reading First, which allowed them to implement many of his instructional ideas in early childhood classrooms. I was his research assistant at that time. I remember that we developed numerous workshops on dramatic play; and we delivered props to selected teachers in Arizona. We drove hundreds miles from Yuma to Phoenix, AZ, doing many workshops on play and literacy. This was the happiest moment in my scholarly life and a very sad personal moment to see his battle with the cancer.

At the very beginning of the 2000s, the second landmark book on play and literacy was published entitled *Play and literacy in early childhood: Research from multiple perspectives* (Roskos & Christie, 2000). These two researchers, Kathy and Jim, who tried to understand the deeper meaning of play in literacy development brought together the scholars who pushed play and literacy research onto the next level using more sophisticated research methodologies. They called this time the second generation of play and literacy research. Building on Jim's 1991 collection, they offered a next round of play and literacy research grouped by three theoretical perspectives - cognitive, ecological, and sociocultural- perspectives. What is unique about this book is that they included critical commentaries from distinguished play scholars such as AD Pellegrini, James Johnson, and Artin Goncu, that followed by each set of studies. This book illustrated once again the fertility of play for children's literacy development; and it presented stronger evidence for the link between play and literacy. Included in this book were studies by Rowe, Fein, Bergen, Einarsdottir, Dunn, Neuman, Roopnarine, etc. This book offered rich theoretical foundations for play and literacy and applied strategies; and the book cautioned that sound evidence must be used to influence the policy environment of early literacy education.

However, the 21st century had a very different educational environment with a big shift to standard-driven instruction and accountability of schools in the US. Under the No Child Left Behind (NCLB) initiative, it was a heyday for early literacy research as the federal government funded a large number of early reading projects using scientifically-based-reading research. The downs of this movement was that some programs decreased play time and focused on a literacy based curriculum using explicit and direct instruction over play-based instruction. There was a concern on inappropriate use of play and literacy instruction. In 2001, Kathy and Jim wrote an article to warn about this in Young Children entitled "On not pushing too hard: A few cautionary remarks about linking literacy and play." In this article, they cautioned that too much focus on literacy in play could interfere with children's play and became stumbling blocks to the literacy learning that might flourish in play. Teachers need to be mindful not to overstock literacy materials in play settings and avoid becoming too directive in their play intervention.

For the upside, one achievement of play and literacy research during this time was that the literacy-enriched play intervention was recognized as one of three effective evidence-based approaches in the field of early literacy along with storybook reading and phonological awareness instruction (Justice & Pullen, 2003). It was because of prominent scholars like Jim and Kathy who persistently wrote about the foundations of the play and literacy interface and about practical strategies teachers could use to promote literacy learning in play (Roskos & Christie, 2002)

For the downside, the 2000s was a decade of a big alert for play advocates as the disappearance of play was evident in childhood homes and schools (Miller & Almon, 2009); and the scientific value of play was questioned by some researchers (Lillard et al., 2012). In 2007, Kathy and Jim published the second edition of *Play and Literacy in Early Childhood: Research From Multiple Perspectives* (Roskos & Christie, 2007). They carefully addressed this issue in this volume with a mix of old and new generation play and literacy research. They wrote (p. 219):

> We view the current situation as less dire than many play advocates, provided that early educators expand play's role to complement and enhance the new pre-K basics. In the past, play has functioned as a stand-alone activity, isolated from the rest of the curriculum. Play themes and materials were chosen on

their own merit to elicit rich play, with little regard for how this play was connected to what went on during large-group circle time and small group instruction. This needs to change. We believe that if play is to thrive in the current educational environment, a considerable amount of classroom play needs to be closely connected or networked with the academic curriculum. This can be accomplished by linking play environments and activities with the standards-based content taught in large-and small group settings (p. 219).

This idea caused a big shift for early childhood educators. Jim and his colleagues in Arizona implemented this idea successfully in their Arizona Centers for Excellence in Early Education project. Traditional play-based practices were isolated from the main curriculum and did not fit with the new emphasis on basics and standards. Thus, they advocated for a blended curriculum that networked play activities and academic goals and standards. In the commentary of the chapter, Jim Johnson supported the idea of a blended curriculum and also cautioned against letting standards lead to a neglect of the complex cognitive-affective processes that underlie learning. This book stimulated deeper conversations around complex issues on the play and literacy nexus within the new challenging educational context. Included in this volume were the studies by Smith, Sawyer, Rowe, Dunn, Han, Neuman, Hall, Bodrova, and Leong.

Between 2010 and 2015, Jim and Kathy together wrote several theoretical review articles including reporting meta- analysis on research on play and literacy, reminding us that this area of research is a robust field and needed to be continued. Jim's last publication (Christie & Roskos, 2015) offered the urgent call to address the need for more, better, and richer play and literacy research. They spelled out the challenges facing play and literacy researchers at the time, such as policy shift, demand for experimental evidence, and the need for better theory. They affirmed that the best way to promote play-based education in early childhood is to reinvigorate play and literacy research and to double down on efforts to find a firm connection between play and early literacy skills. They also urged play and literacy researchers to move beyond traditional theories of Piaget and Vygotsky and to embrace new theories such as dynamic systems theory and connectionism and addressed the need for more applied research.

CONCLUSION

Arguably, James F. Christie, was the leading scholar in this history of play and literacy research. He inspired many new researchers to continue this line of study. His influence can be seen in many recent studies including those by Pyle (Pyle & Poliszczuk, 2018), Weisberg (Weisberg et al., 2013), Meacham (Meacham et al., 2016), myself (Han et al., 2010), and so on. His contribution and influence will last in the play and literacy research and in early childhood education. His legacy and role in play and literacy research will be remembered forever.

REFERENCES

Christie, J. (1978). The effects of later appearing syntactic structures on children's oral reading errors, *Reading Improvement,* 15(2), 154–156.

Christie, J. (1980a). Syntax: A key to reading comprehension. *Reading Improvement,* 17(4), 313–317.

Christie, J. (1980b). The Cognitive significance of children's play: A review of selected research. *Journal of Education,* 162(4). 23–33.

Christie, J. (1980c). Play for cognitive growth. *Elementary School Journal,* 81(2), 115–118.

Christie, J. (1982). Sociodramatic play training. *Young Children,* 37(4), 25–32.

Christie, J. (1983). The effects of play tutoring on young children's cognitive performance. *Journal of Educational Research,* 76(6), 326–330.

Christie, J., & Johnsen, E. P. (1983). The role of play in social-intellectual development. *Review of Educational Research,* 53(1), 93–115.

Christie, J. (1987). Play and story comprehension: a critique of recent training research. *Journal of Research and Development in Education,* 21(1). 36–43.

Christie, J., Johnsen, E. P., & Peckover, R. (1988). The effects of play period duration on children's play patterns. *Journal of Research in Childhood Education,* 3, 123–131.

Christie, J. (Ed.). (1991). *Play and early literacy development.* Albany, NY: State University of New York Press.

Christie, J. & Enz, B. (1992). The effects of literacy play interventions on preschoolers' play patterns and literacy development. *Early Education and Development,* 3, 205–220.

Christie, J., & Roskos, K. (2015). How does play contribute to literacy? In James E. Johnson, Scott G. Eberle, Thomas S. Henrics, & David Kuschner. (Eds.). *The Handbook of the Study of Play,* 417–424. A joint publication NY: The Strong, and MD: Rowman & Littlefield.

Christie, J. & Stone, S. (1999). Collaborative literacy activity in print-enriched play centers: Exploring the "zone" in same-age and multi-age groupings. *Journal of Literacy Research,* 31(2), 109–131.

Christie, F. & Wardle, F. (1992). How much time is needed for play? *Young Children,* 47(3). 28–32.

Collier, R. G. (1979). Developing language through play. *Elementary School Journal,* 80, 89–92.

Dansky, J. L. (1980). Make-believe: A mediator of the relationship between play and associative fluency. *Child Development,* 51, 576–579.

Dansky, J. L., & Silverman, I. W. (1973). Effects of play on associative fluency in preschool-aged children. *Developmental Psychology,* 9, 38–43.

Enz, B., & Christie, J. (1997). Teacher play interaction styles: Effects on play behavior and relationships with teacher training and experience. *International Journal of Early Childhood Education,* 2, 55–69.

Fink, R. S. (1976). Role of imaginative play in cognitive development. *Psychological Reports,* 39, 895–899

Golomb, C., & Cornelius, C. B. (1977). Symbolic play and its cognitive significance. *Developmental Psychology,* 13, 246–252.

Guthrie, K., & Hudson, L. M. 91979). Training conservation through symbolic play: A second look. *Child Development,* 50, 1269–1271.

Han, M., Moore, N., Vukelich, C., & Buell, M. (2010). Does play make a difference? How play intervention affects the vocabulary learning of at risk preschoolers. *American Journal of Play,* 3(1), 82–105.

Hutt, C. (1971). Exploration and play in children. In R. E. Herron 8k B. Sutton-Smith (Eds.), *Child's Play.* New York: John Wiley & Sons

Iannotti, R. (1978). Effect of role-taking experiences on role taking, empathy, altruism, and aggression. *Developmental Psychology,* 14, 119–124

Justice, L., & Pullen, P. (2003). Promising interventions for promoting emergent literacy skills: Three evidence-based approaches. *Topics in Early Childhood Special Education,* 23(3), 99–113.

Lieberman, J. N. (1965). Playfulness and divergent thinking: An investigation of their relationship at the kindergarten level. *Journal of Genetic Psychology,* 107, 219–224.

Lieberman, F. N. (1977). *Playfulness: Its relationship to imagination and creativity.* New York: Academic Press.

Lillard, A., Lerner, M., Hopkins, E., Dore, R., Smith, E., Palmquist, C. (2012). The impact of pretend play on children's development: A review of the evidence. *Psychological Bulletin.* Advance online publication. Doi: 10.1037/a0029321

Lovinger, S. L. (1974). Sociodramatic play and language development in preschool dis advantaged children. *Psychology in the Schools,* 11, 313–320.

Meacham, S., Vukelich, C., Han, M., & Buell, M. (2016). Teachers' responsiveness to preschoolers' utterance in sociodramatic play. *Early Education and Development,* 27(3), 318–335.

Miller, E., & Almon, J. (2009). *Crisis in the kindergarten: Why children need to play in school.* College Park, MD: Alliance for Childhood.

Morrow, L. (1990). Preparing the classroom environment to promote literacy during play. *Early Childhood Research Quarterly,* 5, 537–544.

Neuman, S., & Roskos, K. (1992). Literacy objects as cultural tools: Effects on children's literacy behaviors in play. *Reading Research Quarterly,* 27, 203–225.

Pyle, A., Poliszczuk, D., & Daniel, E. (2018). The challenges of promoting literacy integration within a play-based learning kindergarten program: Teacher perspectives and implementation. *Journal of Research in Childhood Education,* 32(2), 219–233.

Rosen, C. E. (1974). The effects of sociodramatic play on problem-solving behavior among culturally disadvantaged preschool children. *Child Development,* 45, 920–927.

Roskos, K., & Christie, J. (2000). *Play and literacy in early childhood: Research from multiple perspectives.* Mahwah, NJ: Lawrence Erlbaum Associates.

Roskos, K., & Christie, J. (2001). On not pushing too hard: A few cautionary remarks about linking literacy and play. *Young Children,* 56(3). 64–66.

Roskos, K., & Christie, J. (2002). "Knowing in doing": Observing literacy learning in play. *Young Children,* 57(2). 46–55.

Roskos, K., & Christie, J. (2007). *Play and literacy in early childhood: Research from multiple perspectives, 2nd edition.* Mahwah, NJ: Lawrence Erlbaum Associates.

Roskos, K., & Christie, J. (2011). Mindbrain and play-literacy connections. *Journal of Early Childhood Literacy,* 11(1), 73–94.

Rowe, D. (1998). The literate potentials of book-related dramatic play. *Reading Research Quarterly,* 33, 10–35.

Russ, S. (2003). Play and creativity: Developmental issues. *Scandinavian Journal of Educational Research,* 47:3, 291–303.

Saltz, E., Dixon, D., & Johnson, J. (1977). Training disadvantaged preschoolers on various fantasy activities. Effects on cognitive functioning and impulse control. *Child Development,* 48, 367–380.

Smilansky, S. (1968). *The effects of sociodramatic play on disadvantaged preschool children.* New York: John Wiley & Sons.

Smith, P. K., & Syddall, S. (1978). Play and non-play tutoring in preschool children: Is it play or tutoring which matters? *British Journal of Educational Psychology,* 48, 315–325.

Stone, S. & Christie, J. (1996). Collaborative literacy learning during sociodramatic play in a multiage (k-2) primary classroom. *Journal of Research in Childhood Education,* 10(2), 123–133.

Sutton-Smith, B. (1968). Novel responses to toys. *Merrill-Palmer Quarterly,* 14, 151.

Sylva, K., Bruner, J. S., & Genova, P. (1976) The role of play in the problem-solving of children 3–5 years old. In J. Bruner, A. Jolly, & K. Sylva (Eds.), *Play its role in development and evolution.* New York: Basic Books.

Vandenberg, B. (1981). The role of play in the development of insightful tool-using strategies. *Merrill- Palmer Quarterly,* 27, 97–10.

Vukelich, C. (1994). Effects of play interventions on young children's reading of environmental print. *Early Childhood Research Quarterly,* 9, 153–170.

Weisberg, D., Zosh, J., Hirsh-Pasek, K., & Golinkoff, R. (2013). Talking it up: Play, language development, and the role of adult support. American Journal of Play, 6 (1), 39–54.

Yawkey, T. D. (1980). An investigation of imaginative play and aural language development in young children, five, six and seven. In P. F. Wilkinson (Ed.), *In celebration of play.* New York: St. Martin's Press.

Zammarelli, J., & Bolton, N. (1977). The effects of play on mathematical concept formation. *British Journal of Educational Psychology,* 47, 155–161.

Chapter Two

The Book-Play
Paradigm in Early Pedagogy

Kathleen A. Roskos

INTRODUCTION

Storybooks and play are staples of early childhood in most places around the world. It is hard to imagine one without the other in some shape or form. Children enjoy stories from books and carry their meanings into their own play, using the language of books on their own terms. It was Margaret Meek who said that "successful early readers discover that the story happens like play . . . because they know that a story, like the house play under the table, is a game with rules (Meek, 1982, p. 37). Stories are at the heart of learning to read and write but imaginative play is at its soul—that intellectual energy to do it for the pure joy of it.

This chapter takes a fresh look at links between book reading and play that nurture early literacy development and skills in the preschool years. Evidence of play-learning links is not new, observed in children's play as early as the 16th century (Johnson, Christie & Yawkey, 1999, p. 313). What is new (relatively) is capitalizing on these links for purposes of teaching literacy, which now begins earlier in modern societies than ever before. Accompanying a deeper understanding of play-literacy relationships is an emerging book-play paradigm that is becoming increasingly defined and more deliberate in early literacy teaching, perhaps in response to higher literacy expectations in the early years.

The chapter traces the history of the paradigm, from its roots in Smilansky's work (1968) to the thematic fantasy play (TFP) strategy as the forerunner of the current book-play model in early childhood pedagogy. It next synthesizes research on the design and implementation of the model in early childhood classrooms as an evidence-based practice that supports learning outcomes aligned to early learning standards. A final section discusses the future of the paradigm in an increasingly digital learning environment, exploring links between digital books and play. The chapter also comments on the role of professional education in helping teachers learn how to use the paradigm effectively in classrooms.

A LOOK BACK

Smilansky's seminal work, *The Effects of Sociodramatic Play on Disadvantaged Preschool Children* (1968), is the foundation of a book-play paradigm in early literacy teaching. It researched what Jerome Kagan (1996) refers to as a "pleasing idea", that is the power of play in early learning. Smilansky theorized that sociodramatic play, as complex play, provides a lens on cognitive functioning, distinguishing more from less skilled children, particularly in relation to their language use. She observed that children from middle income households played more (social pretend) and used more complex language than peers from low income homes, mirrored later in Hart and Risley's classic study of children's everyday talk in homes across income groups (1995). Moving from observation to investigation, she then tested the effects of sociodramatic play as an intervention for improving the language skills (syntax, vocabulary, volume) of children from low income homes. She used two imaginative play training procedures that prompted role play, make believe, interaction, play talk, and persistence: guiding play flow from outside the play and modeling by participating in the play to up the ante. Results showed that the training significantly improved play quality; and it was Lovinger's later study that demonstrated its benefits for increasing language use and verbal expression (Lovinger, 1974). But was it the play per se, or the training that helped children learn? In a critical analysis of play training studies, Smith and Sydall (1978) concluded that it is was adult engagement that mattered and not the play in and of itself—an observation borne out in a later study by James Christie (1983).

Still, as a very early prototype of a book-play paradigm, Smilansky's play training seeded several of its emergent design features, namely a common experience to stimulate play; adult modeling; intervening in play activity; and prompting language use. It also gave rise to thematic fantasy play training -- an adaptation of Smilansky's training approach and an important milestone in the evolution of the book-play paradigm. Saltz and Johnson (1974) introduced thematic fantasy play (TFP) as "a type of dramatic play somewhat akin to Smilansky's sociodramatic play" (p. 624), but also of a different stripe. Whereas role taking in sociodramatic play is spontaneous, TFP structures role play around a play theme or plot based on folk tales or favorite books. Children are provided opportunities to enact story sequences and required to imagine and perform behaviors following along with the story narration. In some respects, TFP resembles story drama made popular by David Booth in the 1980s (Kukla, 1980). Story drama is anchored in a story read whole or in part, discussed and then enacted by the players as the story is read. Similar to TFP, it is driven by a shared story, but different in that story drama, after repeated reading, encourages improvisation on the story elements whereas in TFP children are guided to enact scenes and roles as described in the story, i.e., to transition from "symbolic story form into behavior form" (Saltz & Johnson, 1974, p. 624).

An initial test of TFP as an intervention technique to improve the cognitive skills and impulse control of low income children showed promising results (Saltz & Johnson, 1974). It outperformed an alternative technique (dimensionality training), significantly increasing social play skills, role taking ability, story memory and story comprehension. Especially helpful in this early research is the careful description of TFP implementation that improved the technique, namely, simpler stories with fewer plot episodes, contiguity of narration with play enactment; minimum props to reduce distraction; established classroom locations for story scenes; adherence to storyline. It is also helpful to learn that TFP was initially hard for young children (preschool age), and required consistent practice. These are important details that lay the foundations of instructional design for purposes of replication and refinement.

Further testing of TFP training occurred over a 3-year period in the same setting to replicate the initial test and to tease out critical variables (fantasy play or verbal stimulation) (Saltz, Dixon & Johnson, 1977). The study involved four conditions—TFP; fantasy discussion; sociodramatic play; crafts—and hypothesized that the effects of TFP are attributable to verbal stimulation as shown by no differences between the three fantasy conditions. Briefly, the hypothesis was not upheld. Results showed the superiority of the TFP and sociodramatic play conditions on most cognitive tasks and impulse control with TFP systematically outperforming sociodramatic play. Play enactment appeared to be the crucial variable in making a difference. This aside, albeit important, the TFP design features are especially salient in the evolution of the book-play paradigm. The study reveals several: (a) stories transitioned from simple to more complex plots over a year's time; (b) implementation involved a 2-step procedure: a read aloud on day one followed by a repeated reading, assignment of roles, etc., and rehearsal (sometimes with teacher as participant) on day two; (c) approximately 4–6 sessions (2 weeks) were spent on each story; and (d) props were kept to a minimum. It is important to note here that the sociodramatic play condition involved similar design elements (e.g., a shared experience), but no pre-determined plot—children were free to improvise. Still—both TFP and sociodramatic play designs were better for improving cognitive functioning (and notably story comprehension) than were fantasy discussion alone or a craft activities. TFP, however was the best. Why? The researchers propose that TFP training demands a higher degree of imagination (distance from reality or decontextual-ization); is strongly plotted; and involves themes relevant to conflicts and problems of children. TFP, in short, creates cognitive demand in a structured play frame that is personally meaningful.

The potential of TFP tilted toward early literacy in a pivotal study conducted by Pellegrini and Galda (1982), which directly linked it to story comprehension. Their study compared three distinctly different modes of story reconstruction randomly assigned among K–2 grade "typical" children—TFP, discussion and drawing. The results, in a nutshell, showed the benefits of TFP for improving children's story comprehension, especially for kindergarteners and first graders who rely on action to stimulate verbal retellings. Still, it remained unclear whether it was fantasy reenactment, retellings, or adult tutoring that accounted for gains in story comprehension. From a design perspective, however, the structuring of TFP is notable. A traditional folk tale is read aloud; play roles are assigned; the adult stimulates and prompts "acting out" the story; individual children are asked to retell the story. In short, a read-prepare-play-retell structure is established and repeated for purposes of developing story comprehension. This "organizing" framework moved a book-play approach closer to an early literacy instructional model. In a follow up study, Pellegrini (1984) attempted to tease out the TFP design elements that made a difference, using both adult-directed and peer-directed TFP conditions. Adult-directed and peer-directed thematic-fantasy play were equally effective in facilitating children's immediate story recall, implying that adult tutoring was not an essential element, but that children could "act out" the story on their own. Neither adult-directed nor peer-directed TFP, however, demonstrated sustaining effects when compared with simple questioning about the story one week later. This finding raises the efficiency of TFP as a possible early literacy practice. For purposes of teaching early literacy, other techniques may be equally as effective, but take less instructional time.

In a series of studies that closely examined TFP implementation among larger samples of primary grade children, ages 5–9 years, TFP's design elements were further tested and clarified (Williamson & Silvern, 1991). A synthesis of the results indicated that (a) the technique worked better with younger (kindergarten -grade one) than older children (grade 2 +); (b) adult-directed and peer-directed play were equally effective; (c) story familiarity made a difference—unfamiliar stories benefitted more from adult guidance; and (d) practice with TFP improved the play quality, which in turn facilitated story comprehension. As a result of these studies, design details of who-what-when of TFP were further defined for implementation as an intervention.

Proposing an alternative to adult or peer-directed TFP, Rowe (1998) introduced the concept of book-related dramatic play as a type of TFP that supports young children's story comprehension. She described book-related dramatic play as "spontaneously initiated and directed by children," involving explorations of books and writing in literacy-rich early childhood settings. Book-related play, in short, is not taught, but emerges naturally. She conducted two naturalistic studies that gave rise to the concept, one involving 16 typical preschoolers at a school site and the other a case study of her son from birth to age 4 at home. Qualitative analyses of considerable observational data revealed dramatic play with books (re-enactments; reading/writing in connection with book play); exploratory play (with language; with book-related props) and constructive play (finding/making props for play). The richness of the data yielded a strong working hypothesis: that book-related play served a purpose in early literacy development (processes) and skills (content). Considerable research of literacy-related play followed the trail of this hypothesis, examining the literacy-play relationship in early word recognition (e.g., phonological awareness) and comprehension (e.g., narrative text structure). (See, for example, Roskos, Christie, Widman & Holding, 2010.) The thick description also advanced the book-play paradigm in at least two important ways. It pointed to the centrality of the book as a "leading activity" of play—a play "tutor," so to speak (similar to an adult tutor), and it more firmly linked literacy and play in the early childhood curriculum. Reading books and playing with their meanings, it appeared, was functional in early literacy learning, a domain itself becoming more deeply understood by the end of the 20th century.

EMERGENT EVIDENCE-BASED PRACTICE

The turn of the century ushered in a new awakening to the preschool and kindergarten years as an appropriate time to teach early literacy processes and skills that lay the foundations of conventional literacy achievement (NELP, 2008). Learning to read and write, research showed, begins very early in life and thrives in rich teaching contexts of home and school. Shared book reading, rooted in the bedtime story routine, emerged as one of the most promising early literacy teaching practices (Bus, 2001; Mol & Bus, 2011). And in this context, the design of the book-play paradigm shifted to relationships between shared book reading and indoor play in early childhood classrooms. The basic instructional framework was simple: read aloud/discuss books around a theme or topic and provide related props for spontaneous play in activity centers—a framework adaptable to most early childhood curriculums (e.g., *Creative Curriculum* [Dodge, Colker & Heroman, 2002]). Implicit in the framework is a theory that children naturally transfer story meanings and language from books to their play, and in the process learn emergent literacy skills, such as story comprehension and writing.

This framework, reflective of the discovery ethos in early education, however, lacked sufficient structure for the explicit, systematic and sequential instruction that early literacy learning demands. Here, the concept of educational play (Johnson, Christie & Wardle, 2005) or more recently guided play (Weisberg, Hirsh-Pasek & Golinkoff, 2013), provides a better fit for the book-play paradigm and one more closely aligned to the earlier body of research on TFP. Guided play is adult-assisted yet child-led play in the school context. In Bruner's words (2008), the adult deliberately "leads from behind" to help children learn important academic concepts and skills in a playful way.

In early literacy education, the effects of guided play on improving children's vocabulary is of keen interest among several researchers. In their Read-Play-Learn project (an intervention to increase vocabulary knowledge of low income preschoolers), Hadley, Dickinson and colleagues (2016), for example, describe a book-guided play method conducted by intervention specialists. The book reading procedure consists of four steps: (i) draw attention to a new word while pointing to a picture of it; (ii) define the word in child-friendly terms; (iii) use gesture to reinforce meaning; and (iv) provide an example different than used in the book. In subsequent readings, phonological and lexical features of the words are reinforced through verbal exchanges. Each book reading is followed by a 10-minute play session with replica toys that matched book characters and other props. While the content of play sessions is not fully described, the authors share that the intervention specialists used play scripts to scaffold the play activity toward usage of target vocabulary words. Analyses of pre/post test data from 240 preschoolers showed significant increases in depth of knowledge for all word types (nouns, verbs, adverbs, adjectives). Along these same lines, Han, et. al (2010) and more recently LaGamba (2018) provided teachers with scripts to help them "play with" children after book reading to enact pretend play scenarios using book-related props associated with target words. Both studies showed the benefits of guided play for increasing children's vocabularies on target words. Across these studies, two design features of the book-play paradigm are consistent with prior TFP research: book-based props and scripts as scaffolds to achieve educational goals. It's also important to note here a distinct shift in research perspective from either/or to both/and, i.e., not the historical either adult or play, but rather both adult facilitation and play as agents of change.

Taking another tack, Hassinger-Das et al. (2016), combined book reading with game play. Book reading followed a similar procedure as that used in the Hadley and colleagues' research work, but the play consisted of a vocabulary board game where each player had an individual game board. The game play allowed the adult to ask questions when a child landed on a space with a target word. Questions ranged from low cognitive demand (recall) to high cognitive demand (making inferences). Again, the book-play intervention proved successful in increasing children's receptive and expressive word knowledge for taught words. A related line of research also demonstrates the value of game play as an alternative to sociodramatic play when implementing the paradigm (Lenhart, Brueck, Liang, & Roskos, 2019). Board games that involve recall or matching afford a more tightly controlled play opportunity than dramatic enactment of story elements. In the Lenhart et al. study, game play activity immediately following explicit word instruction in shared book reading increased the number of words recalled, supporting the repeated exposure principle of word learning: the more often a word is used, the more likely it is to be remembered. As a design feature in the paradigm, board game play has several advantages. It has clear rules and boundaries; it focuses talk around game content; it has clear goals (to win); it incentivizes learning; it is efficient. It, in short, gamifies learning words from books.

Together these studies report the beneficial effects of the book-play paradigm for increasing young children's vocabulary, which, in time, may facilitate reading achievement (Sénéchal, Ouellette, & Rodney, 2006). Considerable research shows the long reach of vocabulary knowledge on children's future reading comprehension; children's vocabulary at age 3 years predicts reading comprehension at grade 3 (Hart & Risley, 2003). They also focus research more squarely on oral language skills that directly impact early literacy acquisition, i.e., phonological awareness, listening comprehension, and reading comprehension. Shared reading is an excellent source of oral vocabulary, and when linked to guided play affords multiple exposures to new words across multiple contexts and, as a result, creates opportunity to expand vocabulary knowledge beneficial for hearing sounds in words, making inferences, and text comprehension. The paradigm, in sum, emerges as a promising evidence-based practice in early literacy pedagogy.

A "WORKING" PRACTICE GUIDE

An historical account of the TFP to the current interactive reading-play framework, traces the origins and evolution of the book-play paradigm as an instructional intervention in early childhood literacy. It describes a well-grounded knowledge base that demonstrates the positive effects of connecting storybooks with children's play in deliberate, explicit, and systematic ways to develop their narrative comprehension skills and vocabulary—the building blocks of conventional literacy (NELP, 2008) and future reading comprehension (Cain & Oakhill, 2006; Justice, Mashburn, & Petscher, 2013). What follows is a "working" guide for practice that draws on the best available evidence so far as well as professional expertise. It is organized into a set of recommendations for the book-play paradigm as a promising evidence-based practice. Each recommendation is summarized and how to carry it out is briefly described.

Recommendation #1: Select a Book Purposefully to Support Narrative Comprehension and Vocabulary

The heart of the book-play paradigm is a good story. Good stories have well-developed themes, engaging plots, suitable structure, memorable characters, well-chosen settings, and an appealing style. To ensure a "good" story, studies of TFP training often used folktales as a source for book reading because they appeal to children's imagination, use literary language and provide a text structure that is memorable for purposes of enactment. Recent predictable stories in early literacy programs, such as *Mrs. Wishy Washy* (Cowley, 1997), also work well. Good stories contain new words that extend children's vocabulary knowledge beyond its current level. They expose children to book language that develops syntactic awareness and special usage, such as idioms, metaphors and similes. Fantastical stories and related toys, in particular, may lead to increases in definitional vocabulary, i.e., knowledge of a given word's meaning (Weisberg, Ilgaz, Hirsh-Pasek, Golinkoff, Nicolopoulou, & Dickinson, 2014).

Folktales, fairy tales and predictable books are good choices for implementing the book-play paradigm. Numerous sources provide quality titles, including print book sources (e.g., Kiefer & Tyson, 2013) and internet sites, such as *Great Web Sites for Kids* sponsored by the American Library Association. Several blog sites, such as Digital Storytime (http://digital-storytime. com/), provide reviews of digital storybooks that can stimulate story drama and puppet play. Appendices A and B of the Common Core State Standards offer another valuable resource for book selection, especially at K–1 levels (Appendices A and B are available at the http://www.corestandards.org/ ELA-Literacy/). Appendix A of the Common Core State Standards describes quantitative and qualitative measures for assessing text complexity, which is a key indicator of cognitive demand related to the development of listening and reading comprehension. It is important to actively engage young children in book-play activities that advance their oral language skills as a foundation for written language development. Appendix B lists titles of text exemplars in the read aloud stories category.

Recommendation #2: Teach a Play Method Purposefully to Support Narrative Comprehension and Word Learning

Currently the research evidence supports two guided play methods for implementing the book-play paradigm: enactment and game play. Of the two, enactment is less structured than game play, and thus more complex to "tutor" than game play. The rules are less clear and interactions are more spontaneous. Enactment involves pretending, which asks the player to decontextualize, i.e., to mentally change the here and now, you and me, this and that, i.e., to act "as if." It involves role-taking and setting/object substitution. To work well it usually revolves around a problem or a goal, i.e., the baby is sick or a vehicle needs to be fixed. The adult tutors the play by suggesting a problem, modeling roles (including language) and maintaining play flow via questioning and prompting. Story drama is an excellent entrée into more improvisational enactments of book themes or plots because it follows the story as is. Both a training and an improvisational approach involve a four-part contingent teaching procedure (Wood, Bruner, & Ross, 1976) outlined in Table 2.1.

Game play provides clear rules for player participation and constrains language to the goals of the game (e.g., to name matching pictures or words). In this respect it involves less pretend and improvisation whereas enactment is more imaginary and open-ended. Its parameters, however, are more amenable to direct teaching of early literacy skills. Specifically, research shows

Table 2.1.   Contingent Teaching Procedure

Contingent Teaching Procedure	
Steps	Teaching Action
Get Set	Select a book or an old favorite (predictable books work well)
Give Meaning	Read the book at least two times
	Discuss the setting, characters, plot, resolution
	Model how to act out a role, including language
Build Bridges	Establish setting (assign spaces in the classroom)
	Select props
	Assign roles
Step Back	Read book aloud
	Guide children's story enactment

Hints: During initial enactments, the teacher should take on one of the roles and model how to act out part of the story. If several children want to have the same role, children can "share" the role and take turns playing the character. After a few performances, encourage children to improvise and experiment with their own variations of the story.

the benefits of game play for increasing children's learning of target vocabulary in books. Games can vary from simple games like *Go Fish,* where
children are asked to "fish" for and name target words on picture cards, to
board games where a player's position is tracked in relation to others using a
token or avatar to represent the player. A roll of the dice is used to move
spaces on the board; the space limits what can be done in a particular move.
Each space affords a teachable moment.

The hard part of game play is designing a game that matches book-based
vocabulary to early literacy skills, i.e., word meanings, phonic elements (e.g.,
sounds; syllables); rhyming words; synonyms/antonyms. The Hassinger-Das
et al. game design (2016), for example, used questioning to scaffold word
learning at each space; Lenhart et al. (2019) used word recall; word matching
and picture talk as design features. Oodles of sources are available on the
internet that show how to make board games, which can make game design
easier for teachers. Even the children can help make games for books, creating tokens and picture cards. An online article by Bank Street College of
Education is a good place to start (http://www.readingrockets.org/article/six-
games-reading).

Recommendation #3: Implement the Book-Play Paradigm Routinely

To realize the benefits of uniting books and play in early literacy development, children need time and opportunity to listen to stories and play with
them. They need to experience it as a routine. Regular use of the book-play
paradigm not only builds early literacy skills, but also develops children's
turn-taking and communication skills that support social interaction and collaboration. For maximum effects on children's early literacy learning, the
teacher needs to plan ahead for the integration of books with play methods.
This process begins with the end in mind when matching a particular book to
a particular play method. The first step is to identify what children will learn
aligned to early literacy expectations (e.g., new vocabulary). The next is to
decide what evidence will show that children are actually learning skills
keyed to expectations. This is where selecting a play method is important.
Enactment supports direct observations of story comprehension skills (e.g.,
story sequence) and language use whereas game play is more suited to assessment of vocabulary, word meanings and word awareness. The final step
is to schedule the book-play activity into an instructional sequence that supports larger early literacy curriculum goals. Ms. Madrid, for example, uses
puppet play with *The Three Billy Goats Gruff* to help her pre-kindergarteners
practice retelling the story, including story features of setting, goal, characters, plot events, and resolution. She uses video recordings of children's
retells to progress monitor their story comprehension skills over the prekindergarten year.

Recommendation #4: Establish an Engaging and Motivating Play Environment

Effective implementation of the book-play paradigm is contingent on a quality play environment where children feel they belong. Quality, in turn, is the result of many little things embedded in the physical and social environment of play spaces. By design, the physical play environment should be of sufficient space and include clear signage, ample materials, accessible storage and appeal (Neuman & Roskos, 2007; Vukelich, Enz, Roskos, & Christie, 2019). The social play environment should be predictable, create a welcoming mood, support participation and contain enough content to challenge children and extend their world experience (Neuman & Roskos, 2007). It is the well-designed, thoughtful, caring play environment that helps children to feel successful, make choices and collaborate productively with peers. It is where they can enact stories they hear and imagine them in their own minds on their own terms; it is where they can play games with others in friendly competition, demonstrating what they know and learning from peers; it is where they can be (comfortably) at their best—where, as Vygotsky observed, they can be "a head taller" than themselves (1966, p. 102).

A LOOK AHEAD

A history of the book-play paradigm covers a half-century of research on its origins and evolution. It shows how the longstanding (and pleasing) idea of play as a mechanism for learning has merged with our deepening understandings of early literacy development to inform early literacy pedagogy. History looks back, but it also projects the future. And in the case of the book-play paradigm it points in at least two new directions for study and research—the role of digital books/apps in the model and improving implementation in early literacy teaching, which is largely a matter of better professional education. A brief sketch of each follows as starting points for a continuing history.

Digital books offer new, exciting possibilities for a book-play model. Digital books are like paper books in that they can tell a good story, but they are also different in important ways. Digital books do not require adult presence; they can be listened to and enjoyed solo or with a peer. Digital books can enhance stories in ways paper books cannot; they can enliven a story with film-like qualities—animations, characters' voices, sound effects and zooming in on illustrations to emphasize text. Digital books can be re-visited at will, listened to over and over making it easier to remember story elements of setting, character, plot and resolution.

Not only this. Digital books can be coupled with digital play that need not involve an adult or peer. The digital story *Fierce Grey Mouse* (Bourgonje, 2011), for example, contains a matching game where children can match pictures of characters; there is also a coloring book with the text illustrations. The story is available in multiple languages. Many digital books for young children include game play, some with games embedded in the story itself, which as research shows may support children's story comprehension and vocabulary (Smeets & Bus, 2012; Verhallen, Bus, & de Jong, 2006). Apps, too, such as Puppet Play (WeeSchool, Inc., n.d.), can be used to enact digital stories for purposes of retelling them and improvising them.

In brief, the book-play paradigm is virtual more than real; it can be solitary more than social. It affords a media rich learning environment, nurtures digital skills and offers multimodal literacy experiences that may be of special benefit to some children. Evidence is growing as to what a digital book-play paradigm might mean for early literacy, as well as social play skills, although the focus is more often on playful behaviors in digital book reading rather than on play as an activity for rehearsing and reinforcing early literacy learning as an integral part of it. We don't know, for example, about differences between a digital book read aloud + play or a paper book read aloud + play. It's unclear how interactive features of digital books effect play activity either in a solo or social condition. Mostly, early digital book studies point to playfulness as a distractor in the digital reading experience, but when might it be an enhancer that promotes early literacy skills? Questions along these lines are increasingly important as access to digital books expands in homes and educational settings. How to integrate digital books into the early learning environment, including play, are growing and pressing problems of early literacy practice.

Another new research direction involves using what we already know more often and more productively. The call for play-based learning is a first move in this direction (Singer, Golinkoff, & Hirsh-Pasek, 2006). In their Mandate on Playful Learning in Preschool, Hirsh-Pasek, Golinkoff, Berk, and Singer (2009) make recommendations for policy and practice that return play to "its evidence-based, rightful place in early education—center-stage in the curriculum" (p. 67). Without more implementation research, however, ambitious recommendations and resets may fall short of desired educational goals. Not only evidence of play's vital role in learning, but also evidence of how play-based learning can be implemented effectively and efficiently in real world settings is very needed. This requires "new eyes" on implementation strategies that work to build educators' knowledge and skill for integrating play into early literacy pedagogy successfully. The book-play paradigm provides a small-scale example in the larger field of play-based learning. What do teachers need to know and be able to do to implement the model in everyday practice? What does effective preparation and training for implementing the model look like? What are strategies that support implementation in diverse settings? What are examples of teacher education curriculums and professional development programs that "teach" play-based methods well, including the book-play paradigm? Presently, scientific answers to these questions are fuzzy and loosely defined. It is challenging indeed to center-stage a book-play paradigm in early literacy pedagogy without hard evidence that it can be implemented with fidelity across a wide range of early childhood educational settings. A scan of the Council for the Accreditation of Educator Preparation (CAEP, 2016) Elementary Teacher Preparation Standards (initial licensure) (caepnet.org.) provides a quick glimpse of the tremendous challenge facing those who wish to advance play-based policy and practice, containing a mere two (vague) references to play as pedagogy in instructional planning in the early grades.

FINAL REMARKS

The book-play paradigm is one piece of history in a long-running historical account of play's role in learning. Tracing its past gives shape and form to defining its future in research and practice. A scientific knowledge base for implementing the paradigm in early literacy education is building, and the professional endeavor must continue if we are to create, improve, enrich and sustain the best early literacy learning opportunities for young children in a dynamic age.

REFERENCES

Bourgonje, C. (2011). *Fierce Grey Mouse*. Tizio BV. Reviewed at https://www.kirkusreviews. com/book-reviews/chantal-bourgonje/fierce-grey-mouse/.

Bus, A. G. (2001). Joint caregiver-child storybook reading: A route to literacy development. In S.B. Neuman & D. Dickinson (Eds.). *Handbook of Early Literacy Research, V1*. New York: Guilford Publications.

Bruner, J. (2008). Culture and mind: Their fruitful incommensurability. *Ethos, 36*, 29–45. doi:10.1111/j.1548-1352.2008.00002.x.

Council for Accreditation of Educator Preparation (CAEP). (2016). *Elementary Teacher Preparation Standards (Initial Licensure Programs)*. CAEP: Washington, D.C. Retrieved November 20, 2019 from caepnet.org

Cain, K., & Oakhill, J. (2006). Profiles of children with specific reading comprehension difficulties. *British Journal of Educational Psychology, 76*(4), 683–696.

Christie, J. (1983). The effects of play tutoring on young children's cognitive performance. *Journal of Educational Research, 76*(6), 326–330.

Cowley, J. (1997). *Mrs. Wishy Washy*. New York: McGraw-Hill.

Dodge, D. T., Colker, L. J., & Heroman, C. (2002). *The creative curriculum for preschool (4th ed.)*. Washington, DC: Teaching Strategies.

Hadley, E. B., Dickinson, D. K., Hirsh-Pasek, K., Golinkoff, R. M., & Nesbitt, K. T. (2016). Examining the acquisition of vocabulary knowledge depth among preschool-aged children. *Reading Research Quarterly, 51*(2), 181–198.

Han M., Moore N., Vukelich C., Buell M. (2010). Does play make a difference? How play intervention affects the vocabulary learning of at-risk preschoolers. *American Journal of Play, 3*(1), 82–104.

Hart, B., & Risley, T. (1995). *Meaningful differences in the everyday experience of young American children*. Baltimore: Paul H. Brookes Publishing.

Hart, B., & Risley, T. (2003, Spring). The early catastrophe: The thirty million word gap by age 3. *American Educator.* Retrieved January 10, 2019 from https://www.aft.org/sites/default/files/periodicals/TheEarlyCatastrophe.pdf.

Hassinger-Das B., Ridge K., Parker A., Golinkoff R. M., Hirsh-Pasek K., Dickinson D. K. (2016). Building vocabulary knowledge in preschoolers through shared book reading and gameplay. *Mind Brain Education,* 10, 71–80.

Hirsh-Pasek, K., Golinkoff, R., Berk, L., & Singer, D. (2009). *A mandate for playful learning in preschool: Presenting the evidence.* New York, NY: Oxford University Press.

Johnson, J., Christie, J., & Yawkey, T. (1999). *Play and early childhood development,* 2nd ed. New York: Longman.

Johnson, J., Christie J., & Wardle, F. (2005). *Play, development and early education.* NY: Pearson.

Justice, L., Mashburn, A., & Petscher, Y. (2013). Very early language skills of fifth-grade poor comprehenders. *Journal of Research in Reading,* 36(2), 172–185.

Kagan, J. (1996). Three pleasing ideas. *American Psychologist,* 51(9), 901–908.

Kiefer, B., & Tyson, C.T. (2013). *Charlotte Huck's children's literature: A brief guide, 2nd ed.* New York: McGraw-Hill.

Kukla, K. (1980). David Booth: Drama as a way of knowing. *Language Arts,* 64(1), 73–78.

LaGamba, E. (2018, April). *An investigation of read alouds, classroom interactions, and guided play as supports for vocabulary learning in preschool.* Unpublished doctoral dissertation, University of Pittsburgh. Pittsburg, Pennsylvania.

Lenhart, L., Brueck, J., Liang, X. & Roskos, K. (2019). Does play help children learn words?: Analysis of a book play approach using an adapted alternating treatment design. *Journal of Research in Childhood Education,* 33(2), 290–306.

Lovinger, I. (1974). Sociodramatic play and language development in preschool disadvantaged children. *Psychology in the Schools,* 11(3), 313–320.

Meek, M. (1982). *Learning to read.* London: The Bodley Head.

Mol, S. E., & Bus, A. G. (2011 January). To read or not to read: A meta-analysis of print exposure from infancy to early adulthood. *Psychological Bulletin,* 137(2), 267–296. doi: 10.1037/a0021890

National Early Literacy Panel (2008). *Developing early literacy: A scientific synthesis of early literacy development and implications for intervention,* Retrieved on April 8, 2009 from http://www.nifl.gov/publications/pdf/NELPReport09.pdf

Neuman, S.B., & Roskos, K. (2007). *Nurturing knowledge: Building a foundation for school success by linking early literacy to math, science, art and social studies.* New York: Scholastic.

Pellegrini, A. D. (1984). Identifying causal elements in the thematic-fantasy play paradigm. *American Educational Research Journal,* 21(3), 691–701.

Pellegrini, A., & Galda, L. (1982). The effects of thematic-fantasy play training on the development of children's story comprehension. *American Educational Research Journal,* 19(3), 443–452. doi:10.2307/1162724

Roskos, K., Christie, J., Widman, S., & Holding, A. (2010). Three decades in: Priming for meta- analysis in play-literacy research. *Journal of Early Childhood Literacy,* 10(1), 55–96.

Rowe, D. (1998). The literate potentials of book-related dramatic play. *Reading Research Quarterly,* 33, 10–35.

Saltz, E., & Johnson, J. (1974). Training for thematic-fantasy play in culturally disadvantaged children: Preliminary results. *Journal of Educational Psychology,* 66(4), 623–630.

Saltz, E., Dixon, D., & Johnson, J. (1977). Training disadvantaged preschoolers on various fantasy activities: Effects on cognitive functioning and impulse control. *Child Development,* 48(2), 367–380.

Sénéchal, Monique., Ouellette, G., & Rodney, D. (2006). The misunderstood giant: On the predictive role of early vocabulary to future reading. In D. K. Dickinson & S. B. Neuman (Eds.), *Handbook of early literacy research.* Vol. 2 (pp. 173–182). New York: Guilford Press.

Singer, D., Golinkoff, R. M., & Hirsh-Pasek, K. (Eds.) (2006). *Play=learning: How play motivates and enhances children's cognitive and social-emotional growth.* New York, NY: Oxford University Press.

Smeets, D. J. H., & Bus, A. G. (2012). Interactive electronic storybooks for kindergartners to promote vocabulary growth. *Journal of Experimental Child Psychology,* 112, 36–55. doi:10.1016/j.jecp.2011.12.003.

Smilansky, S. (1968). *The effects of sociodramatic play on disadvantaged preschool children.* New York: Wiley.

Smith, P.K., & Sydall, S. (1978). Play and non-play tutoring in preschool children: Is it play or tutoring which matters? *British Journal of Educational Psychology,* 48(3), 315–325.

Verhallen, M., Bus, A., & de Jong, M. (2006). The promise of multimedia stories for kindergarten children at risk. *Journal of Educational Psychology,* 98(2), 410–419.

Vukelich, C., Enz, B., Roskos, K. & Christie, J. (2019). *Helping young children learn language and literacy, 5th ed.* New York: Pearson

Vygotsky, L.S. (1966). Play and its role in the mental development of the child. *Soviet Psychology,* 12(6), 62–76.

WeeSchool, Inc. (n.d.). *Puppet Play app.* https://itunes.apple.com/us/app/puppet-play/id665031692?mt=8.

Weisberg, D.S., Ilgaz, H., Hirsh-Pasek, K., Golinkoff, R., Nicolopoulou, A. & Dickinson, D. K. (2014a). Shovels and swords: how realistic and fantastical themes affect children's word learning. *Cognitive Development,* 35, 1–14.

Weisberg, D., Hirsh-Pasek, K. & Golinkoff, R. (2013). Guided play: where curricular goals meet playful pedagogy. *Mind, Brain and Education,* 7(2), 104–112.

Williamson, P., & Silvern, S. (1991). Thematic-fantasy play and story comprehension. In J. Christie (Ed.), *Play and early literacy development* (pp. 69–90). Albany, NY: State University of New York Press.

Wood, D. J., Bruner, J. S., & Ross, G. (1976). The role of tutoring in problem solving. *Journal of Child Psychiatry and Psychology,* 17(2), 89–100.

Part II

Play and Books

Chapter Three

"I Wrote a Mona Lisa!"

Preschoolers' Play During
Traditional and Digital Writing

Renée Casbergue and Julie Parrish

Sitting side by side with a researcher to create an e-book page for a digital book, 4-year-old Edyn selected a picture of himself drawing on an iPad in the library center of his preschool classroom and inserted it onto a blank page using the iPad Book Creator app. When prompted to write about what was happening in the picture, Edyn instead drew a picture of a smiling girl to the left of the page with a line from her head to the photograph and wrote his text using linear scribbles beneath the photo. When he was finished drawing and writing, he read his page aloud. "It says 'Mia loves Edyn (last name).' She's thinking about something. She wants to give him a Paw Patrol *toy."*
(Figure 3.1)

In a study of the traditional (paper/pencil) and digital writing of 38 preschool children as they created their own eBooks, we quickly recognized that children's preoccupation with play often overcame their adherence to our conceptions of the format and content of the books they were to create. Our study was designed to investigate differences in children's written and oral language as they wrote, read their written pages, and elaborated on their creations. (Those results were reported in Casbergue, Parrish, & Skinner, 2018, and Casbergue, Parrish, Skinner, & Burstein, 2018.) We were also intrigued, however, by the ways children like Edyn brought their ideas about play to the writing task, and we reexamined their drawings, writing, oral responses, and field notes about their process for evidence of how play was manifested in the children's efforts. The analysis reported here was designed to explore the manner in which children's play was evident in the e-books they produced.

WRITING AND PLAY

That children approached their writing and drawing playfully is not surprising. A large body of literature has documented the connection between literacy and play. Early observations of children in preschool settings (Jacob, 1984; Roskos, 1987) revealed that many children quite naturally incorporate reading and writing into their dramatic play. A wealth of early studies focused on children's emergent literacy and play was gathered in Christie's (1991) landmark book, *Play and Early Literacy Development*, demonstrating conclusively across many settings how intertwined children's literate behavior is with their play.

While much of that early work focused on children's play in classroom centers, especially as they engaged in dramatic play spaces enriched with print opportunities (Morrow & Rand, 1991; Neuman & Roskos, 1989; 1990), researchers also examined the reverse—how young children incorporated play into literate activity, with close attention to their writing behaviors in particular. Clay (1977) reported that very young children engaged in "exploring with a pencil" (p. 334), with no intention to encode a particular message—a simple act of discovery and play. In a series of studies, Dyson (1989; 1997; 2002) explored the manner in which children's pretense and superhero play made their way onto children's pages of drawing and writing. Rowe, Fitch, and Bass (2003) explored the interconnectedness of play and writing as they invited children to use toy props to create stories that they then wrote. They noted how children often spoke and respoke their stories during dramatic play, using the props before committing their ideas to print. Rowe and Neitzel (2010) further honed understanding of the connection between writing and play, documenting that children "chose some (writing) activities, materials, and interactions more than others, creating profiles of preferred writing activities based on personal interests that were remarkably consistent with their profiles of play behaviors" (p. 193). They concluded that teachers need to provide a variety of writing experiences that correspond with children's play preferences.

DIGITAL WRITING

More recently, researchers have begun to turn their attention to children's writing in digital contexts, acknowledging that even very young children increasingly have access to tools for digital play. According to Rideout (2017), tablets have seen a surge of use in homes, with 78% of homes with children age 8 and under owning a tablet, almost double the amount of homes that had them in 2013. Tablets are also increasingly found in prekindergarten classrooms, with a wide variety of uses, especially in the literacy and math curriculum (Moore & Adair, 2015; Wells, Sulak, Saxon, & Howell, 2016; Schacter & Booil, 2017). Pagacia and Donahue (2017) documented that literacy and language instruction is one of the most targeted curricular areas for classroom use of mobile devices.

In a study of preschool classroom use of iPads, researchers noted that the devices supported authentic writing, that writing was often multimodal, and that some apps served to fluidly connect reading, writing, speaking, and listening (Beschorner & Hutchinson (2013). Flewitt, Messer, and Kucirkova (2014) studied iPad use in three classrooms, including two for children 3- to 5-years-old, and found that the devices helped adults and children assume the role of an expert writer; that iPad use increased motivation, independence and attention; and that use of the devices enriched communication and collaboration. Neumann (2018) determined that iPads were effective when used to support emergent reading skills such as letter identification, sound/symbol matching, and name writing skills. After studying preschool children's writing and drawing using iPads and more traditional paper and pencil materials, Knight & Dooley (2015) concluded that "both modes benefit and develop a child's drawing and writing skills," and that preschoolers used both modes of writing in complementary ways.

EXPLORING PRESCHOOLER'S WRITING AND PLAY

Given the increasing use of iPads and other digital technology in preschool classrooms, and our observations that there were few differences in children's emergent writing levels (Casbergue, Parrish, & Skinner, 2018) or in their oral language (Casbergue, Parrish, Skinner, & Burstein, 2018) as they participated in drawing and writing activities both on iPads and using traditional paper and markers, we turned our attention to evidence of children's playful approach to the literacy tasks we set before them.

Our study included 38 preschool children from two classrooms as they created digital e-books. One classroom was in a university laboratory preschool serving a mixed income group of children of faculty, staff, and students admitted in the order of application submission. The second classroom was part of a state funded preschool program housed in a public charter school for children in grades PreK-12. This preschool program served low SES families through a parish (county) run lottery. The schools are in the two largest metropolitan areas in the state. Across both classrooms, children ranged in age from 4 years 7 months to 5 years 6 months at the start of data collection in the spring of 2018, with a mean age of 5:2. The sample consisted of an Asian, four African American, seven Latinx, and 26 white children.

We first photographed children at play and working in their classrooms to create a photo bank on iPads from which children could select pictures to include on their digitally created pages. This resulted in multiple images of each child, either individually or among groups of other children, from which they could choose. Using the Book Creator for iPad app, we then worked side by side with individual children to create four eBook pages—two drawn and written on paper with colored markers then photographed and uploaded into the app, and two created directly on the iPad in response to child-selected photos. We structured the task so that at the completion of the study, each child would have a digital book entitled "(Child's name) at School" that could be sent home to parents. For traditionally created pages, we invited each child to draw and write about something he or she liked to do at school. For the digitally created pages, children were asked to look through the library of photographs from their own classroom and select a picture of themselves to import onto their page. They were then encouraged to write about that picture.

Children's read-aloud and oral elaboration about what they had written and drawn and about the photographic content of their pages were recorded within the app upon completion of each page. Each researcher observed the children and took field notes as they drew and wrote about their pictures in each mode. At the end of the six-week study, we had collected 130 sample pages (65 from each condition) and 260 oral language recordings (130 from each condition), the first as children initially read aloud what they had written, and a second as they elaborated on the page as a whole. (Due to absences, some children only completed two rather than four book pages.) Children's drawing, writing, transcripts of the oral language recordings, and field notes were then analyzed for evidence of the ways that play was manifested during children's engagement in writing.

Evidence of three approaches to play within the writing and drawing task emerged from this analysis. First, we documented that children approached the literacy task as if it was a free play activity. Second, we noted that the content of their pages usually revolved around play, whether illustrating their play with friends, or referencing toys and games they enjoyed. Finally, we discovered that some children engaged in dramatic play on their pages, voicing characters as they drew and using marks on their pages to indicate action.

PLAYFUL APPROACH TO THE DRAWING AND WRITING TASK

As we began data collection, we quickly recognized that many children approached the entire literacy task playfully, regardless of the mode of writing. They were eager to join us to work on their books, and often begged to have the next turn as they left free choice center activities to draw and write with us. After we explained how to use the Book Creator app while demonstrating the process as we created their book covers with them, children freely explored the features of the app, with many discovering how to change colors and use the eraser tool on their own.

Many of the children then modified or completely ignored the task as we defined it, as seen in the vignette of Edyn's drawing and writing that opened this chapter. Instead of writing about the photographs they selected and imported into their digitally created pages, many children drew new pictures in the white space around the photo and wrote all around both pictures. Edyn (Figure 3.1) loosely connected his new drawing to the photograph he selected by drawing a line from his drawing to the photo, turning it into a "thought bubble" that allowed him to focus his narrative on his friend Mia and what she was thinking about (wanting to give him a *Paw Patrol* toy).

Parks took a similar approach to his page (Figure 3.2) in which he added drawings on either side of his photograph, but then did write about his activity in the photo (reading aloud his name and the statement that he was "just

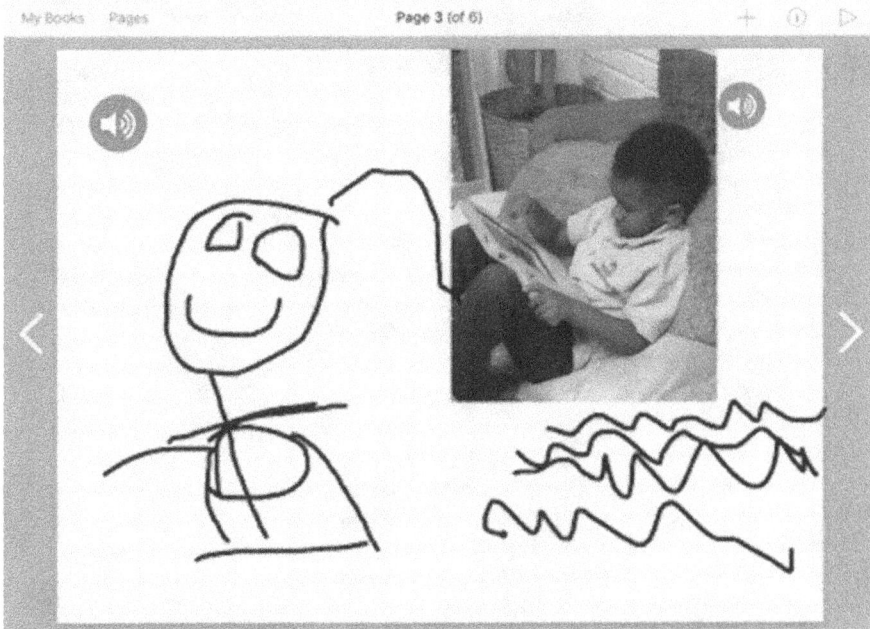

Figure 3.1.   Edyn's drawing. Edyn drew and wrote about Mia thinking of giving him a *Paw Patrol* toy. Created by Renée Casbergue and Julie Parrish

two steps away from the concrete," the final word in that phrase clearly printed with the invented spelling "eKRET."

In a similar vein, rather than drawing and writing about their school activities in the traditional condition, many children drew pictures of their families, friends, and scenes from their homes or communities, with back-yards, playgrounds, and parks figuring prominently. Sasha's page (Figure 3.3) is a good example of this as she drew her family happily together in the park. Sofia also drew her extended family, naming siblings and cousins and including illustrations of them riding scooters and bicycles and playing with baby dolls in their neighborhood (Figure 3.4).

A few children took the opportunity to simply explore shape, line, and color without verbalizing any intended message. This was evident in another of Edyn's digital pages when he drew a series of arched lines beneath the photograph he imported using every color available, creating what appeared to be an inverted rainbow that had no connection to the photograph he had chosen for that page. When asked to read what he had written, he said with some wonder in his voice, "I wrote a Mona Lisa!" Other children produced similar nonrepresentational drawing that experimented with color, line, and

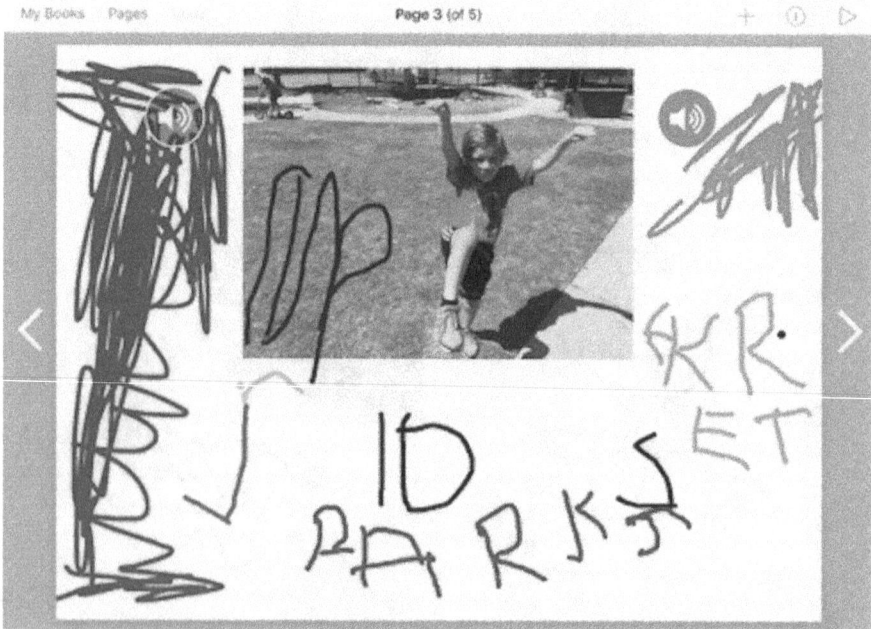

Figure 3.2.   Parks' Drawing. Parks added more drawing around and on top of his photograph in addition to writing about it. Created by Renée Casbergue and Julie Parrish

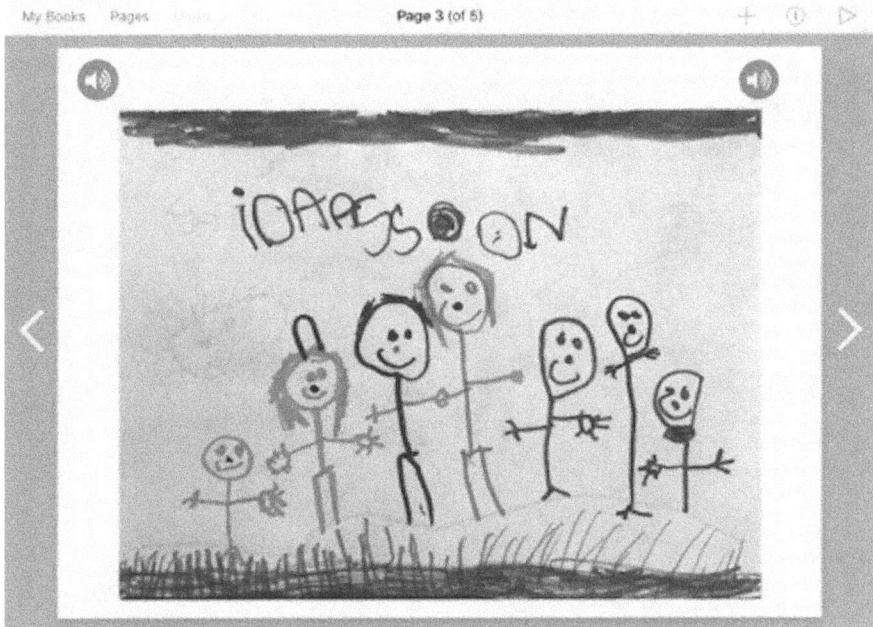

Figure 3.3. Sasha's Drawing. Sasha drew herself with her family at the park. Created by Renée Casbergue and Julie Parrish

shape, clearly engaging in what Clay (1977) referred to as "exploring with a pencil" (p. 334), albeit with markers on paper or colors drawn on the smooth iPad glass using fingers.

These varied responses to our intended task made it evident to us that many children approached the drawing and writing tasks in our research project in the same way they approached other activities in the classroom art and writing centers. That is, they clearly viewed drawing and writing with us as a free choice opportunity for play.

PLAY AS THE CONTENT OF DRAWING AND WRITING

Regardless of whether children adhered to our instructions for producing their pages, the content of their drawing and writing often revolved around play. Just as Edyn used the digital page in Figure 3.1 to draw his friend Mia and speculate that she was thinking of giving him a *Paw Patrol* toy, he used another page to draw a picture of Pinkie Pie (a character and action figure from the *My Little Pony* cartoon series), again with linear scribbles as writing. He read his page saying, "Pinkie Pie loves JoJo, and she was thinking he

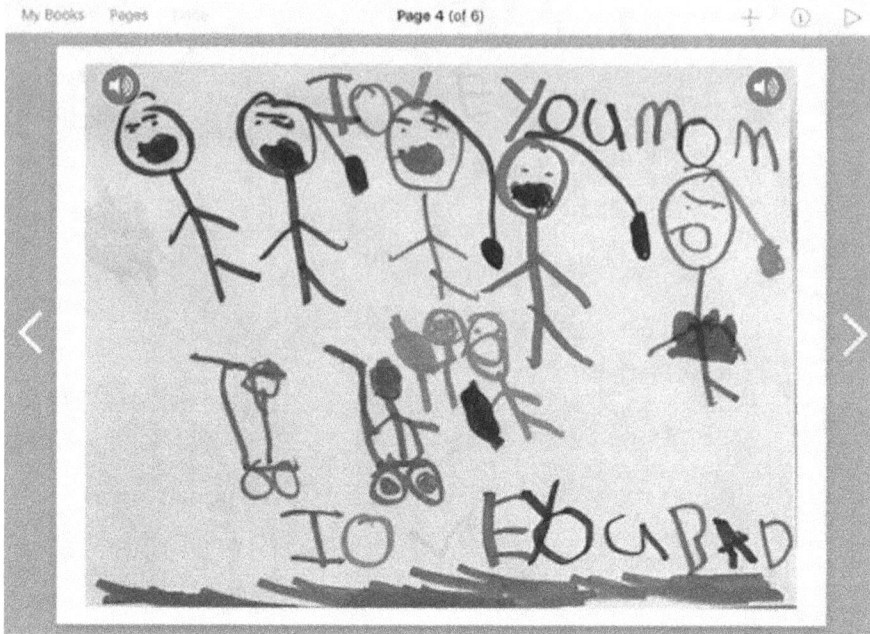

Figure 3.4.   Sophia's Drawing. Sophia drew her extended family and illustrated riding scooters and bicycles and playing with baby dolls. Created by Renée Casbergue and Julie Parrish

wanted a pupcake (cupcake)." On yet another page, he referred to giving his friend a "shimmer shine set." Edyn's preoccupation with toys he liked (or that he anticipated friends might like) was infused into his drawing and writing.

Many children drew and wrote about games they like to play with friends, some realistic and some clearly fantasy. Children wrote about going to the park to play soccer, playing on bicycles with neighborhood children, playing with baby dolls in carriages, and playing board games with classmates and siblings, all realistic play activities. Others wrote about more imaginative or fantastic adventures with friends. For example, Thomas wrote about playing guitars with his friend Parks (who appeared in a photo that depicted both children apparently using long outdoor blocks as pretend guitars) and then Parks following a map to find treasure. On another one of his pages, he drew and wrote about playing baseball with his friends on the water and then surfboarding. On yet a different page, he drew what he described as, "A pirate ship. And that's the captain, and this is where he sees, and (unintelligible) the big boat." Finally, on a digital page with a photograph of him on a tricycle on the school playground, Thomas drew a picture of what he described as "the whole big school (building)" with his friend Sierra inside. Then he elaborated that the photograph showed him and his friend (not visible in the photo) "playing police." Across the four pages of his book, he wrote about play at school in response to two photographs, and drew images of pretend and fantasy play unrelated to the school setting for the other two pages.

Likewise, his friend Parks included fantasy play in his drawings and writing. For example, he described a picture he drew as being inside his house where there are stairs he can slide down directly from his bed into his chair at the kitchen table - where his mother will have his breakfast all laid out. Like Thomas, his drawing and writing for his two digital pages directly accompanied the photographs he selected, one showing him making karate moves on the playground "just two steps away from the concrete" path, and the other showing him building "a Lego underwater race car" with his friend Louie. Like many children, all four of his pages revolved around play, either real or imagined.

A few children adhered even more closely to the tasks we set out for them. Kate, one of the more mature writers among these children, followed the style and format suggested by the cover co-created with a researcher. After selecting a photo of herself at the writing table and watching as the researcher wrote "Kate at School" as the title of her book, her first digital page included a picture of her using a classroom iPad in the library center to take a photo of two of her friends during free choice center time. Using the white space around the photo, she wrote, "Kate on t F tABLt," which she read as "Kate on the tablet," (referring to herself in the third person as on the cover page) and the word LOVE followed by a small heart. Her next page included a drawing of a restaurant with three tables, multicolored chairs, and what she described as fruit on the first table (Figure 3.5). She wrote, "Kate MAD U RASR," that she read as "Kate made a restaurant." This drawing was actually connected to the classroom housekeeping center where she and two friends were pretending to run a restaurant immediately before Kate joined the researcher to work on her book. In a sense, her drawing and writing served as a continuation of that play.

DRAWING AND WRITING AS PLAY ON THE PAGE

While not common among this sample of children, at least two of them engaged in dramatic play on the page, using drawing and mark making to actually enact a dramatic scene they made up as they wrote. The final page of Edyn's book illustrates this phenomenon. While it looks like multiple scribbles, it is possible to see the layers of his drawing beneath the scribbles on

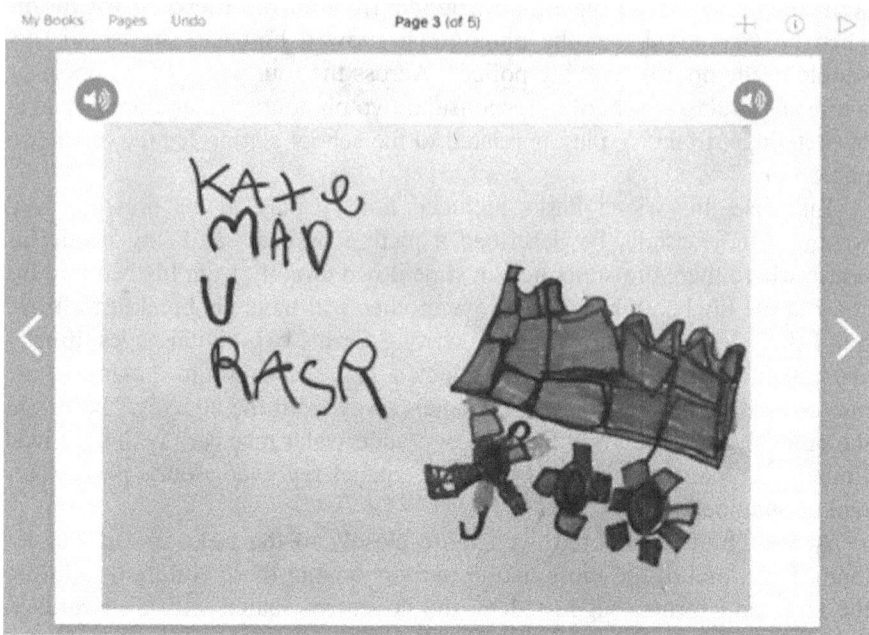

Figure 3.5.   Kate's Drawing. Kate extended her housekeeping play into her drawing and writing. Created by Renée Casbergue and Julie Parrish

this page (Figure 3.6). He drew one figure with a red body on the right of the page before drawing a car at the bottom. He then began drawing lines all over the page while describing a game of "Pinkie go seek." The lines became thicker and more frantic as the game turned into a police chase all over the page. When he elaborated about what he had drawn, he assumed two different voices, his own for "Pinkie" and a deeper voice for the police officer who gave chase. He said in the deep voice, "Police car! There it is. What are you doing?" Then in his own voice, he said sweetly, "I'm taking music. You wanted me to do that, right?" And in his authoritative police voice again he answered, "No, I didn't! We want to take you to jail!"

Similarly, Ben also enacted a mini-drama on two of his pages as he drew and wrote about a character named "Bendy" (presumably from the Xbox action adventure game *Bendy and the Ink Machine* since Ben refers to "chapters," the term used for episodes of this game). Advertisements for the teen-rated game describe it as a "first-person puzzle action horror game." The violent theme of this game is reflected in Ben's drawings (Figure 3.7) that he described as a Bendy trying to turn someone into an inky demon. Like Edyn, Ben narrated action as he used rapid motions of his marker on paper and his

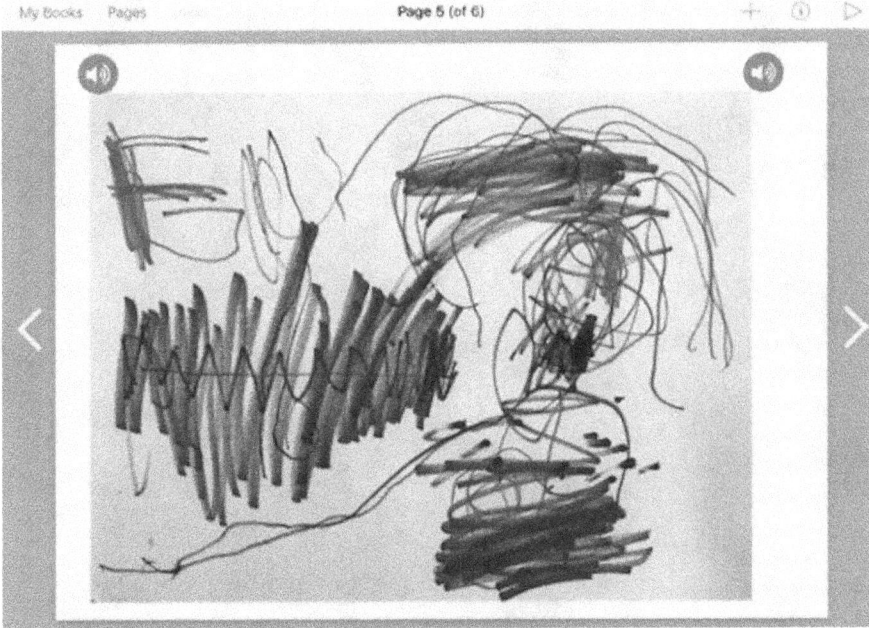

Figure 3.6. Another Edyn's Drawing. Edyn's "Pinkie go seek" and police chase. Created by Renée Casbergue and Julie Parrish

finger on a digital page to capture the chase and eventual conquest. Regardless of the appropriateness of Ben's exposure to a mature video game, like other children, he incorporated play themes with which he was familiar into his drawing and writing at school, in his case bringing that play to life on his pages.

DISCUSSION

As analysis of children's participation in the creation of digital books illustrates, all of the children in this sample incorporated play into their writing and drawing, regardless of the mode of page creation. Whether approaching the prescribed task as an option for free play, incorporating play themes into the content of their drawing and writing, engaging in play on the page, or some combination of each, children's play permeated nearly all of their pages.

In fact, even within the prescribed task of creating pages for their own eBook, children demonstrated behaviors consistent with many of the classifications of play identified by Marsh et al. (2016) from observations of young

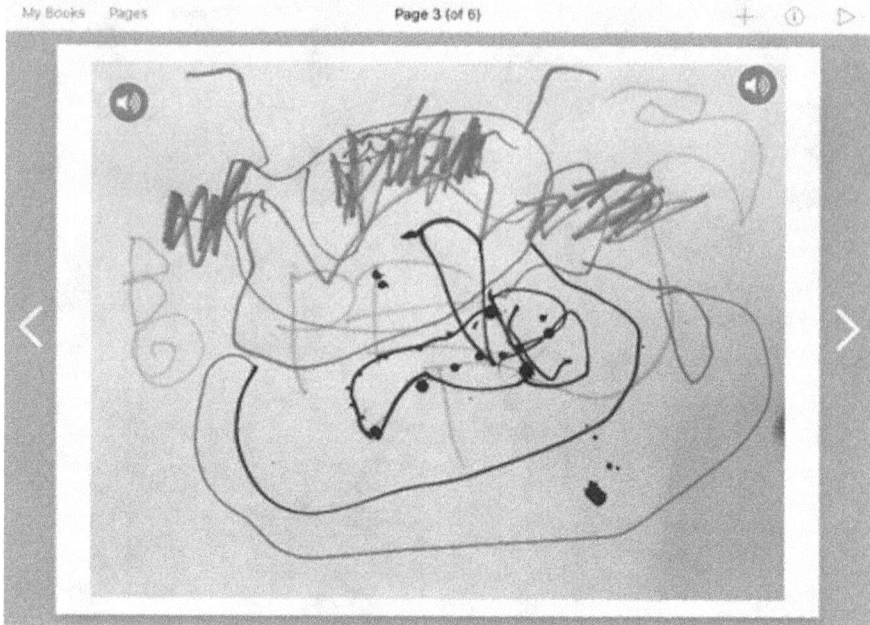

Figure 3.7.   Ben's Drawing. Ben's "Bendy" action drawing. Created by Renée Casbergue and Julie Parrish

children playing with apps on digital devices. Adapted from Hughes's (2002) taxonomy of play, Marsh and her colleagues identified 16 types of traditional play that could be observed in digital contexts. Descriptions of children's drawing, writing, and oral language elaborations from our study illustrated a broad array of play types, including 9 of the 16 identified previously in both traditional and digital contexts, even within the constraints of drawing and writing to create e-book pages (see Table 3.1).

Clearly, the literacy tasks involved in creating an eBook on an iPad did not significantly inhibit children's play experiences, with the exceptions of rough and tumble play, social play, locomotor play, fantasy play, mastery play, object play, and recapitulative play (see Hughes, 2002, and Marsh et al., 2016 for definitions of these types of play). It is likely that some of these additional play types might have been observed had children been encouraged to construct their book pages together, thus inviting more types of play than children might typically engage in individually with an adult present.

These findings should offer some reassurance to those worried that young children's use of mobile apps might displace play and more creative activities (Marsh & Bishop, 2014). As noted by Knight and Dooley (2015) after

Table 3.1.   Play Types and Definitions from Marsh et al., (2016, P. 247) & Examples of Play in Children's Book Creator Writing and Drawing

Type of Play	Definition	Example
Symbolic play	Occurs when children use a virtual object to represent another object	Thomas describing his and Park's use of elongated outdoor blocks as "playing guitar."
Socio-dramatic play	Enactment of real-life scenarios in a digital environment that are based on personal experiences	Children drawing and narrating their pretend play with baby dolls or their playing "police" on tricycles.
Creative play	Play that enables children to explore, develop ideas, and make things in a digital context	Kate writing about making a restaurant.
Communication play	Play using words, songs, rhymes, poetry, etc., in a digital context	Many children's inclusion of words and messages on their pages.
Locomotor play	Involving movement in a digital context	Edyn running from police and Ben fighting off a Bendy.
Deep play	Exploratory play in a digital context in which children encounter risky experiences or feel as though they have to fight for survival	Edyn running from police and Ben fighting off a Bendy.
Exploratory play	Play in a digital context in which children explore objects, spaces, etc. to find out information or explore possibilities	Edyn's experimentation with colors and lines that resulted in him writing "a Mona Lisa."
Imaginative play	Play in a digital context in which children pretend that things are otherwise	Parks drawing and narrating a house in which he could slide straight from his bed into his kitchen chair for breakfast.
Role play	Play in a digital context in which children might take on a role beyond the personal or domestic roles associated with socio-dramatic play	Edyn pretending to be both a music thief and a police officer.

their study of preschoolers' collaborative use of iPads for drawing and writing in teacher assisted small groups,

> Greater awareness of the diverse ways that children can learn to write and draw might lessen the fear around their exposure to digital media. Fears about digital media signaling the end of educational quality and the loss of early childhood innocence begin to dissipate when parents, carers, and educators

experience how children can use digital media without forgetting about or forsaking other toys, games and activities. (p. 62)

This is in keeping with the findings of Marsh et al. (2018) who investigated the extent to which apps for children from birth to age 5 fostered play and creativity among a sample of UK children and families. In that sample, "play and creativity were key drivers for children's use of apps as reported by parents. Parents in the survey reported that their children used tablets and apps for a wide range of purposes, including watching videos on YouTube, making videos, taking photographs, drawing and painting, and playing with virtual avatars and pets" (p. 876).

Our findings go even further, demonstrating that even in the midst of using digital media for the defined task of creating books on an iPad, children maintained a focus on toys and creative expression, and exhibited a wide array of play types, often weaving play into their drawings, writing, and oral narratives.

LIMITATIONS

A significant limitation of this study is that we did not capture video and auditory recordings of children as they created their e-book pages. While their oral reading of their emergent writing and narrative elaborations after the pages were completed provided critical information about the contents of each page, most of the children were very verbal as they completed the drawing and writing tasks, narrating their actions and the identities of people and places represented as they went along. In some cases, it was very clear that their recorded elaborations within the app were limited by the fact that they had carried on a dialog with the researcher while drawing and writing moments earlier. While field notes about what the children said and did as they created their pages provided significant insight, we were unable to capture nuances of embodied meaning making such as gestures and facial expressions.

Examination of children's play in the context of a task that had them work side by side with an adult researcher was also a limitation. There is evidence that writing and drawing is often playful and imaginative when done in collaboration with other children (Dyson, 1989, 2002; Knight & Dooley, 2015; Rowe, Fitch, & Bass, 2003). Future studies of writing and drawing using digital media will be more fruitful when conducted in more naturalistic classroom circumstances in which children often work and play collaboratively.

IMPLICATIONS FOR INSTRUCTION

The growing body of evidence that use of digital media by young children supports their emergent literacy while allowing for continued creativity and play is important for easing educators' and caregivers' hesitation to provide preschool children access to digital devices. High levels of creativity and play within literacy tasks are most likely to occur when children are allowed to pursue them in their own ways and as they are encouraged to incorporate their own ideas. While we initially defined the book creation task for children, we nonetheless followed their lead as they created the book pages. The *children* made the task more open-ended than we envisioned, but did so with no loss of quality in their writing and drawing. More important, being allowed to include their own ideas about favorite activities (whether in or out of school) provided insight into their thoughts about play and clearly served to make their writing more personally meaningful. Thus, we would encourage teachers to provide access to digital media in support of literacy, while also advising that they do so in ways that allow for collaborative endeavors among children with scaffolding from teachers as needed. A key to maintaining play and creativity while supporting literacy most likely lies in the choice of apps offered to children. While there is certainly a place for apps that offer games to help them identify letters and learn letter sounds and other "constrained" literacy skills (Paris, 2005), more open ended apps that allow children to draw, write, and create their own visual content through incorporation of pictures or videos, as in the Book Creator app we used, will allow children to express themselves while using those more constrained skills for the authentic purposes of exploration, expression, and yes, play.

REFERENCES

Beschorner, B., & Hutchinson, A. (2013). iPads as a literacy teaching tool in early childhood. *International Journal of Education in Mathematics, 1*, 16–24.

Casbergue, R., Parrish, M., & Skinner, K. (2018). Preschoolers' book creation: Comparison of digital vs. paper and pencil writing. Paper presented at the Society for the Scientific Study of Reading Annual Conference, Brighton, England, UK, July.

Casbergue. R., Parrish, M., Skinner, K., & Burstein, K. (2018). Preschoolers' oral language in response to their digital vs. traditional emergent writing. Paper presented at the Literacy Research Association Annual Meeting, Indian Wells, CA, December.

Clay, M. (1977). Exploring with a pencil. *Theory into practice, 16*(5), 334–341.

Christie, J. (Ed.). (1991). *Play and early literacy development.* Albany: State University of New York Press.

Dyson, A. (1989). *Multiple worlds of child writers: Friends learning to write.* New York: Teachers College Press.

Dyson, A. (1997). *Writing superheroes: Contemporary childhood, popular culture, and classroom literacy.* New York: Teachers College Press.

Dyson, A. (2002). Writing and children's symbolic repertoires. In S. Neuman & D. Dickinson (Eds.) *Handbook of Early Literacy Research* (pp. 126–141). New York: Guilford Press.

Flewitt, R., Messer, D., & Kucirkova, N. (2014). New directions for early literacy in a digital age: The iPad. *Journal of Early Childhood Literacy,* 15(3), 289–310.

Hughes, B. (2002). *A Playworker's Taxonomy of Play Types.* 2nd ed. London: PlayLink.

Jacob, E. (1984). Learning literacy through play: Puerto Rican kindergarten children. In H. Goelman, A. Oberg, & F. Smith (Eds.), *Awakening to Literacy* (pp. 73–86). Portsmouth, NH: Heinemann.

Knight, L. & Dooley, K. (2015). Drawing and writing on the screen. In M. Dezuonni, K. Dooley, S. Gottenhof, & L. Knight (Eds.), *iPads in the Early Years,* pp. 44–65.

Marsh, J. & Bishop, J. (2014). *Changing play: Play, media and commercial culture from the 1950's to the present day.* Maidenhead: Open University Press/McGraw Hill.

Marsh, J., Plowman, L., Yamada-Rice, D., Bishop, J., Lahmar, J., & Scott, F. (2016). Digital play: a new classification. *Early Years,* (36)3, 242–253. DOI: 10.1080/ 09575146.2016.1167675

Marsh, J., Plowman, L., Yamada-Rice, D., Bishop, J., Lahmar, J., & Scott, F. (2018). Play and creativity in young children's use of apps. *British Journal of Educational Technology,* 49(5), p. 870–882.

Moore, H. C. & Adair, J. K. (2015). "I'm just playing iPad": Comparing prekindergarteners' and preservice teachers' social interactions while using tablets for learning, *Journal of Early Childhood Teacher Education,* 36(4), 362–378.

Morrow, L. & Rand, M. (1991). Promoting literacy during play by designing early childhood classroom environments. *The Reading Teacher,* 44(6), *396–402.*

Neuman, S. & Roskos, K. (1989). Preschoolers' conceptions of literacy as reflected in their spontaneous play. In S. McCormick & J. Zutell (Eds.), *Cognitive and social perspectives for literacy research and instruction* (pp. 87–94). Chicago: National Reading Conference.

Neuman S. & Roskos, K. (1990). The influence of literacy-enriched play settings on preschoolers' engagement with written language. In J. Zutell & S. McCormick (Eds.), *Literacy Theory and Research: Analyses From Multiple Perspectives* (pp. 179–187). Chicago: National Reading Conference.

Neumann, M. M. (2018). Using tablets and apps to enhance emergent literacy skills in young children. *Early Childhood Research Quarterly,* 42, 239–246.

Pagacia, K. A. & Donahue, C. (2017). *Technology and interactive media for young children: A whole child approach connecting the vision of Fred Rogers with research and practice.* Latrobe, PA: Fred Rogers Center for Early Learning and Children's Media at Saint Vincent Vincent College.

Paris, S. (2005). Reinterpreting the development of reading skills. *Reading Research Quarterly,* 40(2), 184–202.

Rideout, V. (2017). *The Common Sense census: Media use by kids age zero to eight.* San Francisco, CA: Common Sense Media.

Roskos, Kathleen. 1987. An exploratory study of the nature of literate behavior in the pretend play episodes of four and five year old children. Unpublished PhD Dissertation, Kent State University.

Rowe, D. W., Fitch, J. D., & Bass, A. S (2003). Toy stories as opportunities for imagination and reflection in writer's workshop. *Language Arts,* 80(5), 363–374.

Rowe, D. W., & Neitzel, C. (2010). Interest and agency in 2- and 3-year-olds' participation in emergent writing. *Reading Research Quarterly,* 45(2), 169–195.

Schacter, J. & Booil, J. (2017). Improving preschoolers' mathematics achievement with tablets: A randomized controlled trial. *Mathematics Education Research Journal, 29(3),* 313–327.

Wells, K. E., Sulak, T. N., Saxon, T. F., & Howell, L. L. (2016). Traditional versus iPad Mediated handwriting instruction in early learners. *Journal of Occupational Therapy, Schools, & Early Intervention,* 9(2), 185–198.

Chapter Four

Children's Literature as a Means to Provide Time for Playful Learning While Meeting Academic Standards

M. Angel Bestwick

Play is vital. Through play, children develop language skills, social skills, cognitive processes, and physical abilities (Brooker, Blaise, & Edwards, 2014; Hynes-Berry, 2012; McNair, Bailey, Colabucci, & Day, 2011; Robinson & Aronica, 2016; L. D. Wood, 2014). "Great thinkers and philosophers including Aristotle, Plato, Rousseau, Freud, Piaget, Vygotsky, and Einstein have put forth their thinking that play is not a frivolity but essential for the development of the mind and human spirit" (Mraz, Porcelli, & Tyler, 2016, p. 10).

Yet play has become less and less a part of children's lives. It has been eliminated in many schools (Genishi & Haas Dyson, 2014; Hynes-Berry, 2012; Robinson & Aronica, 2016; Zosh, Fisher, Kelly, Golinkoff, & Hirch-Pasek, 2013). Teachers feel pressured to increase academic rigor at the expense of play (Hynes-Berry, 2012; L. D. Wood, 2014). "Elementary school schedules in the United States are now largely governed by directives requiring ninety minutes of time-on-task instruction each day in each core academic content area, regardless of the age or grade of students" (Wood, 2007, p. 14). In place of play within some kindergarten classrooms, students are expected to sit for hours completing worksheets delivered through mass-produced curriculum (NAEYC, 2009; Serafini, 2011; Wohlwend, 2018; L. D. Wood, 2014). Contrariwise, effective instruction for primary grades incorporates play (Brooker et al., 2014; NAEYC, 2009; Robinson & Aronica, 2016;).

As a nation, we must move toward recognizing teachers as the professionals they are and empower teachers with agency to make instructional choices for children they teach (Berry et al., 2011; Danielson, 2007; NAEYC, 2009; Robinson & Aronica, 2016). Wohlwend (2018) encouraged schools to permit teachers to design curriculum and instruction in service to their local population of students rather than to foster dependence on curriculum designed for the masses. Genishi and Haas Dyson (2014) stated, ". . . we advocate a view of learning that incorporates play as a standard, not an activity that is allowed only for students whose lessons are well completed" (p. 238). Some teachers, however, lack knowledge about resources available to assist them to include elements of play while meeting curricular demands (NAEYC, 2009; Serafini, 2011). Understanding elements of play and how they apply to instruction can help teachers design learning experiences that are responsive to children's needs while allowing for assessment (L. D. Wood, 2014). This chapter is intended to inspire playful learning by equipping educators with knowledge of quality children's literature titles that depict types of play and to help teachers link children's literature with academic subject areas.

LITERATURE REVIEW

Types of Play

Play is the substance of learning. Play is the medium through which children develop symbolic meaning as a basis for understanding written and spoken words (Genishi & Haas Dyson, 2014; Wohlwend, 2011). Through play, children also develop mathematical competency (Wager & Parks, 2014). Hynes-Berry, (2012) recognized play as "quality intellectual work," and strongly advocated for the implementation of play within school curriculum (pp. 63–65).

Hynes-Berry (2012) identified four types of play: functional or sensory play; constructive play; sociodramatic/imaginative play; and games with rules (Hynes-Berry, 2012). Functional or sensory play begins in infancy and continues through adulthood and is typified by positive sensory stimulation. Piaget (1972) labeled it practice play. This type of play is evident as children play in sand or make noises with objects. Adults exhibit sensory play when doodling or tapping a pen. Constructive play, for both children and adults, involves building or making things (Hynes-Berry, 2012; Zosh et al., 2013). Sociodramatic/Imaginative play, also called symbolic play, is defined by using objects, props, or costumes in a symbolic manner to pretend (Dewey, 1900; Hynes-Berry, 2012; Nilsson, 2010; Piaget, 1972; Welsch, 2008; Zosh et al., 2013). Children manifest imaginative play using natural materials such as leaves, sticks, rocks, and acorns to prepare and serve a "meal." Adults engage in sociodramatic/imaginative play through daydreaming, charades, or when playing simulation games. Games with rules involves using materials in a structured rule-dependent manner (Hynes-Berry, 2012; Piaget, 1972). Young children often invent rule-based games.

Zosh et al. (2013) identified eight domains of play: "adventure, construction, physical, creative, the arts, make-believe, technology, and language play" (2013, p. 98). Of these eight domains, several have overlaps with the four recognized by Hynes-Berry (2012). Make-believe play is like sociodramatic/imaginative play. Language play, which involves communicating and interacting with others through storytelling, expressing emotions, or learning about the world, parallels sociodramatic play (Zosh et al., 2013). Clearly, constructive play is similar to construction play. Creative play may involve painting and drawing, or using other types of materials such as paper, clay, or chalk to create art (Zosh et al., 2013). Music and dance play are subsumed within the arts category. Adventure play is comparable to games with rules. In adventure play, one may use maps to find places or objects, or "go on a scavenger hunt for local 'treasures' . . ." (Zosh et al., 2013, p. 99). Physical play is like many other types of play in that it involves physical movement (Zosh et al., 2013). According to Zosh et al. (2013), physical play involves children using materials to construct something to play upon or in, such as forts, hide-outs, or a child-created playground. Technology play is unlike other play types. Zosh et al. (2013) define technology play as using technology to explore or test scientific ideas. Programming software, geocaching, video games, and robotics are some ways in which one may explore or test scientific ideas (Zosh et al., 2013).

Play, School, and Children's Literature

Accountability measures, standardized testing, and pressure to meet the demands of the curriculum have driven teachers to forsake best practice methods and developmentally appropriate learning. Serafini (2011) expressed how, as accountability through standardized testing grew and took hold across our country, teachers became more dependent on basal readers and heavily scripted curriculum to provide literacy instruction. Consequently, incorporation and utilization of quality children's literature diminished. Children's enjoyment and efficacy as readers have suffered due to the bland offerings and formulaic instructional activities proffered in mass-produced reading curriculum (Allyn, 2017; Gallagher, 2009; Gonzalez, 2017). Constant measurement of children's reading ability for accountability purposes has had detrimental effects on children's confidence as readers (Allyn, 2017). This damaging effect is more pronounced in urban schools (Allyn, 2017; NAEYC, 2009). Allyn (2017) advocated for schools to create safe spaces for children so that they may gain a sense of themselves as readers. Children establish and build reading identities and a sense of self through selecting children's literature of personal interest (Gonzalez, 2017).

Since play is a vital aspect of a child's development, and children spend a great deal of their childhood in school, play should be included in schools. Play and learning are connected. Vygotsky's learning theory including zone of proximal development enfolded play (Mraz et al., 2016; Welsch, 2008). Through teacher modeling and social interactions that involve cooperative play, learners are scaffolded to move along the continuum of the zone of proximal development (Gallas, 2001; Welsch, 2008). A wealth of research exists to show that play is a critical part of learning (Brooker, Blaise, & Edwards, 2014; Dewey, 1900; Gallas, 2001; NAEYC, 2009; Wohlwend, 2011; L. D. Wood, 2014). "Play-based pedagogies expand learning, follow the developing child's lead, and draw from the depth of children's communities, cultural resources, and life experiences as a natural foundation for learning" (Wohlwend, 2018). Therefore, teachers must be aware of the value of play and articulate its benefits to parents, administrators, and other stakeholders (McNair et al., 2011; L. D. Wood, 2014).

Play in school has been banished because of some teachers' perception of lack of time due to pressure to fill the day with didactic teaching and literacy building activities intended to prepare students for standardized tests (Robinson & Aronica, 2016; Wohlwend, 2011). In urban schools, this pressure is more pronounced (Wohlwend, 2013). Allowing play in school does take time, but it is time well invested (Wood, 2014).

Wood (2014) recognized that play must be included in schools and situated play as pedagogy. Melding policy, theory, and practice, Wood (2014) proposed three pedagogical modes of play for schools: Mode A—child-initiated, Mode B—adult-guided, and Mode C—technicist/policy-driven. Child-initiated free play reveals much about a child's cultural background, prior knowledge, and interests, thus offering teachers valuable insight to inform instructional decisions (Mraz et al., 2016). Adult-guided play attends both to a child's interests and attainment of curricular objectives. The technicist/policy-driven mode expects that play "promote specific ways of learning and lead to defined learning outcomes and curriculum goals" (E. Wood, 2014, p. 151).

Book related play. As play is a context for effective learning, children's literature can bridge the incorporation of play, attend to curricular demands, replenish a love of reading, and prepare learners for their future lives. Children's learning and enjoyment of children's literature is enhanced through play (Husbye, 2012; Rowe, 2007; Welsch, 2008). Children's literature, coupled with play, helps children develop understandings about oneself and an understanding of the world (Allyn, 2017; Bishop, 2012; Gallas, 2001; Lin, 2017; Welsch, 2008). "Literacy play levels the field by giving children access to their cultural expertise and time to play the stories they know best, whether classic children's books or popular media" (Wohlwend, 2013, p. 2).

Wohlwend (2011) defined play itself as a literacy. In one kindergarten classroom, students spontaneously reenacted shared reading experiences during playtime (Wohlwend, 2011). One girl pretended to be the teacher, reading from a picture book to a friend. Acting as "teacher," the girl demonstrated understanding of the features of print, thus "reading to play" (Wohlwend, 2011, p. 19). Wohlwend noted that those who pretended to be the teacher strengthened their own reading skills while acting as peer coaches and teaching reading strategies to other children (Wohlwend, 2011).

Gunilla Lindqvist, a play scholar, developed an approach called the "creative pedagogy of play" and "playworlds" (Nilsson, 2010). This approach encompassed forms of drama and literature during which children and adults work together to create and perform stories or poetry. Play is at the center as adults and children work together to build components of a playworld: figures, characters, roles, and plot. Components may be based upon a selected book or a theme important to children such as fear or marginalization (Nilsson, 2010). Hence, teachers have agency to select books with topics appearing in a school curriculum or are of interest to children.

Gallas (2001) studied the role of play and imagination in literacy learning and concluded, ". . . literacy learning as a whole, is an action-embedded activity" (p. 487). Children prepare for literacy learning during imaginative play. "A child mastering play—constructive play, dramatic play—is practicing storytelling: re-creating plot, motive, character, and setting" (Jones, 2011, p. 84). Young learners use book-related play to explore "the most fundamental purpose for literacy, the construction of meaning" (Welsch, 2008, p. 139).

Children's literature-based play results in deeper learning gains and provides teachers with a means for assessment and evidence of learning. Welsch (2000) investigated how two teachers employed book-related play in a primary grade classroom. Teachers selected quality children's literature, gathered props for stories, and filled bins with props to correlate with a selected book. Students had access to the story and props at learning centers. Young learners playfully recounted story events and recreated character traits, thus making powerful and personal connections to the text. Welsch (2008) noted, "book-related pretend play represents a richer method of monitoring students' understanding of stories, moving beyond the typical questions and simple retellings" (2008, p. 145).

Curricular applications. Book related play may be used across the curricular disciplines to deepen learning. *Sheep in a Jeep* by Nancy E. Shaw can prompt learning activities that address science and math standards. Students may explore how far a sheep-filled car will travel using ramps of various heights and the force of gravity (Ansberry & Morgan, 2005; Jackson-Schnoor, 2017). Or, children may learn about inertia and develop a rationale for the importance of wearing seatbelts (sheep fall out of the vehicle when

the jeep comes to a sudden stop), performing Next Generation Science Standards for Forces and Interactions (NGSS Lead States, 2013). Versions of *The
Three Little Pigs* (Galdone, 1984; Guarnaccia, 2010; Scieszka, 1989) can
stimulate STEM-based learning. Paired with this fairytale, students are posed
with a design challenge to construct a strong, wind-proof house for the pigs
(Heroman, 2017; Hynes-Berry, 2012).

Social Studies is another area suitable for incorporating children's literature. The National Council for the Social Studies (NCSS) publishes an annual list of Notable Trade Books for Young People (NCSS, 2017). NCSS'
notable lists contain descriptions of high-quality children's literature titles
with each title's connection to NCSS' Ten Themes of Social Studies (NCSS,
2010). Teachers may use these lists as a basis for selection of children's
literature titles to address curricular goals. A 2016 notable, *Beatrix Potter
and Her Paint Box* (McPhail, 2015), embodies NCSS theme #4, Individual
Development and Identity (NCSS, 2010). Students explore identity through
role play as young Beatrix using student-created puppets after participating
in an interactive read-aloud (Bestwick, 2017). Such book related play helps
children develop empathy, social acuity, knowledge of cultural norms, as
well as understanding about themselves and about the world at large
(Hedges, 2014; Hynes-Berry, 2012; Lin, 2017; Rowe, 2007; Welsch, 2008).

BODY OF WORK

Research began with two questions: (1) What types of play are depicted in
children's literature? and (2) How might children's literature inspire playful
learning in elementary schools? Empirical research related to depictions of
play in children's literature is scarce. Various resources were utilized to
ensure selection of high-quality children's literature that included realistic
depictions play. Searches were performed using the Children's Literature
Comprehensive Database with search qualifiers for books with honors and
awards. Additionally, a local library's countywide database was utilized, as
was the input of knowledgeable librarians. Readings from *The Horn Book
Magazine* were also helpful toward finding play related titles. During atten-
dance at a 2017 weeklong children's literature conference, new titles that
depicted children at play were sought out.

Following a review of research and a reading of a whole host of play
related children's literature titles, eight types of play depicted in children's
literature emerged by melding play theoretical frameworks of Hynes-Berry
(2012), Piaget (1972), and Zosh et al. (2013). Through reading and rereading
play related children's literature, types of play were identified, defined,
coded, and categorized according to the type of play depicted therein (Miles
& Huberman, 1994).

Findings of Types of Play Depicted in Children's Literature

Picture books are a model and an impetus for various types of play. Bader (1976) defined a picture book as "text, illustrations, total design; an item of manufacture and a commercial product; a social, cultural, historical document; and foremost, *an experience for a child*" (p. 1, italics mine). Accordingly, play enhances and deepens a learner's experiences with children's literature. Rowe (2007) demonstrated that young children, without prompting from adults, will naturally playact stories that have been read-aloud to them. Children's book author, Grace Lin, described how as a child, she and her friends would playact their favorite stories written by Laura Ingalls Wilder (Lin, 2017).

Children are better able to relate to realistic depictions featuring humans than to anthropomorphic animals within children's literature (Lombrozo, 2017). Therefore, realistic picture books containing human characters are best for primary grade children.

Eight Types of Play

The eight types of play depicted in realistic children's literature include:

- Sensory play—using one's senses to play with and explore natural phenomena
- Constructive/Maker play—constructing, building, or making things as a form of play or for play
- Sociodramatic/Imaginative play—using one's imagination during play; includes acting out a story, make-believe, pretend
- Games with rules—players engaged in game play with formal rules or self-established rules
- Physical play—physical exertion to build and play in a fort, a hideout, a playground, and so forth
- Adventure play—involves spatial navigation to find a place, treasure, or mystery items, may involve competition
- Arts play—drawing, painting, dancing, making music, and other art forms
- Technology play—using technology to play through physical or virtual means; may replicate the work of scientists, engineers, or inventors

Exemplar Books

This section is intended to provide a review of recent realistic children's books containing depictions of children at play and acts as resource for teachers to incorporate playful learning experiences across the curriculum. One book is highlighted as an exemplar of a particular type of play in conjunction with play-filled learning activities. Lists of other high-quality books that depict play are organized by play type, as shown in Table 4.1.

Educators may decide how best to use these books and ideas to inspire playful learning while attending to students' interests and learning needs.

Sensory Play: Inside Outside by Lizi Boyd (2013)

This ingeniously designed wordless book depicts a young boy's sensory play throughout all four seasons. Double-page spreads alternate between inside and outside views of a young boy's world. The first double-page spread is an illustration of the boy preparing to plant seeds in pots inside, with a cut-out window showing snowmen outside. Outside, the boy builds a snowman, plays in the rain, flies a kite on a windy spring day, rakes leaves in the fall, and plays with a sled in the snow. Inside, the boy paints pictures of birds, cares for a turtle, builds a sailboat, performs a puppet show, and selects appropriate attire for outdoor play. The boy's seemingly ordinary activities are extraordinary events in the life of a child, easily relatable to young children.

Inside Outside (Boyd, 2013) lends itself to a variety of academic disciplines. Students may "read" this wordless book to others by formulating a story to match the illustration, thus attaining Speaking and Listening standards and language play. Teachers may use this book to prompt discussion about weather conditions shown in the book and assist students to make personal connections to the local weather, hence meeting NGSS Weather and Climate standards (NGSS Lead States, 2013). Similarly, National Council for the Social Studies standards for Geography requires that young learners "explain how weather, climate, and other environmental characteristics affect people's lives in a place" (NCSS, 2013). During outdoor expeditions, young children may use sensory play to explore, observe, or record daily weather in science notebooks. Art play may be implemented as students create a wordless inside-outside book to illustrate how local weather affects their lives.

Constructive/Maker Play: This Is My Dollhouse by Giselle Potter (2016)

Imaginative infused constructive play is the silver lining of this tender story. The central character, a young girl [unnamed], narrates the story. Her pride and joy is her dollhouse. She has constructed the dollhouse and its inhabitants from found objects and materials. One day, the girl is invited to play at Sophie's house. Sophie shows off her store bought "perfect" dollhouse. The girls play for a bit, but become quickly bored as little is left to the imagination in this pristine dollhouse. Now the girl is hesitant to invite Sophie to her house to play, as she fears that Sophie would dislike her hand-crafted dollhouse. Sophie does come over to play and loves the dollhouse. The girls play for hours. Once again, the girl feels pride for her dollhouse. This book perfectly depicts constructive/maker play as the girl draws eggs for the doll family's breakfast, makes an elevator for the dollhouse out of a paper cup, and, out of rolled bits of toilet paper, makes popcorn for the dollhouse family. The endpapers and the underside of the dust jacket offer numerous ideas for making one's own dollhouse and furniture out of found materials.

This Is My Dollhouse (Potter, 2016) has applications to several academic subjects. Within NCSS Social Studies (2010) theme #4, Individual Development and Identity, there is opportunity for students to consider how one is similar to and different from others. The girl in the story fears she has nothing in common with Sophie at first, but after getting to know her better, the girl learns the two have much in common. Young children may compare and contrast themselves to the girl, Sophie, or to others. Reading Literature standards may be attained by examining the characters' traits, motivations, and feelings through sociodramatic role play. Application of this story may be extended to address Next Generation Science Standards for Engineering Design (NGSS Lead States, 2013) and maker play. NGSS (2013) standards require students to "define a simple design problem reflecting a need or want that includes specific criteria for success and constraints on materials, time, or cost." Students might create specific home designs that would be suitable for favorite story characters or toys, then build the home using found objects.

Sociodramatic/Imaginative Play: Mudkin by Stephen Gammell (2011)

After a rain fall, a girl declares she is queen over the elements. Mud comes to life under her command and Mudkin is born. The girl and Mudkin create an imaginary kingdom replete with a carriage, castle, and Mudkin-like subjects. This book is semi-wordless; descriptive text contains Mudkin's language which is comprised of mud splotches. Imaginative play is seamlessly portrayed throughout the book. The story ends with the rain's return, washing away Mudkin and the queen's kingdom. Picking up her mud-soaked toys, the girl walks home.

Gamell's illustrations are beautifully rendered in watercolor, thus offering a stimulus for several playful learning activities. Art play meets National Core Arts Standards (2015) by making "art or design with various materials and tools to explore personal interests, questions, or curiosity" (NCCAS, 2015). Students may design a watercolor or mud representations of a Mudkin-like mud-world. To attain NGSS (2013) Structure and Properties of Matter standards through sensory play, students might investigate the properties of soil, water, and mud. During writing, students may verbally translate Mudkin's language to enact "language play" (Zosh et al., 2013, p. 107). Or, students may write and speak descriptions for the wordless sections of the book.

Games with Rules: Dear Primo: A Letter to My Cousin by
Duncan Tonatiuh (2010)

Two cousins, Charlie, living in America, and Carlitos, living in Mexico, are
pen pals. The boys write descriptions of their communities, families, friends,
and daily activities. Carlitos' descriptions are commingled with Spanish
words and labels. Games with rules are interspersed throughout the book, as
Charlie and Carlitos write about fútbol (soccer), basketball, canicas (mar-
bles), and hopscotch. This book provides a window into Mexican culture and
upholds a mirror for learners of Mexican heritage. Tonatiuh's dynamic hand
drawn and digitalized illustrations are inspired by the Mexican Codex (Tonatiuh, 2017). Childhood experiences living in Mexico and the United States
were the impetus for Tonatiuh's book (Tonatiuh, 2017).

   Dear Primo: A Letter to My Cousin (Tonatiuh, 2010) recognizably ap-
plies to instruction of writing letters, as well as other disciplinary content.
Students may employ language play as they write letters to pen pals, friends,
or relatives. This book is perfect for attaining Reading Literature standards
for comparing and contrasting characters or settings. Teachers may offer hula
hoops as a play-like tool for students to use rather than usual Venn Diagram
graphic organizers. During Social Studies, students may role play to attain
geography standards by identifying some cultural and environmental characteristics of Mexico (NCSS, 2013, p. 42). Many students are unfamiliar with
marble games, so teachers may wish to prepare a variety of marble games
and the rules for play within learning centers prior to reading. Students may
also create and write rules for their own marble game.

Physical Play: A Dark, Dark Cave by Eric Hoffman (2016)

A brother and sister use a flashlight to peer into a dark, dark cave in the
opening scene. The pair bravely enter and explore the dark, dark cave and
find bats, reptiles, and other cave creatures. Then a light appears, illuminating a shadow of a giant! The children fearlessly roar in response. Perspective
shifts from inside the cave to the children's room with the chairs and blanket
that comprise the "dark, dark cave." The "giant" is the children's father, who
has come to request that they "find a quiet game." Now cave the becomes a
barn filled with horses and birds.

   Real caves are a natural academic connection to *A Dark, Dark Cave*
(Hoffman, 2016). Teachers may select quality informational titles for student
research on caves. High-quality titles such as *Caves: Mysteries Beneath Our
Feet* by David L. Harrison, *Caves* by Ellen Sturm Niz, *Animals with No
Eyes: Cave Adaptation* by Kelly Regan Barnhill, and *Cave Crawlers* by Pam
Rosenberg will provide a good starting point for a cave "text set" (ReadWrit-
eThink, 2004). After mini-lessons on informational text features, students
may use their knowledge of informational text features to conduct research

on caves and perform Reading: Informational Text standard RI.2.5. and Writing Standard W.2.7. (Common Core Standards Initiative, 2012). An Earth Systems strand from NGSS (2013) require that students "use information from several sources to provide evidence that Earth events can occur quickly or slowly," and to "develop a model to represent the shapes and kinds of land . . . in an area" (NGSS Lead States, 2013). Armed with knowledge of caves, students may create and play in a large model of a cave using blankets, desks, and chairs.

Adventure Play: Sam and Dave Dig a Hole by Mac Barnett (2014)

This Caldecott Honor book depicts two boys and a dog on an adventure to find "something spectacular." Klassen's illustrations show the boys twisty, turn-filled progress toward their goal as they dig deeper and deeper into the Earth. Their path goes in several different directions, while time and again the boys come close to, but do not uncover numerous large gems. The boys grow tired from all the digging and fall asleep. The dog finishes the task and the trio falls through the air, landing in a place that looks very much like home. But, is it? Nevertheless, the boys seem to have found something spectacular.

Sam and Dave Dig a Hole (Barnett, 2014) has relevance to reading, geography, and creative writing. Teachers may employ the "Mapping Storybooks" strategy to inspire students to work collaboratively to create a table-sized map of the path of Sam and Dave's dig (Haywood, 2015). To perform ELA and geography standards with adventure play, students may identify a "spectacular" end point within school grounds, construct a correlated treasure map, then write an adventure story to go along with the map (Common Core Standards Initiative, 2012; NCSS, 2013, p. 41). Adventure play can continue as peers use a friend's map to find "something spectacular."

Arts Play: Trombone Shorty by Troy "Trombone Shorty" Andrews (2015)

Every classroom should have a copy of this visually stunning autobiography. Brian Collier's ink, watercolor, and collage illustrations embody the music, culture, and community spirit that exemplify the life of Troy "Trombone Shorty" Andrews. Troy Andrews grew up in a section of New Orleans that was immersed in music. Young Troy did not have an instrument of his own, so he and his friends made their own instruments and formed a band. This particular life event clearly portrays music play (Zosh et al., 2013). Later Troy found and began to play an old, discarded trombone, becoming forever-more known as "Trombone Shorty."

Students may playfully respond to this biography within several subject areas. To attain Common Core Speaking and Listening standards and National Arts standards, students may listen to songs performed by the band, Trombone Shorty and Orleans Avenue, and create a work of art to represent the music. Kinesthetic learners may respond by dancing to Trombone Shorty's music. Playful science learning may be infused as students create musical instruments and form a band to experiment with sound. During Social Studies, students may explore New Orleans culture and investigate how culture unifies a group of people (NCSS, 2010). Geography concepts may be incorporated as students "describe how human activities affect the cultural and environmental characteristics" of New Orleans (NCSS, 2013, p. 42).

Technology Play: Rosie Revere, Engineer by Andrea Beaty (2013)

Rosie's technology play is described in rhyming verse. "Alone in her attic, the moon high above, dear Rosie made gadgets and gizmos she loved" (Beaty, 2013). The brightly detailed, double-page spread illustration shows Rosie's enormous collection of technology, as well as bits and pieces that may become part of an invention. When Rosie's uncle laughs at the anti-python hat Rosie created for him, she ceases her technology play for months. A visit from Aunt Rose reinvigorates Rosie's technology play. Aunt Rose tells how she unswervingly pursued her dreams, which refreshes Rosie's dream of becoming an engineer. The book's back matter includes a historical note about women's contributions during World War II as symbolized by Rosie the Riveter.

It is important for teachers to provide children with playful experiences so they may "try on" future careers. STEM employers in the United States will need to fill millions of STEM jobs in future years, but employers report that they have difficulty finding qualified citizens to hire for these positions (Bertram & Forbes, 2014). If children have opportunities to learn about STEM careers through technology play, more American children might pursue careers in STEM fields. Heroman (2017) created a design challenge to pair with a reading of *Rosie Revere, Engineer* called "Gizmos Galore" (Heroman, 2017, pp. 51–53). This technology play-based activity challenges students to "take an everyday object and find ways to make it better" (Heroman, 2017, p. 52).

Table 4.1.   Children's Literature Titles That Depict Eight Types of Play

Type of Play	Children's Literature
Sensory Play	*Bringing the outside in* by Mary McKenna Siddals. Illus. Patrice Barton. New York: Random House, 2016. *Float* by Daniel Miyares. New York: Simon & Schuster Books for Young Readers, 2015. *Rain play* by Cynthia Cotten. Illus. Javaka Steptoe. New York: Henry Holt and Company, LLC, 2008. *Shh! We have a plan* by Chris Haughten. Somerville: Candlewick Press, 2014. *Rhoda's rock hunt* by Molly Beth Griffin. Illus. Jennifer A. Bell. St. Paul: Minnesota Historical Society Press, 2014. *This beautiful day* by Richard Jackson. Illus. Suzy Lee. New York: Atheneum/Caitlyn Dlouhy Books. *Wave* by Suzy Lee. San Francisco: Chronicle Books, LLC, 2008.
Constructive/ Maker Play	*Extra yarn* by Mac Barnett. Illus. Jon Klaussen. New York: Balzer + Bray, 2012. *Kite flying* by Grace Lin. New York: Knopf, Borzoi, 2002. *The cardboard kingdom* by Chad Sell. New York: Knopf, 2018. *The carpenter* by Bruna Barros. Layton: Gibbs Smith, 2017.
Sociodramatic/ Imaginative Play	*Birdie plays dress-up* (Board book) by Sujean Rim. New York: Little Brown and Company, 2012. *I am a backhoe* by Anna Grossnickle Hines. Berkley: Tricycle Press, 2010. *Let's do nothing!* By Tony Fucile. Somerville: Candlewick Press, 2009. 9780763634407. *Slightly invisible: Featuring Charlie and Lola with special appearance by Soren Lorenson* by Lauren Child. Somerville: Candlewick Press, 2010. *The adventures of Beekle: The unimaginary friend* by Dan Santat. New York: Little, Brown Books for Young Readers, 2014. *The almost terrible playdate* by Richard Torrey. New York: Doubleday Books for Young Readers, 2016. *The day I lost my superpowers* by Michaël Escoffier. Illus. Kris Di Giacomo. New York: Enchanted Lion Books, 2014. *The troublemaker* by Lauren Castillo. New York: Clarion Books, 2014. *When Stella was very, very small* by Marie-Louise Gay. Berkley: Groundwood Books, 2009.
Games with Rules	*Blackout* by John Rocco. New York: Disney – Hyperion Books, 2011. *Hide and seek* by Anthony Brown. Somerville, MA: Candlewick, 2018. *H.O.R.S.E.: A game of basketball and imagination* by Christopher Myers. New York: Egmont, 2012. *Rulers of the playground* by Joseph Kuefler. New York: Balzer + Bray, 2017.

Physical Play	*Secret tree fort* by Brianne Farley. Somerville: Candlewick Press, 2016. *The fort that Jack built* by Boni Asburn. Illus. Brett Helquist. New York: Abrams, 2013. *The little red fort* by Brenda Maier. Illustr. Sonia Sanchez. New York: Scholastic Press, 2018.
Adventure Play	*Playground* by Mies Van Hout. Translation. Lemniscaat. New York: Lemniscaat USA, LLC, 2015. *The secret box* by Barbara Lehman. New York: Houghton Mifflin Books for Children, 2011.
Arts Play	*Beatrix Potter and her paint box* by David McPhail. New York: Henry Holt and Co., 2015. *Draw!* by Raúl Colón. New York: Simon & Schuster Books for Young Readers, 2014. *Freedom in Congo Square* by Carole Baston Weatherford. Illus. R. Gregory Christie. New York: Little Bee Books, 2016.
Technology Play	*Boy + bot* by Ame Dyckman. Illus. Dan Yaccarino. New York: Knopf Books for Young Readers, 2012. *Doll-E 1.0* by Shandra McCloskey. Boston, MA: Little, Brown, and Company, 2018. *Dot.* by Randi Zuckerberg. Illus. Joe Berger. New York: Harper Collins, 2013. *Little robot* by Ben Hatke. New York: First Second, 2015. *Oh no! Or, how my science project destroyed the world* by Mac Barnett. Illus. Dan Santat. New York: Disney – Hyperion, 2010. *The darkest dark* by Chris Hadfield. Illus. The Fan Brothers. New York: Little, Brown, and Company, 2016.
Variety of Play Types	*A stick is an excellent thing: Poems celebrating outdoor play* by Marilyn Singer. Illus. LeUyen Pham. New York: Clarion Books, 2012. *Play?* by Linda Olafsdottir. Petaluma: Cameron + Company, 2017. *Play! Play! Play!* [board book] by Douglas Florian. Illustr. Christiane Engel. New York: little bee books, 2018. *Toys galore* by Peter Stein. Illus. Bob Staake. Somerville: Candlewick Press, 2013. *What little boys are made of* by Robert Neubecker. New York: Harper Collins Children's Books, 2012.

IMPLICATIONS FOR PRACTICE

While attending to national, state, and local curricular demands, let us not lose sight of the developmental and learning needs of those at the heart of an education system, the children. "These aims have evolved into a work- and not play-based curriculum" (Genishi & Haas Dyson, 2014). Play is the essence of childhood. As a commentary on the state of childhood, Genishi and Haas Dyson (2014) noted that our society looks at children as small adults. As a society, we must move away from the adult expectation that children march lockstep through mandated curriculum—all work and no play—to attain artificially imposed standards. Children have a right to behave and learn in child-like ways.

Play brings joy and so much more into children's lives. American schools may bring back the joy of learning through playful experiences paired with high-quality children's literature. Education officials must look to the well-being of children by releasing the stranglehold placed on teachers by a paradigm of top-down control through accountability policies and permit teachers to have autonomy to act as the professionals they are (Berry et al., 2011; Chen, 2010; Sarason, 1990). Sir Ken Robinson (2016) noted:

> The role of a teacher is to facilitate learning. It may seem unnecessary to say that, but much of what teachers are expected to do is something other than teaching. A great deal of their time is taken up with administering tests, doing clerical tasks, attending meetings, writing reports, and taking disciplinary action . . . When those other tasks distract from that job, the real character of the teaching profession is obscured. (2016, p. 101)

Teachers should be empowered to facilitate instruction based upon local culture, developmental readiness, and learning needs of their students, rather than impelled to act as mindless dispensers of canned curriculum intended for the masses, fearful of failure to attain accountability measures. With professional agency unleased across American classrooms, joyful learning will occur. Exuberant authentic learning, learning that is geared toward student's interests and infused with localized, real-world experiences, inspired by high-quality children's literature paired with play, will bring back the bliss of reading and learning that will equip children for productive future lives.

REFERENCES

Allyn, P. (2017). *Every child a super reader.* Presented at the Once Read, Never Forgotten: Creating Readers One Book at a Time annual Children's Literature Conference, Winchester, VA. Conference website: su.edu/childrenslit.

Andrews, T. & Collier, B., (2015). *Trombone Shorty.* New York: Abrams Books for Young Readers.

Ansberry, K., & Morgan, E. (2005). *Picture-perfect science lessons: Using children's book to guide inquiry, 3–6.* Arlington, VA: National Science Teachers Association.

Bader, B. (1976). *American picturebooks from Noah's Ark to the Beast Within* (First Edition edition). New York: Macmillan Pub Co.

Barnett, M. & Klaussen, J., (2014). *Sam and Dave dig a hole.* Somerville: Candlewick Press.

Beaty, A., & Roberts, D. (2013). *Rosie Revere, engineer.* New York: Abrams Books for Young Readers.

Berry, B., Barnett, J., Betlach, K., C'de Baca, S., Highley, S., Holland, J. M., . . . Wasserman, L. (2011). *Teaching 2030: What we must do for our students and our public schools--now and in the future.* New York, NY: Teachers College Press.

Bertram, V. M. D., & Forbes, S. (2014). *One nation under taught: Solving America's science, technology, engineering, and math crisis* (Kindle Edition). Amazon Digital Services: Beaufort Books.

Bestwick, A. (2017). Beatrix Potter and her paint box lesson plan. *Social Studies Research and Practice*. Vol. 12, No.2, 2017, pp. 232–242. West Yorkshire, UK: Emerald Publishing Limited. DOI 10.1108/SSR–05-2017–0026.

Bishop, R. S. (2012). Reflections on the development of African American children's literature. *Journal of Children's Literature*, 38(2), 5–13.

Boyd, L., (2013). *Inside outside.* San Francisco: Chronicle Books.

Brooker, L., Blaise, M., & Edwards, S. (2014). *The SAGE handbook of play and learning in early childhood.* London: SAGE Publications Ltd.

Chen, M. (2010). *Education nation: Six leading edges of innovation in our schools.* San Francisco, CA: Jossey-Bass.

Common Core Standards Initiative. (2012). Common Core State Standards Initiative | Home. Retrieved August 18, 2012, from http://www.corestandards.org/.

Danielson, C. (2007). *Enhancing professional practice: A framework for teaching* (2nd ed.). Alexandria, VA: Association for Supervision and Curriculum Development.

Dewey, J. (1900). *The school and society. The child and the curriculum.* University of Chicago Press.

Galdone, P. (1984). *The three little pigs* (Reprint edition). New York, NY: HMH Books for Young Readers.

Gallagher, K. (2009). *Readicide: How schools are killing reading and what you can do about it.* Portland, ME: Stenhouse Publishers.

Gallas, K. (2001). "Look, Karen, I'm running like Jell-O:" Imagination as a question, a topic, a tool for literacy research and learning. *Research in the Teaching of English*, 35(4), 457–492.

Gammell, S., (2011). *Mudkin.* Minneapolis, MN: Carolrhoda Books.

Genishi, C. & Haas Dyson, A. (2014). Play as a precursor for literacy development. In L. Brooker, M. Blaise, & S. Edwards (Eds.), *The SAGE handbook of play and learning in early childhood* (pp. 228–239). London: SAGE Publications Ltd.

Gonzalez, J. (2017, December 3). *How to stop killing the love of reading* [Podcast]. Retrieved June 11, 2018, from https://www.cultofpedagogy.com/stop-killing-reading/.

Guarnaccia, S. (2010). *The three little pigs: An architectural tale* (5.2.2010 edition). New York: Harry N. Abrams.

Haywood, A. (2015, 14). *Mapping storybooks.* Retrieved January 15, 2015, from http://education.nationalgeographic.com/education/activity/mapping-storybooks/.

Hedges, H. (2014). Children's content learning in play provision: Competing tensions and future possibilities. In L. Brooker, M. Blaise, & S. Edwards (Eds.), *The SAGE Handbook of Play and Learning in Early Childhood* (pp. 228–239). London: SAGE Publications Ltd.

Heroman, C. (2017). *Making and tinkering with STEM: Solving design challenges with young children.* Washington, DC: National Association for the Education of Young Children.

Hoffman, E. & Tabo, C. R., (2016). *A dark, dark cave.* New York: Penguin Random House, LLC.

Husbye, N. E. (2012). Critical lessons and playful literacies: Digital media in PK–2 classrooms. *Language Arts*, 90(2), 82–92.

Hynes-Berry, M. (2012). *Don't leave the story in the book: Using literature to guide inquiry in early childhood classrooms.* New York: Teachers College Press.

Jackson-Schnoor, D. (2017, 30). *Hands on learning—Connecting STEAM to children's literature.* Presented at the Once Read, Never Forgotten: Creating Readers One Book at a Time annual Children's Literature Conference, Winchester, VA. Conference web site: su.edu/childrenslit.

Jones, E. (2011). Play across the life cycle from initiative to integrity to transcendence. *Young Children*, 66(4), 84–91.

Lin, G. (2017). *The mirrors and windows of your child's bookshelves.* Presented at the Once Read, Never Forgotten: Creating Readers One Book at a Time annual Children's Literature Conference, Winchester, VA. Conference web site: su.edu/childrenslit.

Lombrozo, T. (2017). *In children's storybooks, realism has advantages.* Retrieved December 6, 2017, from https://www.npr.org/sections/13.7/2017/08/14/543405845/in-children-s-storybooks-realism-has-advantages.

McNair, J. C., Bailey, A. R., Colabucci, L., & Day, D. (2011). Children's Literature Reviews: Play-themed children's literature for early childhood classrooms. *Language Arts, 89*(1), 65–69.

McPhail, D. (2015). *Beatrix Potter and her paint box.* New York: Henry Holt and Co.

Miles, M. B., & Huberman, M. (1994). *Qualitative data analysis: An expanded sourcebook* (2nd ed.). Thousand Oaks, CA: Sage Publications, Inc.

Mraz, K., Porcelli, A., & Tyler, C. (2016). *Purposeful play: A teacher's guide to igniting deep & joyful learning across the day.* Portsmouth, NH: Heinemann.

NAEYC. (2009). Developmentally appropriate practice in early childhood programs serving children from birth through age 8. National Association for the Education of Young Children. Retrieved from http://www.naeyc.org/positionstatements/dap.

NCCAS. (2015). Home | National Core Arts Standards. Retrieved October 8, 2015, from http://www.nationalartsstandards.org/.

NCSS. (2010). *National curriculum standards for Social Studies: A framework for teaching, learning, and assessment.* Silver Spring, MD: National Council for the Social Studies.

NCSS. (2013). *Social studies for the next generation: Purposes, practices, and implications of the college, career, and civic life (C3) framework for the social studies state standards* (NCSS Bulletin 113). Silver Spring, MD: National Council for the Social Studies.

NCSS. (2017). Notable Social Studies Trade Books for Young People. Retrieved July 31, 2017, from https://www.socialstudies.org/publications/notables.

NGSS Lead States. (2013). Next Generation Science Standards. Retrieved July 31, 2017, from https://www.nextgenscience.org/.

Nilsson, M. E. (2010). Creative pedagogy of play: The work of Gunilla Lindqvist. *Mind, Culture, and Activity, 17*, 14–22. https://doi.org/10.1080/10749030903342238.

Piaget, J. (1972). *Play, dreams, and imitation in childhood.* New York: Basic Books.

Potter, G., (2016). *This is my dollhouse.* New York: Schwartz & Wade Books.

ReadWriteThink. (2004). Creating text sets for your classroom. NCTE/IRA. Retrieved from http://www.readwritethink.org/files/resources/lesson_images/lesson305/creating.pdf.

Robinson, K., & Aronica, L. (2016). *Creative schools: The grassroots revolution that's transforming education* (Reprint edition). New York: Penguin Books.

Rowe, D. W. (2007). Bringing books to life: The role of book-related dramatic play in young children's literacy learning. In K. A. Roskos & J. F. Christie (Eds.), *Play and Literacy in Early Childhood* (2nd ed., pp. 37–63). New York: Lawrence Erlbaum Associates, Inc.

Sarason, S. B. (1990). *The predictable failure of educational reform: Can we change course before it's too late.* San Francisco, CA: Jossey-Bass.

Scieszka, J. (1989). *The true story of the 3 little pigs!* (1st edition). New York, N.Y., U.S.A: Viking Books for Young Readers.

Serafini, F. (2011). Creating space for children's literature. *The Reading Teacher, 65*(1), 30–34.

Tonatiuh, D. (2010). *Dear Primo: A letter to my cousin.* New York: Abrams Books for Young Readers.

Tonatiuh, D. (2017). *Modern codex.* Presented at the Once Read, Never Forgotten: Creating Readers One Book at a Time annual Children's Literature conference, Winchester, VA. Conference web site: su.edu/childrenslit.

Wager, A. A., & Parks, A. N. (2014). Learning mathematics through play. In L. Brooker, M. Blaise, & S. Edwards (Eds.), *The SAGE handbook of play and learning in early childhood* (pp. 216–227). London: SAGE Publications Ltd.

Welsch, J. G. (2008). Playing within and beyond the story: Encouraging book-related pretend play. *Reading Teacher, 62*(2), 138–148.

Wohlwend, K. E. (2011). *Playing their way into literacies: Reading, writing, and belonging in the early childhood classroom.* New York, NY: Teachers College Press.

Wohlwend, K. E. (2013). *Literacy playshop: New literacies, popular media, and play in the early childhood classroom.* New York, NY: Teachers College Press.

Wohlwend, K. E., (2018). Playing to our strengths: Finding innovation in children's and teachers' imaginative expertise. *Language Arts,* 95(3), 162–170.

Wood, C. (2007). *Yardsticks: Children in the classroom ages 4–14* (3rd ed.). Turners Falls, MA: Northeast Foundation for Children.

Wood, E. (2014). The play-pedagogy interface in contemporary debates. In L. Brooker, M. Blaise, & S. Edwards (Eds.), *The SAGE handbook of play and learning in early childhood* (pp. 145–156). London: SAGE Publications Ltd.

Wood, L. D. (2014). Holding on to play: Reflecting on experiences as a playful K–3 teacher. *YC Young Children,* 69(2), 48–57.

Zosh, J. M., Fisher, K., Golinkoff, R. M., & Hirsh-Pasek, K. (2013). The ultimate block party: Bridging the science of learning and the importance of play. In *Design, Make, Play: Growing the Next Generation of STEM Innovators* (pp. 95–118). New York, NY: Routledge.

Chapter Five

Responsive Play

Exploring Language and Literacy
Through Play as Reader Response

Tori K. Flint

Play in the school setting is a highly contested issue in today's often-restrictive academic environments. Although many early childhood educators advocate the use of play in their classrooms, emphasize the importance of play for children's learning and development, and align play with language and literacy learning, play in US preschool and kindergarten settings is diminishing in favor of academically structured activities while children in primary and elementary grades are rarely afforded any opportunities to learn through play in their classrooms (Paley, 2004; Rowe, 1998; Wohlwend, 2011). Play in these classroom contexts has been devalued and curricular emphasis has been placed mainly upon academic skills, meeting content standards, and explicit instruction (Mandel, Morrow, Berkule, Mendelsohn, Healey, & Cates, 2013).

In this chapter, I will discuss a study conducted in a first-grade classroom in which I analyzed young children's play as a form of reader response and I will make the case for valuing play in the classroom context as a generative source of language and literacy learning and as a vehicle for meaning making.

TRANSACTING WITH STORIES

In her highly influential 1938 text, *Literature as Exploration*, Louise M. Rosenblatt responds to the formalist theories of the New Critics, which promoted "close readings" of texts and rejected all forms of reader interpretation. The New Critics' view that meaning resides only within the text and that the reader is merely a *passive* recipient is countered by Rosenblatt's transactional theory, which suggests that the reader is an *active* agent in meaning making (Rosenblatt, 1978). Meaning, then, is not constructed until the reader transforms the text by infusing it with intellectual and emotional meanings (Rosenblatt, 1938). In this sense, reading is a two-way, transactional process between reader and text; wherein readers bring "past experiences of language and of the world to the task" (Rosenblatt, 2001, p. 268) in order to construct meaning.

Framing the transactional theory within a classroom context, Lawrence R. Sipe (2008) offers a theory of literary understanding that is relevant to contemporary young children with diverse backgrounds. Sipe's (2008) framework suggests that, in the classroom, children respond to text in various ways, that these responses reveal that children are engaged in many different types of literary meaning-making, and that these types of meaning-making are instantiations of the foundational aspects of literary understanding.

Sipe (2008) notes that play as a response to literature might be categorized within the *personal* facet of literary understanding. According to Sipe, within the personal facet, story book characters elicit children's connections to their own play and pretend experiences. Pantaleo's (2008) study of first and fifth-grader's responses to contemporary picture books similarly supports play as personal response to literature, as her research reveals how children's reading work closely resembles play as they construct meaning and respond to text. These studies suggest that children's connections to story characters, influenced by their reservoirs of knowledge and experience, can prompt playful responses to texts.

PLAY, LANGUAGE, AND LITERACY CONNECTIONS

As children draw on various aspects of their past experiences to inform their reading transactions, they also connect their various languages and literacies to play. In contemporary times, literacy includes multiple modes (Kress, 2003, 2009): reading, writing, drawing/art, digital constructions, popular culture, artifacts, affective modes, etc. In each of these modalities, children draw from their social and cultural resources as they connect literacy and play. The links between play and children's literacies is a topic that has been investigated on a number of fronts in recent years (Bodrova & Leong, 2007; Christie & Roskos, 2013; Corsaro, 2003; Owocki, 1999; Paley, 2004; Wohlwend, 2011, 2013a, 2013b).

On one front, researchers interested in language development have examined sociodramatic play with preschool children, wherein children enact self-selected/created, pretend scenarios using personal knowledge from their own lives. These researchers have determined that play of this sort prompts children to use language to convey meaning and/or interpret ideas (Bodrova, 2008; Heath, 1983; Riojas-Cortez, 2001) and is a valuable tool within the field of early childhood education.

Christie and Roskos (2013) suggest that much research has also been done on *play process*, finding positive links between play and literacy in the areas of emergent writing and linguistic skills (Pellegrini, 1985; Pellegrini, Galda, Dresden, & Cox, 1991). Christie and Roskos (2013) further suggest that much research has been done on *play environment*. Focusing on literacy-enriched play centers, researchers have examined preschool and kindergarten settings wherein literacy is infused into dramatic play centers/stations. Recent studies indicate that there is an increase in children's use of literacy materials and engagement in literacy acts (Einarsdottir, 2000; Kendrick, 2005; Kress, 1998) when they transact in these types of centers. Vukelich (1994) further revealed that kindergarten children's ability to read print embedded within literacy-rich play centers was increased.

Other researchers have additionally demonstrated that children's learning and meaning making is informed as they utilize play to engage in literacy activities (Bergen & Mauer, 2000; Flint, 2010, 2018; Kendrick, 2005; Saracho, 2002, 2003; Saracho & Spodek, 1998, 2006). Play-literacy transactions within various play environments have been found to promote young children's literacy acquisition and development (Strickland & Morrow, 1989). These studies suggest that children's play is a "dominant behavior of childhood" (Gaskins, 2014, p. 34), is essential for children's learning and development, and as such, can inform their language and literacy learning in the classroom context.

In connecting play and literacy in the classroom setting, drama is often utilized as a space in which stories can come to life through role-play. Research conducted on children's spontaneous and dramatic re-enactments of stories (Martinez, Cheyney, & Teale, 1991) have shown that the classroom context, exposure to literature, and opportunities for varied story response positively impacted kindergartener's use of dramatic retellings in the classroom setting.

These, and other investigations, have yielded data suggesting that dramatic centers and spaces for dramatic story retellings help children to enact and practice literate behaviors (Adomat, 2009, 2012; Edmiston, 1993; Morrow & Rand 1991; Neuman & Roskos, 1997; Vukelich, 1991). The framework of dramatic response invites children to engage in critical discussions as they interpret stories in various ways. These studies provide a context for further exploring the ways in which young children similarly utilize play to respond to literature.

PLAY AS READER RESPONSE

A seminal piece of research that highlights play as a form of reader response in the classroom context, Rowe's (1998) 9-month study of 16 preschoolers' literacy behaviors found that book-related dramatic play was a "context for literacy learning . . . and a process of comprehending books, expressing one's reactions, experiencing books in affective and kinesthetic ways, as well as a means of inquiry, and participating in literacy events" (p. 11).

This study investigated the ways that preschoolers connected dramatic play to story book readings. Rowe (1998) found that children utilized play as a means to express their reactions to the events and to the characters within the stories. Her study suggests that children use play in order to participate in reading and literacy events because it connects their personal play worlds to the worlds represented within the texts and allows them to understand and relate to texts in meaningful and familiar ways. Importantly, Rowe also suggests that playing out parts of the stories gave the children great enjoyment while simultaneously allowing them to explore stories and construct meaning(s) through language and play. These findings posit that play serves as an integral part of children's literacy-learning processes. Play affords children the opportunity to explore their connections and tensions with/to texts and to expand upon their literacies.

Wohlwend (2009) similarly found that, even in constrained classroom environments that emphasize print-based exercises and the use of worksheets as learning tools, children are able to negotiate spaces to engage in spontaneous play that contributes to their knowledge construction and meaning making processes. Children insistently make space for play, even within highly constrained contexts, and through their play, children are able to create classroom spaces in which their learning is supported and extended (Flint, 2018; Flint & Adams, 2018).

Responsive Play Theory

Children's play as a form of reader response, their *responsive play* (Flint 2016), is not only a meaningful way for children to respond to books, but is also an important part of their meaning making processes and of their literacy learning as a whole (Evans, 2012; Rowe, 2007). Children utilize and incorporate play in their reading responses in order to make sense of texts and to construct meaning and understanding (Rowe, 2007). Children cultivate their literacy abilities within and through the interconnected links among their talk, play, and stories (Evans, 2012; Flint, 2016, 2018). Through responsive play, children's language and literacy learning is also scaffolded (Vygotsky, 1978) and developed due to the social nature of the reading transactions. By linking their reading experiences to their social play in this capacity, children's learning is fostered and extended in the classroom context. In the responsive play framework, it is within the intersection of children's language(s), literacies, and play wherein knowledge is built upon and expanded, children's understandings are developed, and meaning is ultimately constructed (Flint, 2016).

THE STUDY: CONTEXTS AND METHODS

Purpose

The purpose of this research is to develop deeper understandings about the affordances of play in response to text within a first-grade classroom and to investigate the ways that children utilize play to respond to literature and to construct meaning. This portion of the study is informed by two guiding research questions: (1) What are the affordances of play for responding to text in a first-grade classroom? (2) In what ways do children incorporate and utilize play to make meaning with texts and with each other in the classroom context?

Setting

This eight-month study was conducted in Mrs. Swanson's first-grade classroom in Horizon View K–8 School, located in a semi-rural, suburban area in the Southwestern United States (all names are pseudonyms).

Participants

Students

Included in this research are the 30 students in Mrs. Swanson's class who agreed to participate in the study. They range in ages from 6- to 7-years-old. The children's reading levels, according to Mrs. Swanson, are on a broad continuum from very emergent readers to very fluent readers. Accordingly, students are labeled by Mrs. Swanson as Fluent Readers (students who read beyond the first grade standards, such as reading a range of chapter books, etc.), Early Readers (those who are blending and reading words/sentences/ stories according to first grade standards), and Emergent Readers (readers who may need support in blending sounds together and reading words and sentences). These labels assist Mrs. Swanson as she creates guiding reading groups and prepares materials to scaffold student learning, based on their needs.

Of the 18 girls and 12 boys in Mrs. Swanson's first-grade classroom, one reports (all reports are by parents) being Asian (Vietnamese), eight report being Hispanic or Latinx, five report being bi-racial (two are Hispanic or Latinx and white, two are Hispanic or Latinx and Pacific Islander, and one is Native American and white), and 16 report being white. Several students also receive English language services from the school.

Teacher

This classroom includes a 33-year-old, white, middle-class, female teacher (all self-reported), Mrs. Swanson. At the time of the study, Mrs. Swanson was an experienced first-grade teacher and had been teaching for nearly 10 years.

Classroom Context

The Mandated First-Grade Reading Curriculum

The first-grade curriculum at Horizon View K–8 School has a strong reading focus. Reading is taught according to the Common Core State Standards. In order to teach reading according to these Standards, the first-grade classrooms at Horizon View K–8 School utilize two basal reading sets. These sets aim to provide explicit instruction in the areas of phonemic awareness and phonics and the strategic application of these skills during reading.

Mrs. Swanson's Classroom Reading Curriculum

Although still focused on the Common Core Standards and in alignment with the two mandated programs, Mrs. Swanson supplements the curriculum by reading a variety of picture books and novels to the children in her class. Most often, she chooses books to read that correlate to the focus or theme provided within the mandated materials, but that also add to student learning.

The Reading Centers

Mrs. Swanson draws from the Reading Centers prescribed by the mandated curricula, but also implements her own ideas within the Centers. The classroom Reading Centers include: Read to Self (children read independently), Read with Someone (children read with partners), Work on Writing (children practice writing), Listen to Reading (children read along with books on tablets), Word Work (children work on word building/phonics, etc.), and Read to the Teacher (small groups with the teacher).

Invitations to Play: The Read and Respond Center

In order to observe and analyze children's play in response to literature, I created the *Read and Respond Center*, which was implemented within the framework of the already established classroom Reading Centers, wherein the children were invited to discuss and playfully respond to various children's books. So as to invite creative and playful responses from the children within this Center, I utilized a modified version of Patricia Edmiston (Enciso)'s (1990) Symbolic Representation Interview (SRI). This research method asks children to manipulate paper cutouts while they read. The cutouts represent the students (as readers) as well as the story characters. In her study, this method was implemented with individual readers in order to measure children's active reading engagement. When children use this method of response, they do not have to solely rely upon their "linguistic abilities to express the complex, simultaneous emotions, thoughts, actions, and questions that might be part of [their] reading experiences and transactions" (Enciso, 1996, p. 180). The SRI allows children to more fully express themselves while reading and makes their reading engagement more *observable* to teachers and researchers, providing valuable insights (Flint & Adams, 2018).

My study utilized a modified version of this SRI in which small groups of children were given a story book along with Reader (an image of a mirror-representing the children as readers), Author (an image of a pencil), and Illustrator (an image of a paintbrush) Cutouts, taped to popsicle sticks (see Figure 5.1 top). Children were also provided with Character Cutouts (images of characters from the stories) (see Figure 5.1 bottom). While the standard SRI is focused primarily on evaluating reading engagement, this modified version differs in that it focuses on utilizing the Cutouts as an *invitation* for children to use play as a means of story response, similar to the ways puppets can be used to elicit observable responses from children.

Children were given general instructions for the Read and Respond Center, so that their transactions and their responses were not directed. I informed the children that I was creating a new Reading Center, called the Read and Respond Center, in which they were able to read and respond to books with their friends. I did note that, unlike the other Centers, they *were* allowed to play in this Center, so long as they focused on the book, were reasonably quiet, stayed on the carpeted area where the Center was located, and so long as their play was related to the book somehow (*if* they chose to play). It was also noted that the children did *not* have to use the Cutouts if they did not want to and that play was *not* a requirement of the Center.

After taking into account the children's reading levels using evaluative data provided by Mrs. Swanson, I created groups of approximately three students (though this number sometimes fluctuated between two-four) that generally included a reader from each level (Emergent, Early, and Fluent) and began observations and filming. These groups were fluid and changed often, based on which students the teacher was with during Reading Center rotations. Children rotated to the Read and Respond center independent of the classroom literacy centers, but during the same time, allowing ample opportunity for reading and response.. Generally, students were in the Read

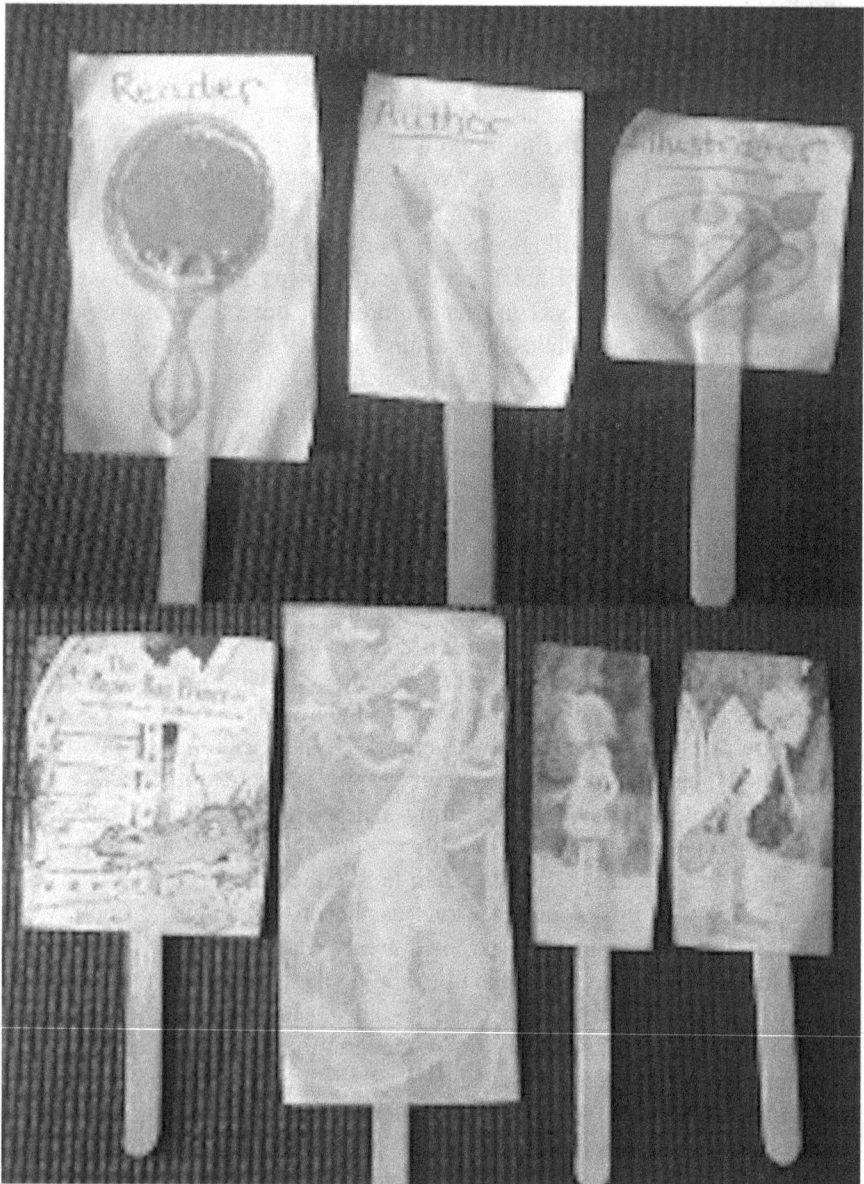

Figure 5.1.   Cutouts for Reader, Author, and Illustrator (top) and Sample Characters from *The Paper Bag Princess* (bottom). Created by Tori K. Flint

and Respond Center for approximately 15–20 minutes but not all students rotated to the Center each day.

Books Utilized in the Read and Respond Center

All students need to find their lives and cultural experiences reflected within the books they read in their classrooms (Short, Lynch-Brown, & Tomlinson, 2014). So that the children participating in the Read and Respond Center could find personal and cultural connections with the books they were reading together, and so that these books might allow for rich language and play responses, diverse books were used that reflected multiple identities. The books highlighted in this chapter include *Tuesday*, by David Wiesner, a mainly wordless picture book about frogs that mysteriously fly through a town at night, *The Paper Bag Princess* by Robert Munsch, a story in which traditional gender roles are reversed and the princess saves herself and the prince from a dragon by using her wit, and *Creepy Carrots* by Aaron Reynolds, about a rabbit who loves to eat carrots but then begins to be followed by them.

Data Collection and Analysis

Qualitative data, including classroom observations and detailed field notes, video-recorded/audio-recorded transactions and conversations, interviews, transcriptions, home visits, and artifact collection, were gathered over an eight-month period. Data were analyzed in an ongoing fashion, informed by thematic analysis (Glesne, 2011), the constant comparative method, and grounded theory (Glaser & Strauss, 1967), allowing for the continuous comparison of gathered information and the construction of themes both within and across data sets, and further allowing for the inductive construction of a responsive play theory as data were gathered and analyzed concurrently. Data were viewed from a sociocultural lens, positioning children as essential contributors to the cultural classroom landscape (Bakhtin, 1986; Bruner, 1990; Miller & Goodnow, 1995; Vygotsky, 1978).

FINDINGS AND DISCUSSION: EXPLORING LANGUAGE AND LITERACY THROUGH RESPONSIVE PLAY

The children in this study made story predictions, scaffolded each other's learning, clarified their understandings of story events, made analyses of stories, retold stories in their own words, and extended stories through their responsive play in the classroom context.

Making Predictions

Throughout this study, children often made predictions about what would happen next in a story. In the following vignette, Hunter (Fluent Reader) and Carlos (Emergent Reader) read *The Paper Bag Princess* and play in response to the text.

Hunter: (Begins reading, as the Reader Cutout)

Carlos: (As the dragon, moving the Cutout across the page) Rawww-wrrrrr!

(As the reader) Now I think she'll say, "I'm NOT marrying him."

Hunter: Let me draw her. (As the illustrator, moves the Cutout over the page) Yah, she won't, 'cause look . . . I drew her like she doesn't like him. (Pointing to the illustration, laughs)

In this vignette, Carlos predicts that the princess in the story will say that she will not marry the prince. Taking on the illustrator role, Hunter draws the princess character in the illustration and suggests that Carlos is correct, as he draws the character to look like she does not like the prince, corroborating this prediction.

In the next vignette, Emma (Fluent Reader), Madison (Early Reader), and Chloe (Emergent Reader) also read *The Paper Bag Princess* and make predictions about what the story characters will do.

Emma: I'm gonna be the princess!

Madison: And I'm the prince.

Chloe: We can be whatever we want.

Emma: (Begins reading) She's the reader! (Suggesting that the princess

Cutout is now the Reader)

Chloe: She is gonna trick the dragon!

Madison: Tricky! (Laughs)

In this excerpt, the girls read and play together and Chloe suggests that the princess, who is also the reader in this play scenario, will trick the dragon. Madison echoes this prediction and verifies Chloe's viewpoint when she follows up by noting that the princess is indeed, "tricky."

In several instances, children made predictions about what would happen next in the stories, what would happen if the events took place in "real life" or if they (as themselves *and* as story characters) were "there" at that certain moment, and what they thought that the characters (or themselves as the characters) would do next. In doing so, they assumed agency in the stories as they argued what they would or would not do in relation to the texts (Sipe, 2008). Making predictions and taking agency in these ways helped the students to think about the stories and the sequences of events as they created understandings together. Becoming the characters and participating in the story worlds, children took on active roles as they made predictions and constructed meaning (Pantaleo, 2008) together while they played in response to the stories.

Scaffolding Learning and Clarifying Understandings

Children also focused on making meaning when they clarified their understandings of the stories. In the following excerpt, Alyssa (Early Reader), Carlos (Emergent Reader), and Hunter (Fluent Reader) read *Tuesday* and collaboratively construct their understandings of the story events. Alyssa becomes the illustrator and paints the illustrations on each page as Carlos and Hunter retell the story in their own words as they become the characters and play with/in the scenes.

> Carlos: (Points to the illustration depicting a Detective who is looking at the lily pads which were dropped throughout the town) Who's this guy? (As the frog Cutout)

> Hunter: Prolly a detective trying to solve floating frogs . . . floating frogs, floating out of the book, out of the book! (Using a sing-song pattern and using his hand to pretend a frog is floating out of the pages)

Here, Carlos attempts to clarify story information so as to improve his understanding. In character, Carlos asks about the person on the page and what he is doing. Hunter suggests that the character is a detective, possibly trying to solve the case of the mysterious floating frogs, demonstrating his intertextual knowledge, as he may have seen detective characters in other texts or TV shows. He shares this knowledge with Carlos, simultaneously demonstrating his story comprehension and understanding and supporting/ scaffolding Carlos' comprehension of the story events (Vygotsky, 1978). This helps Carlos to clarify his understanding and then construct story meaning. Hunter uses his imagination to pretend his hand is a frog and floats mysteriously out of the pages, extending his explanation and rejoining the responsive play frame.

Similarly, Tuan (Fluent Reader), Noah (Emergent Reader), and Diego (Early Reader) read *Creepy Carrots* and clarify their understandings as they read and play together.

Tuan: (As the rabbit) I'm running for my life!

Noah: (Low voice, as the reader) Ahhh, creepy carrots!

Tuan: (Scary voice, as a creepy carrot) Ahhh, ohhhh! Scary! Scary!

Noah: What's that?

Tuan: Those are bottles and cans.

Noah: Wait, why's he cutting the wall?

Tuan: It's so he can (inaudible) . . . so he won't fall.

Noah: He wants to be small?

Tuan: No, he doesn't want to be small; he doesn't want to get hurt from falling.

In becoming the characters in this tale through responsive play, the boys negotiate meaning and understanding. During the reading, Noah asks what some things are (in the illustration) and Tuan suggests that they are bottles and cans. Needing further explanation, Noah asks Tuan why the rabbit is cutting a hole in the wall. Tuan answers, but is misunderstood; Noah thinks that Tuan has said that it is because he wants to be small. Tuan clarifies that it is because he does not want to get hurt from falling off of the wall. Together the boys interpret the illustrations and the text and construct a mutual under-standing of the story events and then demonstrate this understanding through their imaginative retelling and their responsive play. As the children in these vignettes reinterpret the stories and create meanings and understandings together, they also build upon and practice their literacy skills and scaffold each other's learning in relation to illustrations, characters, and story events as they play in response to the books.

Analyzing Stories

While scaffolding each other's understanding, children also practiced their literacy skills by analyzing story structures and features of illustrations as they responded to and reinterpreted the books through responsive play. In this vignette, Julieta (Early Reader) and Mariana (Emergent Reader) analyze the story structure of *Tuesday* as they prepare to reinterpret the story through play. The girls decide they should act out the story after they flip through the book.

Julieta: (Picking up the book) K, let's act!

Mariana: How bout we make it from first, next, then last?

Julieta: First the guy with the sandwich.

Mariana: No, first the frogs. (Flipping to the beginning of the story to show Julieta how it begins)

Julieta: Let's use sticks to put it.

(The girls then read through the story and place the Cutouts in story sequence on the carpet to prepare for their "acting" out of the story)

Julieta: First, second . . . (Placing Cutouts in story sequence, in a line on the carpet)

Mariana: First, next (Pointing to the order and checking with the text) . . . we need the last.

Julieta: Last, pigs.

Mariana: Can we read the book first?

Julieta: Yah.

Mariana: If I need help, you're gonna help me.

Julieta: Yah.

Mariana: So all the pages that don't have words, we're gonna act it out.

(The girls then begin to read the story from the beginning and act out each page/scene/illustration using the ordered Cutouts that they prepared)

In this vignette, the girls decide to respond to the text by reinterpreting and acting out the story together. After briefly flipping through the book, they use their knowledge of story sequence and structure (first, next, last) in order to negotiate and setup their playful reenactment and retelling of the story. They analyze the text and the story sequence as they carefully read through the book together so that they can prepare and order the Character Cutouts for their eventual responsive play. This shows great planning and engagement with the text. These types of explicit negotiations, or *metaplay*—"out-of-play" talk in which children propose new ideas and/or modify/suggest modifications of their play—allows children to clarify story structure and story comprehension in relation to the sequence of events (Sawyer & DeZutter, 2009).

Metaplay, in this regard, occurred in several of the observations. This type of talk, in which the children must use language to explicitly negotiate in order to play together, has been studied in depth (Pellegrini, 1984, 1985; Pellegrini & Galda, 1993; Rowe, 1998; Sachs, Goldman, & Chaille, 1984; Williamson & Silvern, 1991). Findings of this research suggest that metaplay of this sort can often be related to story recall, story reproduction, and story comprehension (Pellegrini, 1984; Sawyer & DeZutter, 2009; Williamson & Silvern, 1991).

Retelling Stories

Owocki (1999) suggests that "dramatic retelling" is the "act of retelling a story or a part of a story using masks, costumes, puppets, props, pantomime, or language and gesture" (p. 35). In this study, children often used the Character Cutouts as a type of character representation and also utilized language and gesture to *become* characters while playing in response to books. When children transform their understandings from one sign system (written language, illustrations) to another sign system (oral language, play), they have to reorganize, rework, and recreate their conceptions about what they have read and understood (Owocki, 1999). This process allows for and facilitates children's literacy learning through *transmediation*, the process through which the expression of meanings constructed in one sign system is then represented and constructed through other sign systems (Eco, 1976; Suhor, 1984). As noted within this study, children's book-related play involves the "transmediation of the linguistic and graphic signs from the text and illustrations" (Rowe, 1998, p. 29) through their responsive play as they retell and reenact stories.

In the following excerpt, Collin (Fluent Reader), Madison (Early Reader), and Daniella (Emergent Reader) read *Tuesday*. In this vignette, Collin becomes the author and narrator and retells the story in his own words. Daniella holds the book up for Collin and turns the pages while he reads and Madison uses the various Character Cutouts to reenact the scenes on each page. Collin also intermittently uses the Cutouts to act out the scenes with Madison.

Collin: (Retelling the story) They went into a house. Now turn the page (To Daniella). And there was an old lady sleeping, and the turtles were sticking their tongues out, and changing channels. (Sticks his tongue out)

Madison: (Flying her frogs around the page) Woosh!

Daniella: It's not a turtle.

Collin: It's a toad. I'm by the old lady's face! (He becomes one of the frogs in the illustration).

Daniella: The grandma is sleeping while the frogs eat her up! (Turns page)

Collin: And the toad runs right by a dog. Then the dog was running from a bunch of toads that were smiling.

Madison: (Flying her frogs around the page as if they were being chased by the dog) Ahhhh!

Daniella: (Turns page)

Collin: And then one morning, they started running, because they were supposed to be hibernating, but in the nighttime they loved it.

Daniella: (Turns page)

Collin: And then it was morning, they were jumping so high, they were having fun. Ohhh, they went in the water, look at his legs!

Collin has taken the written texts (though this book has minimal text-it is a mainly wordless picture book) and the illustrations (linguistic and graphic signs) and reorganizes, reworks, and recreates—transmediates—the story through other sign systems (language, gesture, play) as he retells the story in his own words and cooperatively reinterprets and makes sense of it with Madison and Daniella.

As suggested by Rowe (1998), the "transmediation of meanings from books to the medium of dramatic play and back again was often a transformative experience . . . reading created new potentials for children's play" (p. 30). When children read and explore book themes and characters together and retell stories through their responsive play, new potentials for meaning construction are created (Rowe, 1998). When they engage in dramatic retellings through their responsive play, children are able to reinterpret stories, construct knowledge on a personal level, and gain new perspectives as they transform the story ideas from one sign system to another (Owocki, 1999; Short, Harste, & Burke, 1996).

Extending Stories

Within their retellings, when they revisit characters and replay story scenes (Rowe, 1998), children also extend the stories through their responsive play. In one instance, Mateo, reading *Tuesday* with Paige and Lucia, suggests that the frogs are actually "flying up to God," adding to the storyline as the group then plays out this imagined story extension. In another instance, after reading *Creepy Carrots*, Alyssa (Early Reader) and Maya (Fluent Reader) discuss and then play out an alternate ending for the story wherein the rabbit, realizing he was tricked by the creepy carrots into never going near them again, gets revenge on the carrots and eats them all.

> Alyssa: Wait . . . the end will *really* be that they were camping and then they saw the creepy carrots . . . and he gets revenge, and his revenge was to eat them! (Laughs)

> Maya: (Laughs) Yah! Revenge! (Uses the rabbit Cutout to eat the carrot Cutout) Chomp!

> Alyssa: (Laughs)

The Read and Respond Center gives children a space to imagine and play with, in, and through books. Within this space they are able to cooperatively build upon, construct, and recreate their reinterpretations and their understandings of the characters and of the stories, become those characters, and live within and through the stories as they make sense of them (Rosenblatt, 1978). Responsive play thus affords the children opportunities to "enter the story cave" (Booth, 1995, p. 31), join the story experiences as if they were happening at that moment (Enciso & Edmiston, 1997), and demonstrate their understandings and their comprehension of the characters and of the stories as they use their imaginations to extend them.

Children's book-related play allows them to sort through and sort out book meanings (Rowe, 2007). Children are able to make sense of stories, characters, and plots as they revisit, rework, and recreate them through their playful reenactments and responses. Within the responsive play framework, on the first level of understanding and interpretation, children read stories together and make sense of and interpret character motivations, plotlines, etc., as presented within the books. On the second level of understanding and interpretation, having read and interpreted the stories in order to understand what is happening, who the characters are and what they represent, etc., children collaboratively *re*interpret the stories and their meanings as they recreate and demonstrate their understandings through play. Responsive play, in this capacity, provides an arena in which the children are able to rework, and "refine their interpretations of books by revisiting and replaying scenes" (Rowe, 1998, p. 25).

CONCLUSIONS

"A child's play is not simply a reproduction of what he has experienced, but a creative reworking of the impressions he has acquired" (Vygotsky, 2004, p. 11–12). When they played and pretended with books, the children in this study translated their real world perceptions and interpretations of the characters and of the stories into the actions that defined their book-related playworlds. The children constructed and shared their understandings of the stories and the characters by making predictions, scaffolding each other's learning, clarifying their understandings of story events, making analyses of story structures, retelling stories in their own words, and extending stories, through their responsive play. This allowed them to rework various aspects of the stories and their understandings of them in order to create imaginative reinterpretations of the characters and the story events and to construct meaning together in creative, imaginative, and playful ways.

IMPLICATIONS FOR PRACTICE

Responsive Play as a Generative Source of Language and Literacy Learning

This study supports responsive play as a generative source of children's language and literacy learning. As noted in the findings, children demonstrate their sophisticated thinking about complex concepts through their responsive play. The data suggest that children's play in response to literature encourages their use of interpretative strategies and suggests that children move beyond simple comprehension and recall of story events into deeper interpretations and understandings of stories when they respond through play (Rowe, 2007). These findings further support the notions that children's play, language, and literacy are complementary and that children's responsive play should be encouraged in the classroom setting. In utilizing responsive play to practice language and literacy skills, children think about these complex tasks, build upon, and develop these skills. These language and literacy practices correlate to the many academic standards that teachers are required to (and hope to) develop in their students and that are clearly evident in the children's playful responses. As such, children's play can be directly related to their language and literacy learning, when utilized and valued in the classroom context.

For classroom teachers, these findings signal the need to reflect upon their beliefs about utilizing play in instruction and to consider that play, as the work of children (Gaskins, 2014; Paley, 2004), is essential for children's learning and development. Responsive play should be explored as a viable reading response strategy for young children as it encourages the development of their reading and interpretive strategies and promotes their language and literacy learning through cooperative discussions and meaningful responses. The findings also suggest the need to explore play as grounded in the culture of childhood and to encourage teachers, teacher educators, and early childhood researchers to consider play in the classroom context from sociocultural perspectives (Gaskins, 2014; Gonzalez, Moll, & Amanti, 2005). Spaces for this type of learning should be opened up in classrooms for young children as valid routes to learning and understanding.

LIMITATIONS

As the findings of this study are based solely on one first-grade classroom, more extended investigations in various contexts and settings are necessary. Findings suggest that utilizing a longitudinal approach to extend the timeline of this research and to explore children's responsive play in various grade levels, with children of varying reading levels, within various reader pairings/groupings, with bi- and multilingual children, and with children from various backgrounds could reveal new information about the ways in which children connect play, language, and literacy and respond to texts through play in the classroom context. Further investigations could also explore children's responsive play in out-of-school settings.

It should further be noted that as children played in the Read and Respond Center, there were instances in which their talk and play were *not* focused on the book. Since these instances were very rare, they were not included in the findings or discussion presented in this chapter. As these occurrences might shed light on how responsive play might realistically work in a classroom setting, it is important to note these instances, however few, and to suggest that children's "off-task" play behaviors within the responsive play framework be further analyzed.

Responsive play affords children opportunities to improvise, to explore the ambiguities and the possibilities of each story and of each play world that they create as they respond to stories (Wolf, Edmiston, & Enciso, 1997), and gives children opportunities to move beyond simple interpretations and reenactments of stories and to move into more critical reflections and interpretations of texts. This study contributes to the limited research available on children's responsive play in the classroom context and demonstrates the importance of providing children opportunities to respond to stories through play. The findings provide a framework from which educators and teacher educators can draw as they support young children to learn in the way they know best, through play.

REFERENCES

Adomat, D. S. (2009). Actively engaging with stories through drama: Portraits of two young readers. *The Reading Teacher, 62*(8), 628–636.

Adomat, D. S. (2012). Becoming characters: deepening young children's literary understanding through drama. *Journal of Children's Literature, 38*(1), 44–51.

Bakhtin, M. M. (1986). *Speech genres and other late essays* (V. W. McGee, Trans.). Austin, TX: University of Texas Press.

Bergen, D., & Mauer, D. (2000). Symbolic play, phonological awareness, and literacy skills at three age levels. In K. A. Roskos & J. F. Christie (Eds.), *Play and literacy in early childhood: Research from multiple perspectives* (pp. 45–62). New York, NY: Erlbaum.

Bodrova, E. (2008). Make-believe play versus academic skills: A Vygotskian approach to today's dilemma of early childhood education. *European Early Childhood Education Research Journal, 16*(3), 357–369.

Bodrova, E., & Leong, D.J. (2007). *Tools of the mind: The Vygotskian approach to early childhood education.* Upper Saddle River, NJ: Pearson.

Booth, D. (1995) *Storydrama.* Markham, ON: Pembroke Publishers.

Bruner, J. (1990) *Acts of meaning.* Cambridge, MA: Harvard University Press.

Christie, J. F., & Roskos, K. A. (2013). Play's potential in early literacy development. Retrieved from http://www.child-encyclopedia.com/sites/default/files/textes-experts/en/774/plays-potential-in-early-literacy-development.pdf.

Corsaro, W. A. (2003). *We're friends, right? Inside kids' culture.* Washington, DC: Joseph Henry Press.

Eco, U. (1976). *A theory of semiotics.* Bloomington, IN: Indiana University Press.

Edmiston, B. (1993). Going up the beanstalk: Discovering giant possibilities for responding to literature through drama. In R. Hungerford & K. Holland (Eds.), *Journeying: Children responding to literature* (pp. 250–266). Portsmouth, NH: Heinemann.

Edmiston (Enciso), P. (1990). *The nature of engagement in reading: Profiles of three fifth graders' engagement strategies and stances.* Unpublished doctoral dissertation, Ohio State University, Columbus, OH. Retrieved from https://etd.ohiolink.edu/!etd.send_file?accession=osu1487684245466824&disposition=inline.

Einarsdottir, J. (2000). Incorporating literacy resources into the play curriculum of two Icelandic preschools. In K. A. Roskos & J. F. Christie (Eds.), *Play and literacy in early childhood: Research from multiple perspectives* (pp. 77–90). New York, NY: Erlbaum.

Enciso, P., & Edmiston, B. (1997). Drama and response to literature: Reading the story, re-reading "the Truth." In N. J. Karolides (Ed.), *Reader response in elementary classrooms: Quest and discovery* (pp. 69–94). Mahwah, NJ: Lawrence Erlbaum Associates, Publishers.

Evans, J. (2012) "This is me": Developing literacy and a sense of self through play, talk and stories. *Education 3–13: International Journal of Primary, Elementary and Early Years Education, 40*(3), 315–331.

Flint, T. K. (2010). Making meaning together: Buddy reading in a first grade classroom. *Early Childhood Education Journal, 38*(4), 289–297.

Flint T. K. (2016). *Responsive play: Exploring play as reader response in a first grade classroom.* Published doctoral dissertation, The University of Arizona, Tucson, AZ.

Flint, T. K. (2018). Responsive play: Creating transformative classroom spaces through play as reader response. *Journal of Early Childhood Literacy.* Advanced online publication. https://doi.org/10.1177/1468798418763991.

Flint, T. K., & Adams, M. (2018). "It's like playing, but learning": Supporting early literacy development through responsive play with wordless picturebooks. *Language Arts, 96*(1), 21–36.

Gaskins, S. (2014). Children's play as cultural activity. In L. Brooker, M. Glaise, & S. Edwards (Eds.), *The Sage handbook of play and learning in early childhood* (pp. 31–42). London, England: SAGE.

Glaser, B., & Strauss, A. (1967). *Discovery of grounded theory: Strategies for Qualitative Research*. Chicago, IL: Aldine Publishing.

Glesne, C. (2011). *Becoming qualitative researchers: An introduction* (4th ed.). Boston, MA: Pearson Education, Inc.

Gonzalez, N., Moll, L. C., & Amanti, C. (2005). *Funds of knowledge: Theorizing practices in households, communities, and classrooms.* New York, NY: Routledge, Taylor & Francis Group.

Heath, S. B. (1983). *Ways with words: Language, life, and work in communities and class-rooms.* Cambridge, MA: Cambridge University Press.

Kendrick, M. (2005) Playing house: A "sideways" glance at literacy and identity in early childhood. *Journal of Early Childhood Literacy, 5,* 5–28.

Kress, G. (1998). *Before writing: Rethinking the paths to literacy.* London, England: Routledge.

Kress, G. (2003). *Literacy in the new media age.* London, England: Routledge.

Kress, G. (2009). *Multimodality: A social semiotic approach to contemporary communication.* New York, NY: Routledge.

Mandel Morrow, L., Berkule, S. B., Medelsohn, A. L., Healey, K. M., & Cates, C. B. Learning through play. (2013). In D. R. Reutzel (Ed.), *Handbook of research based practice in early education* (pp.100–118). New York, NY: The Guilford Press.

Martinez, M., Cheyney, M., & Teale, W. (1991). Classroom literature activities and kindergart-eners' dramatic story reenactments. In J. Christie (Ed.), *Play and early literacy development* (pp.119–140). Albany, NY: State University of New York Press.

Miller, P. J., & Goodnow, J. J. (1995). Cultural practices: Toward an integration of culture and development. In J. J. Goodnow, P. J. Miller, & F. Kessel (Eds.), *Cultural practices as contexts for development* (pp. 5–16). San Francisco, CA: Jossey-Bass.

Morrow, L., Rand, M. (1991). Preparing the classroom environment to promote literacy during play. In J. Christie (Ed.), *Play and early literacy development* (pp. 41–165). Albany, NY: Statue University of New York Press.

Munsch, R. N., Martchenko, M., & Dann, S. (1980). *The paper bag princess.* Toronto: Annick Press.

Neuman, S. B. & Roskos, K. (1997). Literacy knowledge in practice: Contexts of participation for young writers and readers. *Reading Research Quarterly, 32*(1), 10–32.

Owocki, G. (1999). *Literacy through play.* Westport, CT: Heinemann.

Paley, V. G. (2004). *A child's work: The importance of fantasy play.* Chicago, IL: University of Chicago Press.

Pantaleo, S. (2008). *Exploring student response to contemporary picturebooks.* Toronto, Canada: University of Toronto Press.

Pellegrini, A. D. (1984). Identifying causal elements in the thematic-fantasy play paradigm. *American Educational Research Journal, 21*(3), 691–701.

Pellegrini, A. D. (1985). Relations between preschool children's symbolic play and literate behavior. In L. Galda & A. D. Pellegrini (Eds.), *Play, language, and stories: The development of literate behavior* (pp. 79–97). Norwood, NJ: Ablex Publishing Corp.

Pellegrini, A. D., & Galda, L. (1993). Ten years after: A reexamination of symbolic play and literacy research. *Reading Research Quarterly, 28*(2), 162–175.

Pellegrini, A. D., Galda, L., Dresden, J., & Cox, S. (1991). A longitudinal study of the predictive relations among symbolic play, linguistic verbs, and early literacy. *Research in Teaching of English, 25*(2), 219–235.

Reynolds, A., & Brown, P. (2012). *Creepy carrots.* New York, NY: Simon and Schuster.

Riojas-Cortez, M. (2001). Preschoolers' funds of knowledge displayed through sociodramatic play episodes in a bilingual classroom. *Early Childhood Education Journal, 29*(1), 35–40.

Rosenblatt, L. M. (1938). *Literature as exploration.* New York, NY: Modern Language Association of America.

Rosenblatt, L. M. (1978). *The reader, the text, the poem: The transactional theory of the literary work.* Chicago, IL: SIU Press.

Rosenblatt, L.M. (2001). The literary transaction: Evocation and response. *Theory into Practice, 21*(4), 268–277.

Rowe, D. W. (1998). The literate potentials of book-related dramatic play. *Reading Research Quarterly, 33*(1), 10–35.

Rowe, D. W. (2007). Bringing books to life: The role of book-related dramatic play in young children's literacy learning. In K. Roskos & J. Christie (Eds.), *Play and literacy in early childhood: Research from multiple perspectives* (2nd ed.) (pp. 37– 63). New York, NY: Lawrence Erlbaum Associates: Taylor & Francis Group.

Sachs, J., Goldman, J., & Chaille, C. (1984). Planning in pretend play: Using language to coordinate narrative development. In A. D. Pellegrini & T. D. Yawkey (Eds.), *The development of oral and written language in social contexts* (pp. 119–128). Norwood, NJ: Ablex.

Saracho, O. N. (2002). Young children's literacy development. In O. N. Saracho & B. Spodek (Eds.), *Contemporary perspectives on early childhood curriculum* (Vol. 1) (pp. 111–130). Greenwich, CT: Information Age Publishing.

Saracho, O. N. (2003) Young children's play and cognitive style. In O. N. Saracho & B. Spodek (Eds.), *Contemporary perspectives on play in early childhood* (Vol. 3) (pp. 75–96). Greenwich, CT: Information Age Publishing.

Saracho, O. N. & Spodek, B. (1998). A play foundation for family literacy. *International Journal of Educational Research, 29*(1), 41–50.

Saracho, O. N., & Spodek, B. (2006). Young children's literacy-related play. *Early Child Development and Care,* 176(7), 707–721.

Sawyer, R. K., & DeZutter, S. (2009). Improvisation: A lens for play and literacy research. In K. Roskos & J. Christie (Eds.), *Play and literacy in early childhood: Research from multiple perspectives* (2nd ed.) (pp. 21–36). New York, NY: Lawrence Erlbaum Associates: Taylor & Francis Group.

Short, K. G., Harste, J., & Burke, C. (1996). *Creating classrooms for authors and inquirers.* Portsmouth, NH: Heinemann.

Short, K. G., Lynch-Brown, C., & Tomlinson, C. M. (2014). *Essentials of children's literature* (8th ed.). Upper Saddle River, NJ: Pearson.

Sipe, L. R. (2008). *Storytime: Young children's literary understanding in the classroom.* New York, NY: Teachers College Press.

Strickland, D. & Morrow, L. (1989). Environments rich in print promote literacy behavior during play. *The Reading Teacher,* 43, 178–179.

Suhor, C. (1984). Towards a semiotic-based curriculum. *Journal of Curriculum Studies,* 16(3), 247–257.

Vukelich, C. (1991). Learning about the functions of writing: The effects of three play interventions on children's development and knowledge about writing. Paper presented at: *The 41st Annual Meeting of the National Reading Conference.* Palm Springs, CA.

Vukelich, C. (1994.) Effects of play interventions on young children's reading of environmental print. *Early Childhood Research Quarterly,* 9(2), 153–170.

Vygotsky, L. S. (1978). *Mind in society: The development of higher psychological processes.* Cambridge, MA: Harvard University Press.

Vygotsky, L. S. (2004). Imagination and Creativity in Childhood. *Journal of Russian and East European Psychology,* 423(1), 7–97.

Wiesner, D. (1991). *Tuesday.* New York, NY: Houghton Mifflin Harcourt.

Williamson, P. A., & Silvern, S. B. (1991). Thematic-fantasy play and story comprehension. In J. F. Christie (Ed.), *Play and early literacy development* (pp. 69–90). Albany, NY: State University of New York Press.

Wohlwend, K. E. (2009). Early adopters: Playing new literacies and pretending new technologies in print-centric classrooms. *Journal of Early Childhood Literacy,* 9(2), 117–140.

Wohlwend, K. E. (2011). *Playing their way into literacies: Reading, writing, and belonging in the early childhood classroom.* New York, NY: Teachers College Press.

Wohlwend, K. (2013a). *Literacy playshop: New literacies, popular media, and play in the early childhood classroom.* New York, NY: Teachers College Press.

Wohlwend, K. (2013b). Play, literacies, and the converging cultures of childhood. In J. Larson and J. Marsh (Eds.), *The SAGE handbook of early childhood literacy* (pp. 80–110). London, England: SAGE.

Wolf, S., Edmiston, B., & Enciso, P. (1997). Drama worlds: Places of the heart, head, voice, and hand in dramatic interpretation. In J. Flood, S. B. Heath, & D. Lapp (Eds.), *Handbook of research on teaching literacy through the communicative and visual arts* (pp. 474–487). New York: Macmillan.

Part III

Classroom Dynamics

Chapter Six

Play and Emerging Literacy

A Comparative Analysis of Kindergarten and Mixed-Age (K–2) Children's Scaffolding During Symbolic Play Transformations

Sandra J. Stone and Brian A. Stone

INTRODUCTION

In our current educational system children are segregated by age as an efficient way to deliver a sequential curriculum by grade. That withstanding, early childhood advocates recommend play environments for all early childhood classrooms whether populated by children of same- or mixed- ages. In play contexts research suggests that mixed-age groupings of children benefit all children cognitively, socially, and emotionally due to the developmental differences and the nature of expert/novice scaffolding, which expanded age differences provide (Gray, 2013; Stone & Burriss, 2019). This chapter discusses a study that highlights the scaffolding that occurred in a mixed-age classroom and in a kindergarten classroom of same-age children with a focus on symbolic play transformations as a precursor to emerging literacy. A primary mixed-age classroom of five-, six-, and seven-year-olds was compared with a kindergarten classroom of five-year-olds. The same-age grouping was a group of kindergarteners who played with their same-age peers in the context of a kindergarten classroom. The mixed-age grouping consisted of kindergarteners, first graders, and second graders in a mixed-age classroom. An additional focus of the study was on the two sets of kindergarteners: those mixed with the older children in the K–2 classroom versus those who played with only same-age peers in the kindergarten classroom.

Symbolic play collaboration among children in same-age and mixed-age groupings results in engagement in both groupings. However, this study demonstrates that symbolic play when it occurs in mixed-age groupings provides more opportunities for children of all ages in the grouping to engage broadly across three types of symbolic play. This is surmised to be due to the presence of expanded age differences, which affords greater opportunity for more direct scaffolding of younger children's play by older children, more so than in a same-age grouping with limited age difference. This study highlights the benefit of mixed-age groupings (K–2) over a same-age grouping (K) as it relates to the social nature of learning through scaffolding in the area of symbolic play transformations. In addition to exploring the benefits of mixed-age groupings, this study also considered the symbolic play transformations and scaffolding of the same-age kindergarten group in comparison to the kindergarten children in a mixed-age group of five-, six-, and seven-year-olds. Data on responses to scaffolding are also reported and discussed as important classroom dynamics in support of quality symbolic play as factors that promote literacy during the early years.

THEORETICAL FRAMEWORK

Theoretical and research evidence for the benefits of multiage groupings have been reported over the years (Goodlad & Anderson, 1987; Gray, 2011, 2013; Katz, Evangelou & Hartman, 1993; Rooparine & Johnson, 1983; Stone, 2004, 2010, 2017; Stone & Burriss, 2019; Stone & Stone, 2018). The benefits of mixed ages include all areas of whole child development: social, cognitive, emotional, moral, physical, and aesthetic (Stone & Burriss, 2019; Stone & Stone, 2018). Gray (2013) believes that we deprive children of "powerful learning opportunities" when "we segregate children by age, in school . . ." (p. 204).

Advocates of mixed-age groupings assume that the younger children benefit from the older children's scaffolding. Vygotsky (1976) envisioned a "zone of proximal development," the distance between the child's actual and potential development in which adults or more capable peers can enhance this zone. In the context of social interactions, adults or more capable peers can "stimulate the children to use more sophisticated approaches to tasks . . . through the process of 'scaffolding'" (Meltzer, 1991, p. 179). "Experts" can provide more sophisticated approaches causing "novices" to consider other possibilities simply by modeling, directing, questioning, and scaffolding during collaboration (Stone & Burriss, 2019).

Based on Vygotsky's "zone of proximal development" (1978), Christie and Stone (1999) envisioned the zone for literacy development as a place where a child will use an emerging literacy skill "only with the help of others . . . If temporary assistance of scaffolding is provided, the child is able to engage in literacy activities that he or she could not do alone. This, in turn, extends the child's knowledge and skills to higher levels" (p. 110). Differences in cognitive maturity levels invite, compel, and challenge children to consider different perspectives as mixed-age children interact socially in play. Also, in understanding the nature of scaffolding, expert and novice roles are not firmly set and the zone varies according to each child's needs, interests and developmental levels; however, previous research has indicated that mixed-ages provide greater differences in perspectives than do same-age groupings, enhancing the expert and novice relationship (Christie & Stone, 1999; Goldman, 1981; Stone & Stone, 2017, 2018).

For example, researchers have found that the "scaffolding" process, through social interactions or collaboration, significantly impacts the child's problem-solving ability (Tudge & Caruso, 1988). Other studies (Christie & Stone, 1999; Stone & Christie, 1996) have shown that in collaborative learning opportunities with older students, kindergartners in the mixed-age classroom engaged in proportionately more literacy activity than their counterparts did in the same-age kindergarten. Multiage groupings have also resulted in more complex fantasy narratives than have resulted in same-age kindergarten groupings, and without compromising the quality of the play (Christie, Stone, & Deutscher, 2002). Combining "experts" in symbolic transformations with "novices" broadens the possibilities of novices' engaging in symbolic play as experts scaffold for novices (Stone & Stone, 2017, 2018).

Symbolic play, one of the most significant cognitive developments of young children, signals the development of representational thought in that the child is now able to represent objects and events *symbolically* (Gardner, 1979; Pellegrini, 1985). Abstract thought is developed through the process of representation. Symbolic play begins to emerge at 18 months and starts to decline around age six years (Johnson, Christie, & Wardle, 2005; Kelly & Hammond, 2011). As five- and six-year-olds are most often emerging into literacy at these ages, symbolic play is a critical foundational function to this process. Both literacy and symbolic play require the "ability to use words, gestures or mental images to represent actual objects, events or actions" (Isenberg & Jacobs, 1983, p. 272). Symbolic play provides a foundation for emerging literacy development with symbolic play being first-order symbolism and literacy (reading and writing) being second order symbolism (Vygotsky, 1976, 1978). The mental process is similar for both orders (Stone & Stone, 2015). Five-year-olds, in particular, benefit from becoming "fluent," so to speak, in symbolic play transformations as they engage in transformations scaffolded by experts who are older, ages six and seven. Children progress in representing the world abstractly through play as a block "stands for" a car, a child "stands for" a character such as "mom," or a gesture or word (s) "stands for" an object or event such as "we are driving to a pizza place." As Stone & Stone (2015) suggest, "Without abstract thought, children would not be able to represent the world symbolically such as using drawings for objects, letters for sounds, or multiple letters for words" (p. 5). Without abstract thought, developed naturally through symbolic play, children would not be able to become literate. Thus, symbolic play is critical to the development of emerging literacy in young children (Isenberg & Jacobs, 1983; Schrader, 1990; Stone & Burriss, 2016).

Research (Frey & Kaiser, 2011) has shown that adults engaged in the play of children with disabilities can increase the diversity and complexity of symbolic object play. Children can also play a crucial role in enhancing symbolic representations for one another by collaborating with their peers within their zones of proximal development (Broadhead, 2006).

Recent research has investigated the types and effects of scaffolding of symbolic play transformations used by children in informal, kindergarten play groups (Stone & Stone, 2015). Stone and Stone (2015) found that kindergarteners scaffold symbolic play for one another through collaboration within the social context of play. Research to date has not been conducted comparing the scaffolding of symbolic play transformations of same-age kindergarten with mixed-age (K–2) groupings.

The purpose of this study is to investigate the relation of the social context (same-age kindergarten children to mixed-age children K–2), to the amount and types of scaffolding of three types of symbolic transformations. The aim is to see if enhancing the expert/novice relationship through the presence of more age differences impacts play engagement. In addition, other comparisons between the kindergarteners in the same-age grouping and the kindergarteners in mixed-age grouping are made, including kinds of scaffolding behaviors and responses to scaffolding behaviors.

The three types of symbolic transformations are: (1) *Object transformations* where a child imagines properties or gives identities to objects; (2) *Roles*: functional, relational, character, and peripheral; and (3) *Ideational* where the child uses language, gestures or mental images (independent of objects) to create the fantasy (Copple, Cocking, & Matthews, 1984; Elder & Pederson, 1978; Shotwell, Wolf, & Gardner, 1979; Watson & Jackowitz, 1984). Ideational transformations are the most complex of the three types of transformations, because this transformation requires that the child represent objects and events *symbolically* without a concrete object or role to "stand for" a fantasy (Stone & Stone, 2015). As Stone and Burriss (2016) note, "The thought represented in the brain can stand alone without the support of a substitute object" (p. 61).

This study addressed the following questions:

1. Does the age difference, a proxy for expert versus novice, in mixed-age groupings (K–2) within an informal classroom play context, in this case the home center, provide more social opportunities for children to use symbolic play transformations than do the same-age kindergarten groupings?
2. Do Mixed-age (K–2) children scaffold more during the symbolic play transformations for one another than do same-age kindergarten children?
3. What types and amounts of scaffolding are used by mixed-age children in comparison to same-age kindergarten children during symbolic play transformations?
4. What are the outcomes of the scaffolding types used by both groupings?

METHODS

This descriptive mixed-methods study used quantitative methods to gather, process and analyze the data (Creswell & Creswell, 2018). Qualitative aspects of the methodology included obtaining the data through observations of children's play captured by video, transcription of the video observations, and analyzing the transcribed data by identifying particular themes as both researchers interpreted the meaning of the data (Bogdan & Biklen, 2016; Creswell & Creswell, 2018). The first principal investigator completed the coding in agreement with the second investigator. The quantitative aspect included arranging the observations numerically to identify trends and then using percentages for comparing trends within both groupings; and this was done by both investigators.

DATA SOURCE

The mixed-age classroom included 10 kindergarteners (5 female, 5 male), seven first graders (3 female, 4 male) and 10 second graders (7 female, 3 male). The same-age kindergarten grouping was composed of 22 children (10 male, 12 female). The children in both groupings were from low-income families, representing diverse ethnic backgrounds, including Anglo, Hispanic, Indian, Native American, African American and Pacific Islander. The teacher was an experienced teacher (18 years) who had taught in self-contained kindergarten and primary grade classrooms before teaching in the primary multiage classroom (Christie & Stone, 1999; Stone & Christie, 1996).

Due to a change in the school personnel and programs, the mixed-age teacher moved to a kindergarten program the following year but used her same classroom with the exact room arrangement and educational strategies for both groupings. The primary mixed-age classroom was observed the first year of the study and then compared with the same-age kindergarten classroom the second year. The language arts approach of these classrooms used shared book, modeled writing, and guided reading strategies for literacy. Daily, open-ended play, approximately one -hour choice centers, including the home center option, were provided for the children when they were not engaged in small group guided reading.

For both groupings, the home center contained play furniture, books, writing materials, and domestic props. Fifteen hours of free play for each grouping was videoed over a period of four weeks during April and May for the two-year study. The camera was positioned so that it only covered the home center. A detailed transcript was made of the action and dialogue that occurred in the home center during each session for both groupings.

Symbolic transformations for each grouping were coded by social context (solitary, parallel or collaborative). Next, the transcripts were studied, organized, and then analyzed for the three types of symbolic transformations (roles, object, ideational). As children scaffolded transformations for one another, scaffolding categories were identified. Two researchers examined relationships among the coding variables and refined the coding categories. The data were then sorted in order to determine frequency counts for the different coding categories and to search for relationships between categories. The data from the frequency counts assisted in determining trends in each grouping.

RESULTS

Composition of Play Groups

For this study, 10 mixed-age and 10 same-grade kindergarten play groups were randomly selected from a total of 40 play groups in each classroom with the criteria that each play group contained three to four children and each mixed-age play group contained at least one kindergartener, first grader, and second grader. In both groupings, the children chose which play center in which they wanted to participate; thus, the play groups in the home center were determined by participation of the children, and not controlled by the teachers or researchers. Since the play groups varied by children's choices, play groups varied with respect to how much participants played together over time. When play members of a given group changed, a new playgroup was designated. Only the playgroups in the home center were observed in this study.

Social Context

Symbolic transformations occurred in three social contexts:

1. Solitary –conducted independently of other children.
2. Parallel—conducted jointly with one or more other peers but no help is given.
3. Collaborative—conducted with other peers; help given.

The table 6.1 reports the frequency of social context where symbolic transformation occurred in each group.

For mixed-ages, collaborative play (667 events) was by far the most common context for symbolic transformations, about 84%. About 10% of the symbolic transformations occurred in parallel situations. Solitary symbolic transformations were minimal at 6%.

For same-age kindergarten, collaborative play (630 events) was also the most common context for symbolic transformations, about 85%. 13% of the symbolic transformations took place in parallel play. Solitary symbolic transformations were minimal at 2% (Stone & Stone, 2015).

Both groupings were similar in all areas of percentages for trends in social context, highlighting the commonality of children choosing to play with each other regardless of same-age or mixed-age groupings. The preference for collaborative play by children was predictable but yet remarkable to see, within the framework of symbolic transformations.

Symbolic Transformations

Symbolic Transformations were categorized as *Object*, *Role*, or *Ideational* with the following definitions:

1. *Object Transformation*: Transforming an object into another object.
2. *Role Transformation*: Transforming him or herself into another character.

Table 6.1. Frequency of Social Context for Symbolic Transformation

Play Groups	Solitary	Parallel	Collaborative
Same-Age Kindergarten (10 groups)	13	101	630
Mixed-Ages (10 groups)	45	79	667

3. *Ideational Transformation*: Using language, gestures, or mental images (independent of objects) to create the pretend play.

Table 6.2 shows the frequency of types of symbolic transformation in the
Mixed-age groups and the Same-age Kindergarten group.

There were 992 symbolic transformations in the 10 Mixed-age grouping.
Object Transformations accounted for 450 events, approximately 45%. *Role
Transformations* consisted of 153 events, approximately 15%. *Ideational
Transformations* occurred 389 times, approximately 40%. Percentages of
trends *within groups* were used as comparisons. Particularly, for example,
kindergarteners in each group varied in number: 3–4 children in each K play
group, whereas there were only 1–2 kindergarteners in each mixed-age play
group.

There were 739 symbolic transformations in the 10 same-age kindergart-
en playgroups. *Object Transformations* (494) were the most common for the
kindergartners, accounting for 67% of the transformations. *Role and Ideational Transformations* were comparable with 17% for roles and 16% for
ideational (Stone & Stone, 2015).

Comparing the trends in both groupings, there were more *Object Transformations* in the same-age kindergarten grouping (65%) than in the mixed-
age grouping (45%). There was minimal difference in *Role Transformations*
(kindergarten—17%; mixed-ages—15%). However, there was a greater difference in *Ideational Transformations* in the Mixed-age grouping (40%)
compared to the same-age kindergarten grouping (16%).

**Table 6.2. Frequency of Types of Symbolic Transformation in Mixed-Age
Groups and Same-Age K groups**

Play Groups (N)	Object Transformation	Role Transformation	Ideational Transformation	Total
Mixed Age Grouping (10)				
KDG	165	32	18	215
1 grade	123	40	76	239
2 grade	162	81	295	538
Mixed-Age Group				
Total	**450**	**153**	**389**	**992**
Same-Age KDG (10)	**494**	**129**	**116**	**739**

Mixed-ages

Results of mixed-age players who *initially* engaged in or scaffolded the three types of play transformations are shown in Table 6.2. For object play, kindergarteners engaged in and/or scaffolded at a score of 37% (165), first graders engaged in and/or scaffolded at a score of 27% (123), and second graders engaged in and/or scaffolded at a score of 36% (162). Role play transformations were engaged in and/or scaffolded by kindergarteners at a score of 21% (32), first graders at a score of 26% (40), and second graders at a score of 53% (81). Ideational play transformations were engaged in and/or scaffolded by kindergarteners at a score of 5% (18), first graders at a score of 19% (76), and second graders at a score of 76% (295).

Object play was mostly shared by all three age levels (37%, 27%, 36%). Second graders were the primary engagers and/or scaffolders of the role play at a score of 53% with kindergartens and first graders sharing the balance of engaging/scaffolding roles (21%, 26%). However, second graders were dominant in engaging/scaffolding Ideational transformations at a score of 76% with first graders with a 19% score and kindergarteners at 5%.

Object Transformation is demonstrated in the following script from the mixed-age grouping. Ginger (2), Joe (1), and Ashley (K) are pretending to cook dinner at the home center. Ginger (2) is transforming a book (object) into a "recipe" book for Joe (1). Together they check the book and add pretend ingredients into a pot. All three children are working together in "object transformations" to prepare dinner.

> Ginger (2): I found it [referring to the recipe from the transformed reading book—sharing the book with Joe (1)].
>
> Ashley (K): Here's the butter bowl (plastic dish).
>
> Ginger (2): We need a big bar (butter) (to Joe). Where's that butter thing? [Ashley (K) points to the refrigerator and Ginger (2) gets the big bar (pretend butter)].

Ginger (2) is *modeling* reading the recipe book with Joe (1), Ashley (K) is *assisting* Ginger (2) and Joe (1) with the butter bowl and butter for the recipe. All are *engaged* in several object transformations. The children transform objects including a book, a plastic dish, and a bar into a recipe book, a butter bowl, and butter. *Modeling* and *assisting* were the scaffolding strategies used in this example.

Role Transformation is indicated in the following script. Ginger (2), Joe (1), and Ashley (K) begin setting up play in the home center. Ginger (2) puts on an apron, Ashley (K) goes to the cupboard, and Joe (1) helps Ginger (2) with her apron.

Ginger (2): [to Joe (1)] I'm the Momma; you're the Daddy. Ashley, do you want to be the Mom?

Ginger (2) assumes the role of mother, *directs* Joe (1) to be the Dad, and *invites* Ashley (K) to also be a Mom. Joe (1) *engages* in being the Dad by putting on a hat. Ashley, as a mom, gets things from the cupboard and takes care of the baby. All children *engage* in the "role" transformations, transforming themselves into the roles of mom, dad, and another mom. In this example, *directing* and *inviting* are the scaffolding strategies used by the seven-year-old *directing* a six-year-old and *inviting* a kindergartener to engage in role transformations.

Ideational Transformation occurs when Kristy (2), Amy (2), Ashley (K) and Cecilia (1) are pretending to drive to purchase pizza. They use language (independent of objects) to create the pretend play.

Kristy (2): So where we gonna go first?

Amy (2): Chuck E. Cheese

Kristy (2): So let's go.

Ashley (K): I'm gonna stay home in the bed.

Kristy (2): I'm driving the car.

Cecilia (1): I'm drivin'.

Amy (2): "Brian" is driving (made-up person).

Kristy (2): OK. OK (to Cecilia).

Cecilia (1): Who's that?

Kristy (2): He's your husband.

Kristy (2) is *inviting* Amy (2) to go on the trip and *directing* Amy (2) and Cecilia (1) that they are driving to a pizza place. Kristy is *informing* them that she is driving. Cecilia (1) then *informs* them that she is driving; but Amy (2) makes the final decision by *informing* them that Brian (made-up person) is driving. All are *engaged*, including Ashley (K) who joins the cross-age peer conversation by saying she is staying home. Three scaffolding strategies were used in this example: *Inviting, directing* and *informing*. Kristy (2), a seven-year-old is the primary scaffolder in this event, followed by Amy (2).

Same-Age Kindergarten

Object Transformation in the same-age Kindergarten grouping is demonstrated in the following script (Stone & Stone, 2015, p. 8).

Renee: Put your real gloves on.

Nina: Where are they?

Renee: I'll go get them.

(Renee traces around Nina's hand to transform paper into a paper glove.)

In this transformation, Renee uses the *Directing* strategy and the outcome
is *Engagement*.

Role Transformation, demonstrated by Shauna, Renee, Justine, and Nina,
occurs as they play doctor (Stone & Stone, 2015, p. 8). Renee *directs* Shauna
to be a daughter, not an uncle. Nina *negotiates* she is the doctor, not a mom.
Renee *directs* Shauna to be Justine's daughter. The strategies of *directing*
and *negotiating* produce the outcome of *Engagement*.

Renee: Tell your mom (to Shauna) that you have to take (a pill). Shauna,
you're not her uncle . . . And I'm sick. Tell your mom (to Nina) that you
have to take (a pill).

Nina: No, I'm a doctor (identifying herself as the doctor, not the daughter).

Renee: OK . . . Shauna, act like you're Justine's daughter.

Ideational Transformation takes place when Danny has the idea of "moving." Without using objects or activities, Danny *directs* Shauna and Holly to
pretend like they are moving. Shauna *engages* with the idea, but Holly did
not at first and then changes her mind (Stone & Stone, 2015, p. 8).

Shauna: I'm Holly's kitty cat.

Danny: And act like we moved.

Holly: You're our cat!

Danny: And act like we moved. Holly! And act like we moved.

Holly: No, I said, "No."

Danny: Can we move? Because, because I said so.

Holly: No.

Danny: Fine, then me and my kitty cat are moving!

Holly: OK.

In the three examples, same-age Kindergarteners used *directing* and *negotiating* to engage one another in symbolic play.

SCAFFOLDING TYPES

All symbolic transformations were analyzed for the types and amount of scaffolding. The mixed-age grouping used five different types of scaffolding to help peers engage in symbolic transformations (ST).

1. Modeling—demonstrating a ST for a peer with words or actions.
2. Inviting—asking a peer to join in a ST.
3. Assisting—helping a peer to engage in a ST.
4. Directing—telling a peer to engage in a ST.
5. Informing—telling a peer about a ST.

The same-age Kindergarten children also used the above five different types of scaffolding, but used *Negotiating* in place of the *Informing* strategy that was used by the Mixed-age grouping. *Negotiating* was defined as attempting to establish agreement with a peer on a symbolic transformation.

Examples of Mixed-age (K–1–2) scaffolding and outcomes include the following:

Modeling (K–1–2)

David (2): Here, Crystal [*modeling* for Crystal (1) as he gives her the phone, that the call is for her].

Amy (2): Give me that. It's your father, David [Amy (2) gives the phone to David. Crystal *observes*].

Inviting (K–1–2)

Mazen (K): Would you like to order something? [Holding a pad of paper and *inviting* Joshua (1) and David (2) to order food at the table in a pretend restaurant. Both boys *decline*.]

Assisting (K–1–2)

Ginger (2): Stephen, you're the little boy. We're going out for pizza, maybe.

Stephen (1): OK [Ginger (2) *assists* him to put on the play suit jacket]. What am I going to do? Can I go with you? [Stephen (1) *engages* in the play.]

Directing (K–1–2)

Ginger (2): OK. Mama, set the table. [Ginger (2) *directs* Ashley (K) to set the table. Ashley (K) *engages* in setting the table.]

Informing (K–1–2)

Ginger (2): [Ginger (2) *informs* Jessica (K)] She's my mother [referring to Cecilia (1)].

Jessica (K): She can be mine too. We can pretend that we are twins [Jessica (K) *engages*].

Examples of same-age kindergarten (K) scaffolding include the following:

Modeling (K)

Brittany (K): This is my room [picking up book from the floor, sits down by crib and looks at book, *modeling* her room transformation].

Frances (K): [Frances *observes* as Brittany transforms the play center into her own room.]

Inviting (K)

Danny (K): Christian, how 'bout if we be two dads and two moms? [*inviting* Christian to be one of the dads].

Christian (K): No way! [Christian *ignores* the invitation.]

Assisting (K)

Cassie (K): Oh! [as she *assists* Renee to fix the shawl as a place for the baby.]

Renee (K): Cassie, I have to hold this like this [holding a pad above the highchair near the wall].

Cassie (K): OK. [Cassie continues to fix the area under the shawl and Renee *engages* by moving the shawl back and forth playing with it.]

Directing (K)

Christian (K): [handing a pretend dollar to Brittany] Here is a dollar. Gimme a sandwich; a hamburger [*Directing* Brittany to give him a pretend hamburger.]

Brittany: It isn't a hamburger. It's a cookie [Brittany *engages*, but identifies her pretend food as a cookie].

Negotiating (K)

Danny: Here is the money.

Holly: OK. Fix the jacket?

Danny: No. Here's the money. And here's the change.

Holly: For the jacket?

Danny: [handing the money to Holly] I want the suitcase. [Holly is *negotiating* with Danny to fix or buy the jacket, but he decides on buying the suitcase instead. Danny *engages* in the play.]

The examples from both groupings demonstrate how scaffolding for one another is a common course of play. Players scaffold for one another to keep the play going for the personal benefit of each player in the play experience. Engaging one another means children can enjoy the play together. Scaffolding becomes an attribute of the collaborating process.

Amount of Scaffolding

Table 6.3 provides the frequency of different types of scaffolding by symbolic transformation types in mixed-age group and same-age kindergarten group.

In the mixed-age groups, ideational play was the most common transformation with 43% (351), followed by Object play at 40% (333). Role transformations were 17% (143). Modeling was the dominant strategy for Object play at 58% (196). Directing was the dominant strategy for Role transformations at 57% (82). Modeling was the dominant strategy for Ideational play at

Table 6.3. Frequency of Different Types of Scaffolding by Symbolic Transformation in Mixed-Age Group and Same-Age Kindergarten

	Modeling	Inviting	Assisting	Directing	Informing	Total
Mixed-Age Groups						
Object	196	27	8	100	2	**333**
Roles	36	15	3	82	7	**143**
Ideational	122	102	18	107	2	**351**
Total	**354**	**144**	**29**	**289**	**11**	827
Same-Age KDG						
					Negotiating	
Object	215	41	3	64	14	**337**
Roles	44	14	0	46	5	**109**
Ideational	53	20	1	29	3	**106**
Total	**312**	**75**	**4**	**139**	**22**	**552**

35% (122), closely followed by Directing at 30% (107). Informing and Assisting were minimally used.

For the same-age kindergarten groups, Object play was the most common transformation at 61% (337). Role transformations were at 20% (109) and Ideational transformations were at 19% (106). Modeling was the dominant strategy for Object play at 64% (215). Directing was the dominant strategy for Role transformations at 42% (46). Modeling was the primary strategy for Ideational transformations at 50% (53).

Object and Role transformations were comparable in both groupings. However, Ideational transformations were significantly more in the mixed-age grouping. Mixed-ages scaffolded Ideational transformations 42% (351) of the time out of all the play types, while same-age kindergarten scaffolded Ideational transformations only 19% (106) out of all the play transformations. Interestingly, both groups predominately scaffolded using the modeling strategy for object transformations, directing for role transformations, and modeling for Ideational transformations.

Outcomes of Scaffolding Types

Categories for scaffolding types were coded for each type of transformation. Four outcome types were identified.

1. Engages-Child actually participates in scaffolded transformation.
2. Observes-Child observes but does not participate in scaffolded transformation.

3. Ignores-Child ignores the scaffolded transformation.
4. Disengages-Child stops playing.

Table 6.4 reports the amount of the types of outcomes of scaffolding in the mixed-age and the same-age group. The mixed-age group's scaffolding strategies resulted in 67% engagement (629) and 25% observing (249), and only 6% who ignored the scaffolding (57) and 1% who disengaged in the play (6).

In the same-age kindergarten classroom, the outcomes of scaffolding strategies resulted in 62% engagement (407) and 26% observing (173), and only 9% who ignored the scaffolding (61) and 3% who disengaged in the play (17).

In comparing mixed-age kindergarteners to the kindergarteners in the same-age kindergarten, the mixed-age kindergarteners had both the six-and seven-year-olds as scaffolders for symbolic transformations, particularly ideational transformations, enriching the possibilities of more complex ideational play exposure and engagement than their counterparts did in the same-age kindergarten.

CONCLUSION

This descriptive and qualitative comparative study addressed the following questions:

Question 1 asked if the social age difference (expert/novice) in the mixed-age grouping provided greater social opportunities for scaffolding symbolic play transformations than expected in a same-age kindergarten. The majority of transformations occurred in a collaborative, social context: 667 events (84%) in the mixed-age grouping and 630 events (85%) in the same-age Kindergarten group. Both play groups benefitted by scaffolding symbolic transformations for one another. However, the social age difference in the mixed-age grouping provided opportunities players of every age to engage more broadly in the three types of symbolic play transformations, but partic-

Table 6.4.   The Outcomes of Scaffolding in Mixed-Age and Same-Age Group

	Mixed-Age Group	Same-Age K Group
Engage	629	407
Observe	249	173
Ignore	57	61
Disengage	6	17
Total	**941**	**658**

ularly in Ideational transformations. By virtue of greater age differences, more experts could participate in the expert-novice relationships in the mixed-age grouping, thus providing more scaffolding of Ideational play (mixed-ages, 40%; same-age Kindergarten, 16%). The mixed-age kindergartners, particularly, had more exposure to, and thus engagement in, ideational transformations than had kindergarteners in the same-age kindergarten group.

The five-year-olds in the mixed-age kindergarten group are more advantaged than are ones in the same-age kindergarteners by having greater opportunities for playing with more sophisticated older players. As Vygotsky (1976) suggests, more capable peers can enhance the zone of proximal development within the expert/novice relationship. The social interactions of older children can "stimulate the children to use more sophisticated approaches to tasks through the process of 'scaffolding'" (Meltzer, 1991, p. 179). The older children, who were six and seven years of age, were able to scaffold using more straightforward approaches such as "directing" in order to engage the younger five-year-old children. Research suggests that older children in mixed-age groupings are more socially competent than the younger children are, and thus are more skillful in helping novices advance by using more explicit scaffolding strategies such as "directing" (Christie & Stone, 1999; Gray, 2013; Vygotsky, 1976). In addition to greater expertise in symbolic transformations, the display of more direct approaches in scaffolding, provided by older children, is one of the reasons older children can help younger children make symbolic play progress on their road to greater abstraction and literacy.

Question 2 asked if mixed-age children scaffold more symbolic play transformations than do same-age kindergarten children. Results in both groupings show that the mixed-age grouping children exhibited more Ideational Transformations (40%) in contrast to the children in the same-age kindergarten group (16%). In general, same-age kindergarteners mostly used lower level transformations, *Objects* and then *Roles*, but employed substantially less *Ideational* transformations. Mixed-age children provided a greater range of symbolic transformations. Mixed-age kindergarteners were engaged in a higher degree of scaffolding of ideational symbolic transformations by older children in the mixed-age grouping, in comparison to the amount of ideational scaffolding found in the same-age kindergarten group.

Question 3 examined the types and amounts of scaffolding by the two groupings. Both groupings used five different types of scaffolding to engage one another in play. Same-age kindergarten children relied heavily on the strategy of Modeling (67%) which demands less of the child in terms of social interaction; whereas Directing (25%) and Inviting (14%) demand more cognitively sophisticated social interaction. Mixed-age grouping relied on both Modeling (43%) and Directing (40%). The Directing strategy may indicate greater social leadership in the play.

As children become more socially competent with development and experience in social settings, perhaps they are more capable, and thus, more likely to use socially direct strategies. In addition, as children become more competent in making symbolic transformations as a function of development and practice, they may utilize more direct scaffolding strategies such as Directing with novice play partners. While more research is called for, perhaps younger children in mixed-age social contexts benefit from the more direct scaffolding strategies they encounter when playing with older peers. In this study they were engaged twice as often in symbolic transformations in mixed age groupings than in the same-age grouping.

Question 4 examined the outcomes of the scaffolding strategies. Scaffolding was highly successful in engaging children for both groupings. *Engagement* in same-age kindergarten was accomplished 62% of the time, followed by *Observing* at 26%. *Engagement* for the mixed-age grouping was 67% with *Observing* at 25%. *Ignoring* or *disengaging* in play was minimal for both groupings.

The outcomes of engaging each other in play highlights the importance of social play for symbolic transformations for both groupings where children naturally practice and scaffold play transformations. Mixed-age groupings have the added benefit of older children scaffolding for younger children, particularly in the area of Ideational symbolic play, an important literacy precursor.

This research lends support to Vygotsky's (1978) theory of the "zone of proximal development." Vygotsky (1978) suggests that "an essential feature of learning is that it creates the zone of proximal development; that is, learning awakens a variety of developmental processes that are able to operate only when the child is interacting with people in his environment and in collaboration with his peers" (p. 90). Playgroups can provide a natural, social context for experts and novices to interact and awaken learning. Experts and novices were not identified in the same-age or mixed-age groupings, yet it is assumed that some children were experts and some novices. With the development of symbolic play transformations, experts and novices, either by age or development, had the opportunity to scaffold learning for one another indicated by the high percentages of engagement in both groupings. Findings suggested that the heightened availability of experts to novices in mixed-ages, by virtue of age, presented an advantage for scaffolding learning for one another, awakening "a variety of developmental processes" (Vygotsky, 1978, p. 90). All participants, one could make a case, appeared to benefit, even though younger children, particularly the five-year-olds in the mixed-age grouping, one might say, especially benefitted from older children scaffolding for them the more complex Ideational play transformations. In essence, play provided the context and the older children provided the engage-ment through scaffolding, giving the younger children the rich opportunity to *practice* representing objects and events symbolically, and to become good at it (Pellegrini, 1985). The scaffolding is natural and continual as a way to pull "the younger children up to a level that makes" the play more fun for all (Gray, 2013, p. 186).

Mixed-age play contexts also provide opportunities for older children to strengthen or consolidate existing skills such as more sophisticated ideational representation, leadership and nurturing skills, and a deeper understanding of concepts at a higher level (Gray, 2013; Stone & Burriss, 2019). As Gray (2013) discusses "just as older children inspire younger ones to engage in more complex or sophisticated activities than they otherwise would, younger children inspire older ones to engage in more creative activities than they otherwise would" (p. 197). Mixed ages provide a context where younger children lead older children to be more creative in their play (Gray, 2013). Thus, mixed-age play benefits all players, providing a broad range of devel-opment for each player in the learning process. Scaffolding, as a common process of collaborative play, can substantially enhance cognitive and litera-cy development of all players .It is an effective tool to engage one another in play as well as in symbolic play as noted by the scaffolding outcomes in both groupings.

Symbolic play, from objects to roles and then to ideational transforma-tions, is the gradual process of the brain developing abstract thinking, the critical framework for literacy (Stone & Burriss, 2016). Ideational transfor-mations are significant in the hierarchy of symbolic transformations as it solidifies abstract thought. When young children, particularly five-year-olds, have the opportunity to frequently engage in ideational transformations, their development of symbolization and abstract thought will continue its journey to symbolizing with pictures, letters, letters for sounds, groups of letters for written words, and written words for ideas.

Our results suggest that play environments at school, such as the dramatic play area of the home center used in this study, provide a collaborative social context for both same- and mixed-student peer groupings. Specifically pre-pared classroom play environments can support and engage children through the many opportunities they provide for the scaffolding process in simple- to-complex symbolic play transformations in collaborative pretense. This is essential for the development of emerging literacy. Accordingly, instead of substituting academic environments for play, this chapter wishes to close by emphasizing the need for more social play (Stone & Christie, 1996).

Social play contexts combined with having mixed-age learners in schools enhances the expert-novice relationship, resulting in more opportunities for higher levels of social symbolic play, as in the display of ideational transfor-mations in play. Finding ways for strengthening children's abilities for, and use of, representation and abstract thought during play is important to help them become skillful in using symbolic systems in general. Kindergarteners developing ever more symbolic abstract thinking and literacy skills benefit from the opportunity to engage with six- and seven-year-olds, who are developing their symbolic systems including literacy on a somewhat higher plane. Kindergarteners' development is advantaged by their play with experts in the mixed-age grouping. As Gray (2013) suggests, "when children are free to play, they play naturally at the ever-advancing edges of their mental or physical abilities" (p. 155). The mixed-age grouping enhances the younger children's opportunities to advance their mental abilities; whereas the same-age kindergarteners, while still developing, do not have the extra advantage of interacting with a wider range of older experts.

Our results question the narrow, homogenized practice of grouping children by same age. In this chapter we have drawn attention to the idea, supported by data, that individual children in mixed-age groupings can, and do, effectively and comfortably learn from each other how to engage in social pretense at a higher level. It is desirable to provide a broader range of expert-novice learning collaborations through play. As older children show greater social competence to direct and organize play, younger children in a mixed-age grouping can benefit from their older peers' play leadership abilities and use of play facilitation. This dynamic helps both younger and older children and their collaboration. This study offers support for those who argue for transforming educative-social practices, changing classroom environments by deliberately embracing the concept of mixed-age players to increase the diversity of the social nature of learning, as children commonly scaffold learning for each other, providing children with "powerful learning opportunities" through age mixing (Gray, 2013, p. 204).

Limitations

More research information is needed to better evaluate coding reliability; and inferential statistical tests were not reported on these data in this chapter. Additional limitations of this study include: (1) the symbolic levels of understanding of each child was not assessed prior to the study; (2) expert/novice relationships were assumed by age in the mixed-age grouping and not determined by actual experience; older children, six and seven years of age, were assumed to be the experts in symbolic play. Future research can address these and other concerns. It would be valuable to investigate, for instance, scaffolding strategies and consequences with respect to other characteristics of social pretense enactment (and negotiation), such as play plot elaborations and levels of complexity, and to see how scaffolding enactments might be different than scaffolding negotiations in play episodes involving children at different levels. Such work would illuminate further play and peer dynamics for their role in early literacy development.

REFERENCES

Bogdan, R., & Biklen, S. (2016). *Qualitative research for education: An introduction to theories and methods* (5th ed.). New York, NY: Pearson Education.
Broadhead, P. (2006). Developing an understanding of young children's learning through play: The place of observation, interaction and reflection. *British Educational Research Journal,* 32(2), 191–207.
Christie, J. F., & Stone, S. J. (1999). Collaborative literacy activity in print-enriched play centers: The influence of same-age and multi-age grouping. *Journal of Literacy Research,* 32(2), 109–131.
Christie, J. F., Stone, S. J., & Deutscher, R. (2002). Play in same-age and multiage arrangements. In J. Roopnarine (Ed.), *Conceptual, Socio-Cognitive, and Contextual Issues in the Fields of Play* (63–75). Westport, CT: Ablex.
Copple, C. E., Cocking, R. R., & Matthews, W. S. (1984). Objects, symbols, and substitutes: The nature of the cognitive activity during symbolic play. In T. D. Yawkey & A. D. Pellegrini (Eds.), *Child's Play: Developmental and Applied.* Hillsdale, NJ: Erlbaum.
Creswell, J. W., & Creswell, J. D. (2018). *Research design: Qualitative, quantitative, and mixed methods approaches* (5th edition). Los Angeles, CA: Sage Publications, Inc.
Elder, J. L., & Pederson, Dr. R. (1978). Preschool children's use of objects in symbolic play. *Child Development,* 49(2), 500–504.
Frey, J. R., & Kaiser, J. P. (2011). The use of play expansions to increase the diversity and complexity of object play in young children with disabilities. *Topics in Early Childhood Special Education,* 31(2), 99–111.
Gardner, H. (1979). Developmental psychology after Piaget: An approach in terms of symbolization. *Human Development,* 22(2), 73–88. doi:10.1159/0002724.
Goldman, J. (1981). Social participation of preschool children in same-versus mixed-age groups. *Child Development,* 52(2), 644–650.
Goodlad, J., & Anderson, R. (1987). *The non-graded elementary school* (rev. ed.). New York: Teachers College Press.
Gray, P. (2011). The special value of children's age-mixed play. *American Journal of Play,* 3(4), 500–522.
Gray, P. (2013). *Free to learn.* New York, NY: Basic Books.
Isenberg, J., & Jacobs, E. (1983). Literacy and symbolic play: A review of the literature. *Childhood Education,* 59(4), 272–276.
Johnson, J., Christie, J., & Wardle, F. (2005). *Play, development and early education.* Upper Saddle River, NJ: Pearson.
Katz, L.G., Evangelou, D., & Hartman, J.A. (1993). *The case for mixed-age grouping in early education.* Washington, DC: (NAEYC) National Association for the Education of Young Children.
Kelly, R., & Hammond, S. (2011). The relationship between symbolic play and executive function in young children. *Australasian Journal of Early Childhood,* 36(2), 21–27.
Meltzer, L. (1991). Problem-solving strategies and academic performance in learning disabled students: Do subtypes exist? In L. Feagans, E. Short, & L. Meltzer, *Subtypes of Learning Disabilities: Theoretical Perspectives and Research.* Hillsdale, NJ: Erlbaum.
Pellegrini, A. D. (1985). Relations between preschool children's symbolic play and literate behavior. In L. Galda and A. D. Pellegrini (Eds.). *Play, language and stories: The development of children's literate behavior.* Norwood, NJ: Ablex.
Schrader, C. T. (1990). Symbolic play as a curricular tool for early literacy development. *Early Childhood Research Quarterly,* 5(1), 79–103.
Shotwell, J. M., Wolf, D., & Gardner, H. (1979). Exploring early symbolization: Style of achievement. In B. Sutton-Smith (Ed.), *Play and Learning.* New York: Gardner Press.

Stone, S. J. (2004). *Creating the multiage classroom.* Culver City, CA: Good Year Books.

Stone, S. J. (2010). Multiage: A model of education reform—or invention? *Journal of Multiage Education,* 4(1), 13–18.

Stone, S. J. (2017). The essential role of play in school contexts for the well being of children. *LEARNing Landscapes,* 10(2), 305–318.

Stone, S. J., & Burriss, K. (2016). A case for symbolic play: An important foundation for literacy development. *The International Journal of Holistic Early Learning and Development,* 3, 59–72.

Stone, S. J., & Burriss, K. (2019). *Understanding multiage education.* New York, NY: Routledge.

Stone, S. J., & Christie, J. F. (1996). Collaborative literacy learning during sociodramatic play in a multiage (K–2) Primary Classroom. *Journal of Research in Childhood Education,* 10(2), 123–133.

Stone, S. J., & Stone, B. A. (2015). Play and early literacy: An analysis of kindergarten children's scaffolding during symbolic play transformations. *The International Journal of Holistic Early Learning and Development,* 2, 3–16.

Stone, S. J., & Stone, B. A. (2017). *A comparative analysis of kindergarten and mixed-age (K–2) children's scaffolding during symbolic play transformations.* 43rd Annual International Conference of the Association for the Study of Play (TASP), April 2017, Rochester, NY.

Stone, S. J., & Stone, B. A. (2018). *The power of mixed-age play.* 44rd Annual International Conference of the Association for the Study of Play (TASP), February 28–March 3, 2018, Melbourne, Fl.

Tudge, J., & Caruso, D. (1988). Cooperative problem-solving in the classroom: Enhancing young children's cognitive development. *Young Children,* 44(1), 46–52.

Vygotsky, L.S. (1976). Play and its role in the mental development of the child. *Soviet Psychology,* 5, 6–18.

Vygotsky, L. S. (1978). *Mind in society: The development of psychological processes.* Cambridge, MA: Harvard University Press.

Watson, M. W., & Jackowitz, E. R. (1984). Agents and recipient objects in the development of early symbolic play. *Child Development,* 55(3), 1091–1097.

Chapter Seven

Preschool Teachers' Responsive Interactions with Children in Dramatic Play and the Children's Vocabulary Outcomes

Sohyun Meacham and Myae Han

INTRODUCTION

"Learning is active. It involves reaching out of the mind. It involves organic assimilation starting from within. Literally, we must take our stand with the child and our departure from him. It is he and not the subject matter which determines both quality and quantity of learning" (Dewey, 1902, pp. 13–14). Play can be an important context for children's learning (Lillard et al., 2013), since when children play they actualize thoughts from their imagination. When it comes to supporting children's learning through play, as Dewey indicated, following the child's lead is a maxim for teachers. The purpose of this study was to explore this maxim with empirical data. We focused on dramatic play in preschool classrooms where the children engage in pretend play and the teachers assume various roles (e.g., play leader, co-player, stage manager, director, re-director, onlooker; Johnson, Christie, & Wardle, 2005) to support the children's play.

While child-led interactions in play are recommended more, many teachers end up using a lot of teacher-led utterances, which means adult-initiated conversations or one-way statements from teacher to child (de Rivera, Girolametto, Greenberg, & Weitzman, 2005; Girolametto, Weitzman, van Lieshout, & Duff, 2000; Meacham, Vukelich, Han, & Buell, 2016). The existing research has discovered that teachers' responsiveness (the frequency of teachers' repetitions or expansions of children's utterances) during their

interaction with the children in the dramatic play center is positively associated with the frequency of children's verbal responses (Meacham et al.,
2016).

The current study aims to extend the aforementioned research by using
children's vocabulary-outcome measures in addition to their immediate language productivity during the interactions with the teachers. Analyzing interactions of the teachers and their preschoolers, we sought to discover associations between the teachers' responsiveness to children's initiations (e.g., following the children's lead and extending it) and the children's later receptive
and expressive vocabulary outcomes.

As oral language skills in young children before formal literacy instruction are considered to be an important preparation for later reading success
(NICHD Early Child Care Research Network, 2005), vocabulary, as one of
important components of oral language skills (Jean & Geva, 2009; Storch &
Whitehurst, 2002) is emphasized by literacy education researchers. Oral language, including vocabulary, is critical for reading comprehension (Gough &
Tummer, 1986) and predicts later reading achievement (August & Shanahan,
2006). The results of this study can partially support an argument regarding
the teachers' use of responsive language with children in play for later reading development.

Theoretical Perspectives: Teachers and Children in Dramatic Play

Play is seen as a critical experience especially during the early childhood
period. Educators must consider the key impulses of the children in planning
and instruction: children are social, they like to construct, and they like to
investigate (Cunningham & Breault, 2017). In play, these impulses are naturally followed by children, which creates perfect conditions for educative
experiences. Children have the right to accept or reject what adults offer
them during play.

The cognitive and sociocultural perspectives agree that the preschool period is when dramatic play is frequently observed and that dramatic play
supports children's learning and development of general representational
skills (Rowe, 1998). Both perspectives acknowledge the social aspects of
cognitive development. Piaget, from the cognitive perspective, acknowledged that social factors are related to the rate of development (Pellegrini &
Galda, 1993). Vygotskian sociocultural perspectives emphasized that children's interactions with adults and their more capable peers promote their
development (Rogoff & Lave, 1984). Vygotsky's (1978) ideas on the zone of
proximal development explain how young children achieve competencies. In
this zone, children can successfully perform certain actions with adults' or
more capable peers' help that they otherwise would be unable to do at their
current developmental level. Intellectual and linguistic challenges that may

lead children's learning can take place in the zone of proximal development (Rogoff, 1991). This theory has fed approaches that emphasize teachers' assumption of active roles to enhance children's dramatic play (Gupta, 2009).

Although Vygotsky's theory of the zone of proximal development implies the teachers' active participation in the children's development, this is more alluded to than elaborated on (Duncan & Tarulli, 2003), presumably because of his early death. Bakhtinian perspectives shed additional light on teachers' roles in preschoolers' dramatic play (Meacham, 2013). Bakhtin's (1991) theory of heteroglossia and ideological becoming support the extension of teachers' involvement in preschoolers' dramatic play. Heteroglossia means the use of multiple voices in social organization. There are both centripetal and centrifugal dimensions. The centripetal dimensions describe how individuals are pulled in to conform to general social rules. Alternatively, individuals enact social roles in unique ways, which is explained as centrifugal forces. The intermingled functions of centripetal and centrifugal forces make the heteroglossic characteristics of social organization.

Dramatic play has a heteroglossic nature regarding role enactments. Generalized role knowledge (e.g., a doctor in a clinic) and specific role enactments (e.g., a child's specific role enactments of a doctor in a clinic) interact in children's dramatic play. Children are influenced by the centripetal forces of social organization during dramatic play when they become aware of the general knowledge of roles in social organization. At the same time, children are affected by centrifugal forces when enacting social roles in unique, concrete, specific, and particularistic ways employing multiple voices. In this process, children not only learn appropriate language and behavior for adult life but also develop their own creative language and behavior. Teachers' participation in dramatic play can facilitate children's development in both directions: conforming to social rules and expressing unique and creative individual voices.

Role play facilitates children's ideological becoming; however, teacher's participation should be responsive rather than directive. "Ideological becoming" relates to a person's endeavors to develop his or her own voice beyond a discourse initially spoken by others. The discourse is redefined and developed in these endeavors. In dramatic play, preschoolers develop their own voices beyond adult forms of discourse, which was termed "ideological becoming" by Bakhtin. When adults are authoritative and directive with the children, the conversation cannot be internally persuasive, which can hinder the child's ideological becoming.

These theoretical perspectives provide a foundation for looking into teachers' engagement in children's dramatic play. There is a body of empirical literature on this topic. The empirical literature reviewed in the next section advances this line of research by providing fine-grained descriptions of adults' interactions with children and children's language productivity.

Empirical Literature: Teachers' Interactions with Children in Dramatic Play and Children's Language Productivity

Children tend to use pretend talk when they play; i.e., they speak like an imaginary person. Not only children but also their teachers or caregivers use pretend talk. When they do so, they tend to provide the children with linguistic challenges such as advanced vocabulary modeling, expansion of the children's speech, and the use of inferential talk (Gest, Holland-Coviello, Welsh, Eicher-Catt, & Gill, 2006; Tompkins, Zucker, Justice, & Binici, 2013). McLeod, Kaiser, and Hard (2018) examined 53 Head Start teacher-child dyads' vocabulary use in their play sessions. They investigated the relationship between the teachers' vocabulary usage and the children's language productivity. The teachers' total number of vocabulary words (target and sophisticated vocabulary; use of vocabulary development support strategies) and vocabulary supports were positively related to the children's vocabulary use (total number of target words used) within the sessions.

Teachers interact with children in play in different ways, assuming different roles such as play leader, co-player, director, stage manager, and onlooker. Randima Rjapaksha's (2016) qualitative study using observations, interviews, and a reflective journal investigated how the teacher assumed different roles based upon her observation of children's engagement in sociodramatic play. For instance, when the children were not engaging much in the sociodramatic play activities due to their limited experiences, the teacher had to be the play leader. When the children were more deeply engaged in the sociodramatic play activities, the teacher shifted to the co-player role. These findings imply that there is another important layer of teacher responsiveness in addition to being responsive to children's interests: being responsive to their engagement levels.

Not all types of teacher responses are accepted by children. The children's responses to the adults depend on the teachers' behavior and responses during play (Meacham et al., 2016; Gaviria-Loaiza, Han, Vu, & Hustedt, 2017). Gaviria-Loaiza and her colleagues (2017) qualitatively analyzed eleven teachers' roles in facilitating play (e.g., onlooker, stage manager, co-player, play leader, director, and redirector) and the ways the children responded to them. The children's responses to the teachers' behaviors were categorized as ignore/reject, evaluative (resist/question), and acceptance (respond, incorporate, build on) behaviors. When the teachers asked many questions, were not physically close to the child, were overinvolved, provided multiple directions or commands, and/or provided ideas of no interest to the children, the children exhibited ignore/reject behaviors. When the teachers provided unconvincing ideas and/or substantial input in a short period of time, the children were evaluative. While there were several indicators of the teachers' being accepted by the children, the teachers' responsiveness to the children's interests (e.g., showing interest in the children's play, providing input related to their play, letting the children take an active role, and capturing the children's attention) was the overarching aspect. These researchers also found that the teachers' co-player and lead-player roles were more frequently associated than were the other roles with responsive behavior. Relevant to teachers' responsive behaviors, Pursi and Lipponen (2017) interestingly focused on *adults' ability* to build sustained participation in joint play with young children. They determined that this ability is relevant to delicately timed observations, and taking initiative/responding with perceptive and coordinated gestures, gaze, and speech.

In the extant research, teachers' responsiveness to children's interests is a key indicator of a successful interaction with young children in play (Meacham et al., 2016). One notable finding from this line of research is the variability in the teachers' responsiveness (Gaviria-Loaiza et al., 2017; Meacham et al., 2016; Pursi & Lipponen, 2017). Meanwhile, the recent literature is mostly descriptive qualitative studies using relatively small sample sizes. Thus, we still need empirical knowledge about how the variability of teachers' responses to children in dramatic play affects the children's later language outcomes.

There is a line of research that discovered relationships between adults' language inputs in various young children's play-learning contexts (e.g., shared book reading, dramatic play) and the children's language productivity within the interactions (McLeod et al., 2018; Meacham, Vukelich, Han, & Buell, 2013; Tompkins, Bengochea, Nicol, & Justice, 2017); similarly, studies found relationships between adults' language inputs and children's later language outcomes (Bowne, Yoshikawa, & Snow, 2016; Cartmill et al., 2013; Dickinson et al., 2018; Hirsh-Pasek et al., 2015; Toub et al., 2018).

An earlier study by Meacham et al. (2016) examined relations between Head Start teachers' responsiveness to children's utterances in dramatic play and the children's responses to their teachers' utterances. By conducting a sequential analysis which cross-tabbed the 11 teachers' response types (teachers' topic-initiating, following children's initiation by repetition, following children's initiation by extension) in 8,427 utterances and the children's responses (verbal in pretend play, nonverbal in pretend play, verbal not in pretend play, nonverbal not in pretend play, no response), these researchers found that the children responded frequently to the teachers' topic-continuing utterances. They also found that the children responded frequently in the pretend play mode when the teachers extended the children's utterances on topics initiated by the children.

There is one recent study that controlled the teachers' response levels in their experimental grouping. Toub and her colleagues (2018) discovered unique benefits from adult-supported play following shared book-reading. In this study, which was experimental, there were three sets of conditions: free play (only toys were provided), guided play (child-directed play wherein adult's language support was embedded) and directed play (adult-led play that resembled direct instruction, e.g., "adult leading children in a re-enactment of a storybook using figurines," p. 3). All three situations used the same play context with the same toys relevant to the story from the shared book-reading experience, and the adults were only minimally involved with the children's play to supervise for safety reasons. However, the adults were more responsive to the children's interests in the guided-play condition than in the directed play one. They found that guided play and directed play were more effective for target-vocabulary learning than free play was. A second study by the same researchers found that target words taught through play activities were learned better than were ones taught through didactic approaches with picture cards. This finding was particularly salient in the children's expressive vocabulary learning. While this research supports the aforementioned theory regarding play-based learning and adults' involvement in children's play, the findings regarding adults' responsiveness levels are puzzling.

Since we still had only a vague understanding of the relationships between teachers' responsiveness levels in young children's dramatic play and the children's later vocabulary outcomes, we composed the following research question to guide the current study: Are there differences between children's receptive and expressive vocabulary growth in classrooms where teacher-children pretend-play interactions are based on children-initiated topics and comparable classrooms where such interactions are less frequently observed?

METHODS

Modes of Inquiry

In order to address the research question, we utilized a mixed-method approach to analyze video data from the dramatic play centers of 11 preschool classrooms in a Mid-Atlantic state. We first qualitatively analyzed the audio-visual teacher-children interaction data collected from the dramatic play centers to unpack the teachers' responsiveness (teachers' initiating conversation topics vs. following children-initiated ones). The results of the qualitative analysis were quantified by two major measures: (1) the frequency of teachers' utterances when they followed children-initiated topics; (2) the percentage of children's responses in pretense. These measures were used to form groups for comparison of the vocabulary outcomes, which is the quantitative aspect of our mixed methods.

Context

The data were collected in eleven Head Start classrooms with 175 children total. While there were assistant teachers and para-educators, we only collected audiovisual data of the lead teachers' interactions with their children. The teachers' preschool-teaching experience ranged from 6 months to 12 years (M = 7.7 years, SD = 3.56). Their overall teaching experience in all kinds of classrooms varied from 3 to 25 years. Ten teachers held a bachelor of arts degree. One was pursuing one with some college-level credits earned. All of the children in the classrooms were invited to play in the dramatic play center; and we did not control which ones were included in the qualitative data. We randomly chose two sessions of each lead teacher's interactions with the children in the dramatic play centers. In each session, videotaping began when the lead teacher started interacting with the children and stopped when the teacher left the dramatic play center. As the method of qualitative-data collection was naturalistic, we observed the business-as-usual of the dramatic play center, respecting all classroom rules. The dramatic play interactions took place daily during the regular 60-minute-long center time. All teachers were in the same professional-development network and shared instructional coaches. They collaborated on lesson planning and materials preparation. As a result, the dramatic play centers of the classrooms exhibited similar themes. Only "doctor's office" and "post office" settings were observed in our data.

Data

The 11 classrooms were categorized into two groups based on the following two measures of the audiovisual data: (1) teachers' utterances that followed children's interests; (2) children's responses in pretense. Among the 11 lead teachers, 1,923 utterances which were responded to by children were coded as *teacher's initiating* (e.g., when a child said "sick," the teacher said "This is a thermometer. Can you say thermometer?"); or *following child's interests* (e.g., when a child said, "She need a shot," the teacher responded, "She needs a shot to make her feel better?"). Then 597 utterances in the pooled data of the eleven teachers were identified as *following child's interests* (T-Responsive), contingent on the children's verbal response in pretense (CVRP) (e.g., a child pretending to be a doctor told the patient's mother, "Your baby is sick").

Then individual teachers' classrooms were compared to this ratio (597 to 1,923). Based on this benchmark, seven among all of the teachers exhibited higher ratios of T-Responsive & CVRP, while four exhibited lower ones. Based on these results, two groups were formed: the High Responsiveness-Pretense Group ($N_{children}$=109) and the Low Responsiveness-Pretense Group ($N_{children}$=66). A crosstab analysis (2 by 2: High and Low Responsiveness Interaction Groups; High and Low 2 Children's Response-in-Pretense Groups) confirmed that the highly responsive teacher group had more of the highly responsive-in-pretense children than expected.

Repeated Measures ANOVA were used on data for the Peabody Picture Vocabulary Test (PPVT-IV; Dunn & Dunn, 2007: receptive vocabulary) and the Definitional Vocabulary subtest of the Test of Preschool Early Literacy (TOPEL-DV; Lonigan, Wagner, Torgesen, & Rashotte, 2007: expressive vocabulary) for the beginning and end of the school year to compare these two groups of children. Both the PPVT-IV and TOPEL-DV are individually-assessed, standardized and norm-referenced. The PPVT-IV asks the children to point to the visual quadrant that represents the word given by the assessor. The TOPEL-DV asks the children to say the name and definition (function or use) of the visual image on each page of an easel. We compared the two data points of the raw scores to avoid pitfalls from age-based adjustment in standard score conversions, especially for time-based statistical analyses such as Repeated Measures ANOVA or Latent Growth Curve Analysis. Despite the fact that PPVT-IV and TOPEL-DV provide age-adjusted standard scores, we still used raw scores for two reasons. First, when all tested children are in the same classroom (or the same small program) for the same age/grade group, the use of raw scores is usually acceptable (Dunn & Dunn, 2007). Second, the use of raw scores is recommended for analyses with data from different data points because raw scores are more sensitive to changes (e.g., Luu et al., 2009). There were not found any statistically significant differences between the PPVT-IV and TOPEL-DV raw scores between the two groups at the beginning of the school year (PPVT-IV: t (173) = 1.245, p = .214; TOPEL-DV: t (173) = .467).

RESULTS

Table 7.1 presents the means and standard deviations for the two groups for the dependent variable, separately and by time period. Figures 7.1 and 7.2 provide plots from the Repeated Measures ANOVA of the receptive vocabulary (PPVT-IV) and expressive vocabulary (TOPEL-DV) from the pretest (at the beginning of the school year) to the posttest (at the end of the school year) respectively. The PPVT-IV results reveal that the main effect for time was significant (F = 291.324, df[1, 173], p = 0.001). On the other hand, neither the main effect for group or the group-by-time interaction was significant (respectively, F = 1.323, df[1, 173], p = .252; F = .005, df[1, 173], p =

.943). The results from TOPEL-DV revealed a main effect for time ($F = 158.892$, df[1, 171], $p = 0.001$) and the group-by-time interaction ($F = 5.637$, df[1, 171], $p = 0.019$), although there was not a significant main effect for group ($F = 1.761$, df[1, 171], $p = 0.186$).

The interpretation of the above results is as follows. The repeated measures ANOVAs indicated that the expressive vocabulary results favored the High Responsiveness-Pretense Group. The classrooms in that group exhibited a steeper slope from pretest to posttest than the Low Responsiveness-Pretense Group. Meanwhile, there was not a significant difference between the two groups for the receptive vocabulary results.

DISCUSSION

This study investigated the relationships between teachers' responsiveness levels in preschoolers' dramatic play and the children's later receptive and expressive vocabulary outcomes. Based on the existing theoretical and empirical literature, a positive association was hypothesized between teachers' responsiveness to young children's interests during dramatic play and the children's later receptive and expressive vocabulary outcomes.

Our data supported a positive association between teachers' responsiveness and children's expressive vocabulary learning. Children's receptive vocabulary learning did not show a statistical difference between the two

Table 7.1. Means and Standard Deviations for PPVT-IV and TOPEL-DV by Group and Time

Vocabulary Assessment	Time	Group	M	SD
PPVT-IV	Fall	High Responsiveness-Pretense Group	44.31	20.026
		Low Responsiveness-Pretense Group	40.58	21.213
	Spring	High Responsiveness-Pretense Group	60.83	19.966
		Low Responsiveness-Pretense Group	57.18	23.731
TOPEL-DV	Fall	High Responsiveness-Pretense Group	27.11	19.239
		Low Responsiveness-Pretense Group	25.01	20.176
	Spring	High Responsiveness-Pretense Group	39.53	14.223
		Low Responsiveness-Pretense Group	33.80	18.083

Note: M = mean, SD = standard deviation

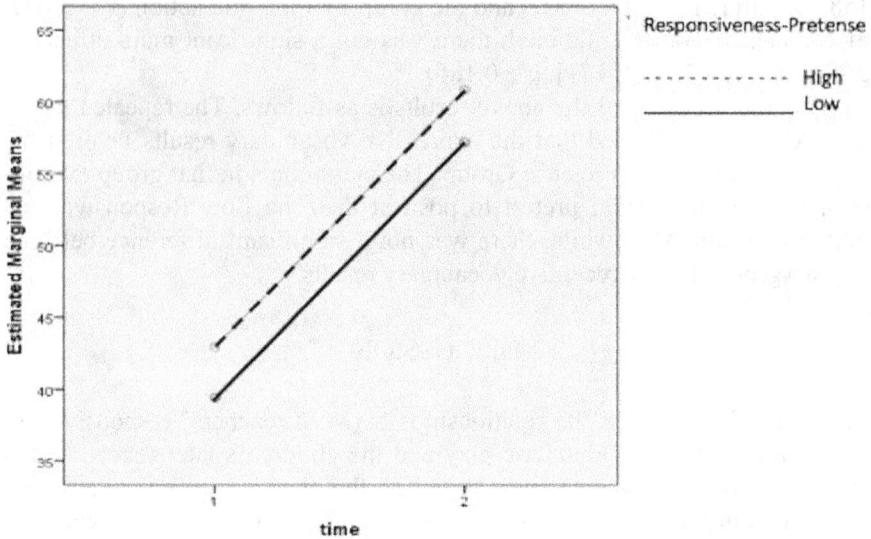

Figure 7.1.   PPVT-IV Plot of Means by Group across Time. Created by Sohyun Meacham & Myae Han

groups based on the teachers' responsiveness levels; instead, the improvement was similar in both groups. This trend was also observed by Toub and her colleagues' (2018), whose recent study determined that play after shared-book reading had a better effect on children's vocabulary learning than did a traditional didactic approach. Their results also indicated that there was a significant difference in expressive vocabulary but not receptive vocabulary. As discussed in Toub et al. (2018), expressive vocabulary learning requires deeper learning and more active processing than does receptive vocabulary learning (Davis, Di Betta, MacDonald, & Gaskell, 2009). This means that learning expressive vocabulary is harder than learning receptive vocabulary. Children may develop receptive vocabulary regardless of how responsive the teachers are in the dramatic play; however, for expressive vocabulary learning to be optimized, the children need more responsive teachers who facilitate the children's dramatic play based on the children's interests. We speculate that teachers' responsive talk can simply help the children speak more. The topics that the children initiate might be what they are familiar with or motivated to talk about. Therefore, they might have things to say about those topics. Moreover, our data indicated that the teachers expanded the children's talk (e.g., when a child said, "She need a shot," the teacher inquired, "She needs a shot to make her feel better?"), which could provide the children a model for more sophisticated speech. While more advanced research meth-

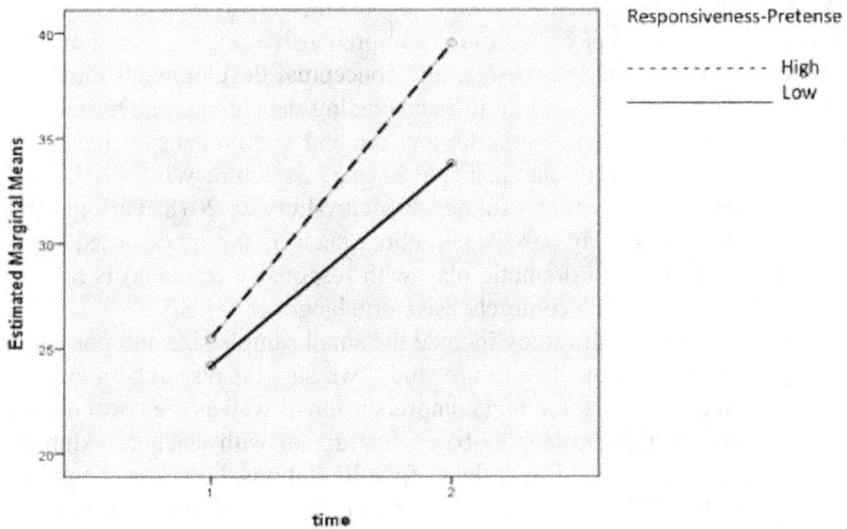

Figure 7.2. TOPEL-DV Plot of Means by Group across Time. Created by Sohyun Meacham & Myae Han

ods should be developed to explain these results, the findings of the current study are still promising news for early childhood educators in an era of standards-driven education, a time when the role of play is diminishing in formal educational contexts. In fact, play-based learning has largely disappeared in early childhood education, particularly in kindergarten (Miller & Almon, 2009). This is due to skepticism about the value of play in academic learning and the assumption that the earlier children read, the more likely they are to be successful in school. This assumption has led schools to focus more on early reading skills, particularly code-based skills such as the alphabet and phonics. As a result, many pre-K and kindergarten classes have changes from play-based to structured instruction using scripted curricula.

The findings of the study have two important implications. First, in order to be responsive to children, teachers need to be free from scripted instruction—it is hard for them to be responsive to children if they are bound to a tight lesson plan. Instead, they should take advantage of child-initiated learning, expand from the children's interests, and build teachable moments. This requires the teachers to be flexible and spontaneous, and the context of play allows them to be like that. If teachers intend to reinforce target vocabulary words within the dramatic play center, we advise them to follow the child-initiated topics, and extend the children's utterances, rather than attempting to teach vocabulary words explicitly. Then the children can use more pretend talk while sustaining their play. Second, the study supports the conclusions of the NELP report (NIL, 2009), in which Dickinson, Golinkoff, Hirsh-Pasek, Neuman, and Burchinal (2009) urged educators to look not only at the code skills but also to pay attention to comprehensive language development, associated background knowledge, and conceptual development. Early oral language development is a key to later reading development. The relationships between oral language skills and reading comprehension have been richly documented, from classical studies (e.g., Storch & Whitehurst, 2002) to recent ones (e.g., Lervåg, Hulme, & Melby-Lervåg, 2018; Parkin, 2018; Tosto et al., 2017). Play-based instruction, such as the model used in our study (guided play and dramatic play with responsive teachers) is an ideal context for learning such comprehensive oral language skills.

The limitations of the study include the small sample size and non-longitudinal data comparison. For future study, we suggest researchers examine longitudinal data on later reading comprehension as well as the vocabulary of children who participate in play-based instruction with teachers exhibiting different response levels. Regardless of the limitations, however, the present study provides additional evidence that play in school supports language learning. Preschool classrooms should continue to take advantage of play, which is children's favorite thing to do.

REFERENCES

August, D., & Shanahan, T. (2006), *Developing literacy in second language learners: A report of the National Literacy Panel on language minority children and youth.* Mahwah, NJ: Erlbaum.

Bakhtin, M. M. (1991). *Dialogic imagination: Four essays by M. M. Bakhtin* (C. Emerson & M. Holquist, Trans.). Austin, TX: University of Texas Press.

Bowne, J. B., Yoshikawa, H., & Snow, C. E. (2016). Relationships of teachers' language and explicit vocabulary instruction to students' vocabulary growth in kindergarten. *Reading Research Quarterly,* 52(1), 7–29. DOI: 10.1002/rrq.151.

Cartmill, E. A., Armstrong III, B. F., Gleitman, L. R., Goldin-Meadow, S., Medina, T. N., & Trueswell, J. C. (2013). Quality of early parent input predicts child vocabulary 3 years later. *Proceedings of the National Academy of Sciences of the United States of America,* 110(28), 11278–11283.

Cunningham, D. & Breault, D. (2017). Educative experiences in early childhood: Lessons from Dewey. In Lynn Cohen & Sandra Waite-Stupiansky (Editors), *Theories of Early Childhood Education: Developmental, Behaviorist, and Critical.* Routledge.

Davis, M. H., Di Betta, A. M., MacDonald, M. J. E., & Gaskell, M. G. (2009). Learning and consolidation of novel spoken words. *Journal of Cognitive Neuroscience,* 21(4), 803–820. DOI: 10.1162/jocn.2009.21059.

De Rivera, C., Girolametto, L., Greenberg, J., & Weitzman, E. (2005). Children's responses to educators' questions in day care play groups. *American Journal of Speech-Language Pathology,* 14(1), 14–26.

Dewey, J. (1902). *The child and the curriculum.* Chicago, IL: The University of Chicago Press.

Dickinson, D. K., Collins, M. F., Nesbitt, K., Toub, T. S., Hassinger-Das, B., Burke Hadley, E., Hirsh-Pasek, K., & Golinkoff, R. M. (2018). Effects of teacher-delivered book reading and play on vocabulary learning and self-regulation among low-income preschool children. *Journal of Cognition and Development,* DOI: 10.1080/15248372.2018.1483373.

Dickinson, D., Golinkoff, R., Hirsh-Pasek, K., Neuman, S., & Burchinal, P. (2009). The language of emergent literacy: A response to the National Institute for Literacy report on early literacy, available at http://nieer.org/wp-content/uploads/2016/08/CommentaryOnNELPreport.pdf.

Duncan, R. M., & Tarulli, D. (2003). Play as the leading activity of the preschool period: Insights from Vygotsky, Leont'ev and Bakhtin. *Early Education and Development. Spcial Issue: Vygotskian Perspectives in Early Childhood Education,* 14(3), 271–292. DOI: 10.1207/s15566935eed1403_2.

Dunn, L. M., & Dunn, L. M. (2007). *PPVT-4: Peabody Picture Vocabulary Test.* Minneapolis, MN: Pearson Assessment.

Gaviria-Loaiza, J., Han, M., Vu, J., & Hustedt, J. (2017). Children's responses to different types of teacher involvement during free play. *Journal of Childhood Studies,* 42(3), 4–19. https://journals.uvic.ca/index.php/jcs/article/view/17890/7533

Gest, S. D., Holland-Coviello, R., Welsh, J. A., Eicher-Catt, D. L., & Gill, S. (2006). Language development subcontexts in Head Start classrooms: Distinctive patterns of teacher talk during free play, mealtime, and book reading. *Early Education & Development,* 17, 293–315.

Girolametto, L., Weitzman, E., van Lieshout, R., & Duff, D. (2000). Directiveness in teacher's language input to toddlers and preschoolers in day care. *Journal of Speech, Language, and Hearing Research,* 43(5), 1101–1114.

Gough, P.B., & Tunmer, W.F. (1986). Decoding, reading and reading disability. *Remedial and Special Education,* 7, 6–10.

Gupta, A. (2009). Vygotskian perspectives on using dramatic play to enhance children's development and balance creativity with structure in the early childhood classroom. *Early Child Development and Care,* 179(8), 1041–1054. DOI: 10.1080/03004430701731654.

Hirsh-Pasek, K., Adamson, L. B., Bakeman, R., Owen, M. T., Golinkoff, R. M., Pace, A., Yust, P. K. S., & Suma, K. (2015). The contribution of early communication quality to low-income children's language success. *Psychological Science, 26* (7), 1071–1083. DOI: 10.1177/0956797615581493.

Jean, M., & Geva, E. (2009). The development of vocabulary in english as a second language children and its role in predicting word recognition ability. *Applied Psycholinguistics,* 30(1), 153–185.

Johnson, J., Christie, J., & Wardle, F. (2005). *Play, development, and early childhood.* Boston: Pearson.

Lervåg, A., Hulme, C., & Melby-Lervåg, M. (2018). Unpicking the developmental relationship between oral language skills and reading comprehension: It's simple, but complex. *Child Development,* 89(5), 1821–1838.

Lillard, A. S., Lerner, M. D., Hopkins, E. J., Dore, R. A., Smith, E. D., & Palmquist, C. M. (2013). The impact of pretend play on children's development: A review of the evidence. *Psychological Bulletin,* 139(1), 1–34. doi:10.1037/a0029321

Lonigan C. J., Wagner R. K., Torgesen J. K., & Rashotte C. A. (2007). *Test of preschool early literacy.* Austin, TX: Pro-Ed.

Luu, T. M., Vohr, B. R., Schneider, K. C., Katz, K. H., Tucker, R., Allan, W. C., & Ment, L. R. (2009). Trajectories of receptive language development from 3 to 12 years of age for very preterm children. *Pediatrics,* 124(1), 333–341. DOI: https://doi-org.udel.idm.oclc.org/10.1542/peds.2008-2587.

McLeod, R. H., Kaiser, A. P., & Hardy, J. K. (2018). The relation between teacher vocabulary use in play and child vocabulary outcomes. *Topics in Early Childhood Special Education.* 39(2), 103–116. DOI: 10.1177/0271121418812675.

Meacham, S. (2013). Preschool teachers' language use in sociodramatic play. [Doctoral dissertation, University of Delaware]. Available from ProQuest Dissertations & Theses Global database. (UMI No. 3594953).

Meacham, S., Vukelich, C., Han, M., & Buell, M. (2013). Preschool teachers' language use during dramatic play. *European Early Childhood Education Research Journal,* 22(5), 250–267. DOI:10.1080/1350293X.2013.789196.

Meacham, S., Vukelich, C., Han, M., & Buell, M. (2016). Teachers' responsiveness to pre-schoolers' utterances in sociodramatic play. *Early Education and Development,* 27(3), 318–335. DOI:10.1080/10409289.2015.1057461.

Miller, E., & Almon, J. (2009). Crisis in the Kindergarten: Why children need to play in school, Alliance for Childhood, https://files.eric.ed.gov/fulltext/ED504839.pdf.

NICHD Early Child Care Research Network. (2005). Pathways to reading: The role of oral language in the transition to reading. *Developmental Psychology,* 41(2), 428–442.

National Institute for Literacy (January 8, 2009). Developing early literacy: Report of the National Early Literacy Panel, http://www.nifl.gov/nifl/publications/pdf/NELPSummary. pdf, p. 218.

Parkin, J. R. (2018). Wechsler Individual Achievement Test-third edition (WIAT-III) oral language and reading measures effects on reading comprehension in a referred sample. *Journal of Psychoeducational Assessment,* 36(3), 203–218.

Pellegrini, A. D., & Galda, L. (1993). Ten years after: A reexamination of symbolic play and literacy research. *Reading Research Quarterly,* 28(2), 163–175. DOI: 10.2307/747887.

Pursi, A., & Lipponen, L. (2017). Constituting play connection with very young children: Adults' active participation in play. *Learning, Culture, and Social Interaction,* 17, 21–37. DOI: 10.1016/j.lcsi.2017.12.001.

Randima Rajapaksha, P. L. N. (2016). Scaffolding dramatic play in the preschool classroom: The teacher's role. *Mediterranean Journal of Social Sciences,* 7(4), 689–694. DOI: 10.5901/ mjss.2016.v7n4p689

Rogoff, B. (1991). Social interaction as apprenticeship in thinking: Guided participation in spatial planning. In L. B. Resnick, J. M. Levine, & S. D. Teasley (Eds.), *Perspectives on socially shared cognition* (pp. 349–364). Washington, DC: American Psychological Association.

Rogoff, B., & Lave, J. (Eds.). (1984). *Everyday cognition: Its development in social context.* Cambridge, MA: Harvard University Press.

Rowe, D. W. (1998). The literate potentials of book-related dramatic play. *Reading Research Quarterly,* 33(1), 10–35. DOI: 10.1598/RRQ.33.1.2.

Storch, S. A., & Whitehurst, G. J. (2002). Oral language and code-related precursors to reading: Evidence from a longitudinal structural model. *Developmental Psychology,* 38(6), 934–947.

Tompkins, V., Bengochea, A., Nicol, S., & Justice, L. M. (2017). Maternal inferential input and children's language skills. *Reading Research Quarterly,* 52(4), 397–416. DOI: 10.1002/rrq. 176.

Tompkins, V., Zucker, T. A., Justice, L. M., & Binici, S. (2013). Inferential talk during teacher-child interactions in small-group play. *Early Childhood Research Quarterly,* 28(2), 424–436.

Tosto, M. G., Hayiou-Thomas, M. E., Harlaar, N., Prom-Wormley, E., Dale, P. S., & Plomin, R. (2017). The genetic architecture of oral language, reading fluency, and reading comprehension: A twin study from 7 to 16 years. *Developmental Psychology,* 53(6), 1115–1129. DOI: 10.1037/dev0000297.

Toub, T. S., Hasinger-Das, B., Turner Nesbitt, K., Ilgaz, H., Skolnick Weisberg, D., Hirsh-Pasek, K., Golinkoff, R. M., Nicolopoulou, A., & Dickinson, D. K. (2018). The language of play: Developing preschool vocabulary through play following shared book-reading. *Early Childhood Research Quarterly,* 45, 1–17. DOI: 10.1016/j.ecresq.2018.01.010.

Vygotsky, L. S. (1978). *Mind and society: The development of higher mental processes.* Cambridge, MA: Harvard University Press.

Part IV

Teacher and Adult Education

Chapter Eight

Re-Learning to Play

Mediating Pre-Service Teachers' Exploration of Drama-Based Instruction

Timothy M. Vetere and Matthew E. Poehner

INTRODUCTION

The field of second language (L2) education has a long tradition of presenting language to learners as comprising lexical lists to be memorized and morpho-syntactic rules to be studied one at a time and mechanically practiced (Lightbown & Spada, 2013). Over the past thirty years, L2 teaching, research, and practice have witnessed a gradual shift toward emphasizing opportunities for learners to use language for meaningful communication even at the earliest levels of language study. While learner personal meanings and creative uses of language are recognized as valuable for developing their L2 abilities, theory in the field has tended to lag behind this advance, with many perspectives attempting to leverage such activity as yet further opportunity for manipulating grammatical structures.

A case in point is drama-based instruction (DBI). DBI, which involves the purposeful integration of the elements of drama into curriculum and instruction (e.g., role-play, improvisation, pantomime, etc.) has been discussed in research as an opportunity for learners to engage in contextualized communication and to see why and how language can be used to express particular meaning, that is, a focus on the relation between language forms and meanings (Darvin, 2015; Di Pietro, 1987; Early & Yeung, 2009). Belliveau and Kim (2013) observe, however, that in actual practice, this relation may be dissolved as drama techniques are often realized through scripted dialogues that are memorized and rehearsed, through role-plays lacking meaningful context, and in the form of warm-up games that precede actual language instruction and practice (Di Naploi & Algarra, 2001; Matthias, 2007).

In addition to sacrificing the potential to integrate language and instruction, the kinds of drama practices in the classroom described by Belliveau and Kim (2013) are also likely to miss one of the major benefits that drama has to offer to all individuals: the development of participants' socio-emotional and cognitive knowledge, a goal that in fact supersedes the production of any formal performance. Properly facilitated, this knowledge manifests itself through personal experience(s) and becomes actively embodied during DBI activities. In short, DBI uniquely opens up possibilities for dynamic interpersonal interactions in diverse imaginary contexts. Teachers and students alike are given the chance to learn, reflect upon, and define their selfhood in relation to others in the world.

This chapter reports on data taken from a larger longitudinal study of a university L2 teacher education program in which DBI was re-theorized as a form of play-based Zone of Proximal Development (ZPD) activity designed to drive instruction (see Vetere, 2018, for the larger study). Vygotsky (1978) argued that imaginative, socio-dramatic play creates contexts in which individuals, with appropriate mediation, achieve in imaginative performance what they are otherwise not yet capable of and that such activity constitutes a ZPD because it is through this performing beyond themselves that their abilities develop further (see also Karpov, 2014). While Vygotsky primarily discussed the developmental value of play for young children, its potential as a ZPD activity has more recently been investigated among older children and adults in a variety of domains (e.g., Holzman, 2009, 2010; Lobman & Lundquist, 2007), including languages (Haught & McCafferty, 2008). The present project drew upon these insights in an effort to reframe L2 DBI for preservice teachers not as an eclectic set of instructional techniques but as a distinct pedagogical methodology emphasizing imagination, creativity, and meaning-making through language.

The present chapter reports the experiences of ten pre-service L2 teachers as they first engaged in dramatic play themselves as part of a teaching methods course and then profiles one participant's early attempts to employ those principles to promote playful ZPD activity during a teaching field experience in a US primary school. Analysis of participant lesson plans and teaching reflections, along with researcher field notes of classroom observations and semi-structured interviews, highlight moments of struggle, confusion, and success as play is "re-learned" and teaching re-conceived.

PLAY, DRAMA, AND THE ZONE OF PROXIMAL DEVELOPMENT

Edmiston (2007) maintains that "fictional situations create what Vygotsky (1967) conceptualized as 'zones of proximal development,' (ZPD), where 'a child is a head taller' and where the often-hidden potentials of children can be revealed" (p. 338). Vygotsky himself conducted research into children's play, and this work has become influential in early childhood education. However, more recently some have sought to extend to other populations Vygotsky's analyses of the developmental benefits to engaging in imagined scenarios where one performs beyond one's current capabilities; that is, the argument that has been proposed, and that provided an impetus for the research reported in this chapter is the potential for forms of play to promote development among adults. In this regard, Holzman (2009, 2010) sees the 'head taller' experience as presenting unlimited possibilities outside of early childhood, and she suggests drama or performance-based activity as, for adults, the developmental analogue to socio-dramatic play in children. Specifically, Holzman (2009) describes performing "in the theatrical sense of the word" as sharing "similarities to the pretend play of early childhood in which children are doing what is familiar to them and, at the same time, doing things that are brand new, things that are beyond them" (pp. 18–19).

In Vygotsky's (1978) formulation, it is stressed that play consists of two necessary components—an imaginary situation and the following of rules (Lantolf & Poehner, 2014; Bodrova & Leong, 2007). Rather than reflecting a child's current cognitive ability, Vygotsky argued that play is an activity that leads, rather than follows, cognitive development in early childhood (ages 3–6).[1] Duncan and Tarulli (2003) explain the developmental significance Vygotsky saw in play as follows:

> leading activity refers to that particular activity through which the most important psychological and social changes occur during a given developmental period. These most important changes are the specific changes that prepare the child for the further challenges of the next developmental stage. (p. 272)

Play, as the leading developmental activity of early childhood, fundamentally changes the child's relationship with his/her present social environment, which in turn requires the need for a new leading activity as the child enters formal schooling and begins to engage in the study of academic content areas. For this reason, one notes in Vygotsky's writings a shift in which play is replaced as a leading developmental activity upon the child's arrival in formal classroom learning contexts, where engagement with abstract conceptual knowledge becomes the driving force of continued development. In this sense, there is a distinction that may be drawn between the ZPD as activity in which a child is a head taller than himself during early childhood and the

ZPD of schooling, wherein the focus is on the relation between the child's everyday knowledge of the world and the conceptual knowledge made available in the classroom.

As mentioned, more recent Vygotskian scholarship has begun to how sharp this distinction must be and specifically how play may continue to hold developmental significance for older children and adults. Bodrova and Leong (2007) express this point as follows

> Vygotskians do not believe that socially oriented play disappears when children reach the age of 7 or 8. Children at 10 and 11 still play socially, but...the older the child, the more time is spent in negotiating roles and actions (rules) and the less time is spent on acting out the script (imaginary situation). (p. 136)

Holzman (2010) speculates that Vygotsky "overlooked some continuity between the two ZPDs [play and school-based learning], in part because he was so concerned with learning in formalized school contexts" (pp. 35–36). She argues that "play might indeed be the highest level of preschool development, but it would be a mistake to infer from this that play's developmental potential is limited to the preschool years" (Holzman, 2009, pp. 52–53). She cautions, however, that this does not mean that older children and adults should simply be directed to engage in open or free play for its own sake; rather, she maintains that the value of play may reside in how it shifts the way in which other activities, including formal learning, are approached. As she puts it, "in order for learning past early childhood to be developmental, it needs to be done playfully" (Holzman, 2009, p. 53).

In our view, drama–including its more formal counterpart, theatre - offers one sort of playfulness in which priority is given to creativity, imagination, and the taking on of 'roles' and identities other than one's own. In this regard, drama, while perhaps more structured and systematic than play during early childhood, holds potential to create contexts in which older children and adults can explore and learn. In the remainder of this chapter, we consider how DBI practices might be leveraged to create play-based ZPDs as a critical feature of pedagogy aimed at promoting learner development through study of another language.

Following our reading of the Vygotskian research literature on play, the following four criteria emerged as central for play-based ZPD activity: (1) an explicit imaginative context; (2) explicit roles to be assumed by participants that follow particular social rules of behavior related to the agreed upon imaginative context; (3) creative imitation of the assumed social roles; and (4) the existence of a conflict or a need to be satisfied in the drama to provide motivation, or a desire to learn and participate in the drama; importantly, the conflict or need must be addressed using targeted academic concepts with feedback and self-reflection provided by the teacher (or in Vygotsky's terms, the *mediator* of the activity). The first three requirements are derived from Vygotsky's definition of a sociodramatic play activity during early childhood while the fourth requirement comes from his outline of a formal learning activity (see Vygotsky, 1978). It is theorized that if a DBI strategy incorporates these requirements learning that leads cognitive development can take place during playful/learning ZPD activity.

To this end, Vygotskian-informed DBI might offer a fundamental reorganization of how teacher-candidates orient to their practice as emerging L2 educators attempting to promote communicative-based standards of language teaching/learning.

(RE)LEARNING TO PLAY

This study began by exploring ten teacher-candidates' original experiences incorporating Vygotskian-informed DBI into their emerging teaching practice during an elementary field experience. The L2 teacher preparation program, where this study took place, leads to a four-year undergraduate degree that qualifies candidates to teach in grades PK–12. During their fifth semester in the program, teacher-candidates are engaged in a supervised field experience that works to develop their language instruction skills in the early grades.

Working in small groups, the field experience requires teacher-candidates to co-construct an eight-week FLEX (Foreign Language Exploration) unit, design and purposefully incorporate instructional materials, write original lesson plans, and co-teach in an after-school world languages program for students in grades 1–5. The students' work in the field experience is complemented by a concurrent three-credit course intended to introduce an array of pedagogical methods and approaches for teaching world languages in the elementary grades. The course instructor (one of the researchers) also served as the field experience supervisor.

The ten teacher-candidates became familiar with a select number of DBI strategies prior to the start of the elementary field experience. These strategies included role-play (assuming a character or persona in an imaginary context), pantomime (physical expression without words), puppetry (giving lifelike characteristics to inanimate objects), and story-telling (i.e., dramatizing or extending the actions described in a story rather than traditional story-reading). Role-play, puppetry, pantomime, and story-telling were discussed in the methods class due to their making an appearance in the course readings. The course text initially positioned DBI instructional tools as a way to link language and action. In this way, DBI was intended to assist in producing contextualized communicative-based learning situations.

DBI strategies, such as role-play, pantomime, puppetry, and story-telling, were described among several pedagogical tools that could help create communicative-based learning experiences. They existed alongside an array of other non-DBI strategies (e.g., games, songs, Gouin Series, Total Physical Response, etc.). In other words, the course textbook presented a Drama-as-Tool orientation to DBI, wherein DBI is conceptualized as a set of instructional tools that support teacher-driven, short-term learning exercises instead of distinct theoretically motivated methodological approach to language teaching and learning (such as in a Drama-as-Methodology framework).

Through class discussions, the essential characteristics to create playful/learning ZPD activity, described earlier, were provided to students and models were given. We wish to note that while DBI strategies were presented in the course readings and were discussed and modeled by the course instructor, the latter presentation specifically followed a Vygotskian theoretical orientation, and this led to what we term a Drama-as-Methodology orientation rather than one of Drama-as-Tool.

When the teacher-candidates began the elementary field experience, their lesson plans tended to incorporate the textbook's approach to DBI in an effort to support L2 learning rather than the way in which DBI had been presented during discussions by their instructor in their methods course. Consequently, DBI strategies, if used, were supportive of a teacher-dominated approach to L2 meaning-making via primarily alternative didactic teaching methods rather than as a unique pedagogical approach grounded in a coherent theoretical view of teaching and learning—a Vygotskian-informed drama-based methodology to L2 teaching and learning.

The course instructor endeavored to mediate the teacher-candidates' awareness and conceptual understanding of the role DBI strategies were playing in L2 instruction. Specifically, he shared observational notes of their teaching practices, engaged in mini-conferences after lessons at the elementary field site, and provided written feedback on participants' blogs and teaching videos during the first five weeks of the elementary field experience. However, in spite of these ongoing attempts at mediation, the teacher-candidates continued to conceptualize DBI-as-Tool rather than DBI-as-Methodology for L2 teaching/learning.

In an attempt to (re)introduce a DBI-as-Methodology orientation, the teacher-candidates were given an in-depth workshop during week six of the eight-week elementary field experience. This workshop more explicitly presented DBI, as informed by Vygotskian-principles, and addressed its potential to create playful/learning ZPD activity that would drive L2 learning and instruction in formal learning environments. It was suspected that the participants perpetual use of DBI-as-Tool may have been a result of the abstract methods they were subjected to when being originally introduced to DBI during their methods course (e.g., generalized anecdotal examples and class discussion vs. detailed modeling with hands-on active participation and critical reflection). The workshop thus intended, through its more conceptual focus, to provide teacher-candidates a stronger framework upon which they could draw to create lessons to support intentional playful/learning ZPD activity; that is learning activities that consisted of the Vygotskian-informed criteria.

The workshop involved an in-depth discussion of the history and purpose of using DBI strategies in the classroom followed by an explicit outline of the four pieces of criteria theorized as being necessary for playful/learning ZPD activity to take place. Participants were then provided a list of terms and definitions of commonly used drama strategies (see Table 8.1). This list contained thirteen commonly used DBI strategies, compiled from the literature across the field of drama in education. It greatly expanded on the previous four DBI strategies that had been discussed earlier in the course (role-play, pantomime, puppetry, and storytelling).

The workshop concluded by providing the teacher-candidates with an opportunity to critically engage in three hands-on DBI activities by involving themselves in playful/learning ZPDs themselves. These activities included a modified alley/gauntlet activity, *tableaux vivants*, and role-play and were chosen to illustrate how DBI could accommodate a range of linguistic demands, variations in participation, and diverse proficiency levels from the perspective of both teachers and learners. By doing this, the flexibility that exists among DBI strategies to address a wide-range of learner needs, teacher skill, and instructional situations was showcased. It was intended that by experiencing a variety of DBI strategies in action from a DBI-as-Methodology perspective, teacher-candidates would trouble their current conceptual understanding of DBI's role in the language classroom.

We now turn to a discussion of one of the teacher-candidates, Max[2], and to his attempt to reconceptualize his work in the field experience following the DBI workshop. Focusing our attention on only one participant permits a more in-depth analysis of the actual application of DBI techniques and the teacher-candidate's reasoning and reflection than would otherwise be possible. However, we do not wish to convey that Max was representative of all the participants in this study. We selected him due to his willingness to experiment with DBI during the field experience and his candor in critically reflecting upon what he perceived to be the benefits and challenges to using it. In this regard, understanding Max's experiences may be informative to future work in this area.

Table 8.1. List of Terms and Definitions of Commonly Used Drama Tools and Techniques

Pantomime	Conveying action, thoughts, and feelings without words; communicating with your body.
Narrative Pantomime	Teacher narrates, coaches, guides a scene while the group pantomimes the action/story.
Improvisation	To create and execute anything extemporaneously, without preparation—"making it up as you go along."
Storytelling	Telling stories—not story reading. Delivering a story in a unique creative way, i.e., puppetry, felt board, dress-up, etc.
Panel/Interview	Students imagine they are an expert on a topic. They are questioned by their peers on the topic.
Soundscape	Atmosphere or mood created by the use of sound.
Alley/Gauntlet	Two lines of people facing each other with space between as an alleyway for participants to 'walk down.'
Tableaux Vivants	Frozen pictures of people to portray a concept that the students can then discuss.
Role-Play	Becoming a character or persona. May include teacher-in-role, student-in-role, and/or writing-in-role.
Side-Coach	Offering guidance, supplying words/phrases, and questioning individuals or the group while they are involved in dramatic play.
Guided Imagery	Teacher narrates, coaches, guides a scene using descriptive words to assist students in forming mental or physically drawn images.
Props	Objects used by the role-player.
Puppetry	Giving life-like characteristics to inanimate objects.

BEING AND BECOMING A LANGUAGE TEACHER: TEACHING AS PLAYFUL PERFORMANCE

Max was a 21-year-old undergraduate teacher-candidate concentrating in French education. When the elementary field experience began, he was focused on improving his use of instructional French in the classroom, which he discussed in his first written teaching reflection:

> My weakest area coming in, I think, was actually having the confidence to use 90%+ French in the classroom setting... On Thursday, I really tried to use a lot more French with the students to sort of transition them into 90%+ mode (Written Teaching Reflection, 10/4/2015).

In an effort to continue meeting this goal, Max challenged himself to read a folktale aloud in the target language during the second week of the elementary field experience. Max self-identified pantomime, storytelling, and narrative pantomiming as the specific DBI strategies he felt he implemented in this particular learning activity. Excerpt 1 illustrates Max's attempt to negotiate meaning among his students, (Thomas, Mitch, Grant, and Eric), using his conceptual understanding of pantomime (double parentheses indicates non-speech activity) See the Table 8.2. Excerpt 1:

Table 8.2. Excerpt 1

Line	Speaker	Utterance[s] and Action[s]	Translation
00	Max	*((Reading))* <L'écureuil effrayé>.	*((Reading))* <The scared squirrel>.
01	Thomas	The squirrel was -	The squirrel was -
02 03 04 05 06 07	Max	*((Continuing to read))* - <Écureuil avait <u>peur</u>> . .hh Qu'est-ce que c'est peur? <u>Peur</u>. J'ai ↑peur. *((Throws both hands in front of face, gasps, and turns head away suddenly))*. >J'ai peur<!	*((Continuing to read))* - <Squirrel was scared> . .hh What is peur? Peur. J'ai ↑<u>peur</u>. *((Throws both hands in front of face, gasps, and turns head away suddenly))*. >J'ai peur<!
08	Mitch	Scared.	Scared.
09	Max	Scared.	Scared.
10	Grant	[The squirrel was scared].	[The squirrel was scared].
11 12 13 14 15 16	Max	[Il a peur]. <Il ne pouvait pas> *((shakes index finger of his left hand back and forth to indicate a negative action))* ma::nge::r *((pantomimes bringing food to his mouth several times))*.	[He was scared]. <He could not> *((shakes index finger of his left hand back and forth to indicate a negative action))* e::at *((pantomimes bringing food to his mouth several times))*.
17	Eric	Eating acorns.	Eating acorns.
18 19	Max	*((Shakes his finger again to indicate a negative action))* Il ne <u>pouvait</u> pas.	*((Shakes his finger again to indicate a negative action))* He could not.
20	Mitch	He couldn't eat	He couldn't eat
21 22 23 24	Max	He (.) <u>couldn't</u> eat. *((Reading))* Il ne pouvait pas *((leans his head towards his left shoulder and closes his eyes))* <u>dormi::r</u>.	He (.) <u>couldn't</u> eat. *((Reading))* He could not *((leans his head towards his left shoulder and closes his eyes))* <u>sle::ep</u>.
25	Mitch	He couldn't sleep.	He couldn't sleep.

In lines 4–6, 15–16, and 22–23 it is possible to see Max's original conceptualization of pantomime as a DBI learning strategy. He employs an Initiation-Response-Evaluation/Feedback (I.R.E/F) pattern of classroom discourse to guide the learners in L2 meaning-making. This teacher-dominated approach to language learning involves Max changing the tone and pitch of his voice while providing complementary non-verbal gestures to hint at the meaning of his L2 speech practices. Max uses his students' L1 responses as his only form of assessing their L2 comprehension. Since Max continues to speak in the target language until the students provide an acceptable translation, they guess L1 interpretations of his pantomimes until a satisfactory response is accepted. When the students do provide a "correct" translation, he uses that moment to discontinue the use of the L2 and provide an evaluative comment in the students' L1. Thus, confirmation, and validation, of L2 meaning-making is only completed through the act of direct translation. As such, the L2 story reading endeavor is a learning exercise targeting the students' L1 deductive reasoning skills through the use of pantomime as a comprehension aide (i.e., Drama-as-Tool orientation).

Similar to how his peers in the teacher preparation program first used DBI strategies in the L2 classroom, it becomes apparent that Max reserved the use of pantomime as a way to assist target language comprehension throughout his learning activity. Without explicit instruction or voiced expectations to use DBI strategies otherwise, Max used drama-based strategies to promote meaning-making through direct translation via teacher-directed comprehension questions rather than as a way to drive L2 instruction through playful/learning ZPD activity.

As Max progresses through the story, he begins to demonstrate a noticeable change in his use of pantomime as seen in Excerpt 2. See the Table 8.3. Excerpt 2:

Table 8.3. Excerpt 2

Line	Speaker	Utterance[s] and Action[s]	Translation
00 01 02 03 04 05	Max	Ou::i. *((Reading))* <↑N'as tu pas> re::marqué? ↓a demandé Écureuil↑. LA LUNE *((extends left arm and points upwards))* est en ↑train de ↑disparaître *((closes left hand into a fist on the word disparaître)).*	Ye::s. *((Reading))* <↑Didn't you> notice? ↓asked Squirrel↑. THE MOON *((extends left arm and points upwards))* ↑is ↑disappearing *((closes left hand into a fist on the word disappearing)).*
06	Thomas	T[he moon disappears].	[The moon disappears].
07	Jack	[The moon disappeared]!	[The moon disappeared]!
08	Gavin	[The moon disappears].	[The moon disappears].
09 10 11 12 13 14 15 16 17	Max	<The moon (.) is disappearing>! *((shakes his fist as he returns his hand to the book. Continues reading))* <Nous devons maintenant> *((points downward with left hand twice on the syllables of the word maintenant))* RASSembler *((takes his left hand and moves it in a circular fashion*	<The moon (.) is disappearing>! *((shakes his fist as he returns his hand to the book. Continues reading))* <We must now> *((points downward with left hand twice on the syllables of the word maintenant))* GATher *((takes his left hand and moves it in a circular fashion towards his chest*

18		*towards his chest as if gathering*	*as if gathering something, or*
19		*something, or beckoning*	*beckoning something to come*
20		*something to come close to him))*	*close to him))* all *((points*
21		toute *((points horizontally with his*	*horizontally with his finger))* the
22		*finger))* la nouritture *((squeezes*	food *((squeezes his left thumb to*
23		*his left thumb to his remaining*	*his remaining five fingers and*
24		*five fingers and places them near*	*places them near his mouth to*
		his mouth to indicate eating)) -	*indicate eating)) -*
25	Mitch	He picked -	He picked
26	Max	>What do you think that means<?	>What do you think that means<?
27	Thomas	P-PICked up a::ll the food?	P-PICked up a::ll the food?
28	Gavin	[Gather]?	[Gather]?
29	Max	*((Points at Gavin))* Ga::ther.	*((Points at Gavin))* Ga::ther.
30		*((Repeats his previous gesture by*	*((Repeats his previous gesture by*
31		*taking his left hand and moving it*	*taking his left hand and moving it*
32		*in a circular fashion to symbolize*	*in a circular fashion to symbolize*
33		*gathering something close to his*	*gathering something close to his*
34		*chest))* all the fo::od >que nous<	*chest))* all the fo::od >that we<
35		<pouvons avant qu'il ne soit trop	<can before it's too late>. Before
36		tard>. Before it's to::o late.	it's to::o late.

In lines 00–05 and 12–24 of Excerpt 2, rather than engaging with pantomime after his L2 utterance, and then initiating a request from the students for an expression of their comprehension in their L1, he begins to use physical actions simultaneously with his speech practices. Max continues to validate students' responses in their L1, but he begins to use physical actions as a way to communicate through the story by embodying the language at the same time. Recalling that pantomime was defined in the workshop as "conveying action, thoughts, and feelings without words; communicating with your body," (see Table 8.1), by adding verbal communication alongside the physical actions Max unknowingly changes the DBI strategy he was using from "pantomime" to "teacher-in-role" who uses physical gestures in character.

As Max continues reading the folktale, a character named Hibou makes an appearance in the story. See the Table 8.4. Excerpt 3:

Table 8.4.   Excerpt 3

Line	Speaker	Utterance[s] and Action[s]	Translation
00	Max	*((Reading; Raises pitch*	*((Reading; Raises pitch*
01		*significantly to create a caricature*	*significantly to create a caricature*
02		*of an old man and slows rhythm*	*of an old man and slows rhythm*
03		*when speaking as Hibou))* Vous	*when speaking as Hibou))* You
04		êtes >↑tous ridicules<, a dit	are >↑all ridicules>, said Hibou.
05		Hibou. >↑Ra::ssemblez-vous<	>↑Ga::ther< *((takes left hand and*
06		*((takes left hand and with a*	*with a sweeping gesture shakes*
07		*sweeping gesture shakes his*	*his index finger at all of the*
08		*index finger at all of the students))*	*students))* ARound *((jabs left*

09	AUtour ((*jabs left index finger at*	*index finger at students))* and
10	*students))* et ((*proceeds to jab left*	((*proceeds to jab left finger at*
11	*finger at students on each*	*students on each syllable for the*
12	*syllable for the remaining L2*	*remaining L2 sentence))* I will
13	*sentence))* je vais vous	>↑TEach< you (.) something
14	>↑APprendre< (.) quelque chose	about the ↓mo::on. >What do you
15	au sujet de la ↓lu::ne. >What do	think he says<?
	you think he says<?	

With Hibou, Max noticeably changes his reading practice. He continued to gesture alongside his L2 utterances, but he also adopted speech patterns that significantly altered his persona. Hibou was described as being both wise and old. As such, Max attempted to present his perception of a "wise and old" character by raising his pitch, fluctuating the prosodic features of the L2, and making his tone drastically more nasal. By incorporating diverse vocalizations and gestures designed to invoke the personality of Hibou (most notably, jabbing his finger on the individual syllables of words spoken by Hibou), Max assumes elements of role-play (specifically, teacher-in-role) into his learning activity. It is unclear why he reserves this shift in vocal performance only during Hibou's speech practices and not with other characters in the story. He does, however, continue to validate students' L1 translations by affirming their responses in their L1 and adopting his normal voice, which maintains the Drama-as-Tool framework.

In using pantomime and teacher-in-role, Max introduces elements of a play activity into his lesson. It is possible to see Max using his imagination and creative imitation (based on his personal experiences) to create identifiable gestures that represent the meaning behind his L2 utterances. Likewise, the students needed to use their imaginations to recognize, interpret, and identify the actions conducted within the pantomime activity. However, the students remained outside of the imaginary context of the story for the duration of the lesson, consciously aware through the I.R.E/F discourse pattern of their continued role as novice L2 learners within the real-world setting of the elementary world language classroom. The imaginative world where the story took place (including the conflicts, conditions, and consequences experienced by the characters) and the world of the classroom remained separate. The students did not have an opportunity to interact with the L2, or imitate Max's modeled behavior(s), in a way that moved beyond direct translation. Thus, while Max used imagination, followed rules/constraints of behavior and creative imitation while engaged on the imaginative plane during the reading of the story, the students did not.

In order for Max to have used pantomime and role-play as a means to create playful/learning ZPD activity, he would have needed to invert his approach to the lesson. Rather than pantomime and role-play being used as tools to comprehend L2 story-reading, L2 story-reading is necessitated because of pantomime and role-play. For example, the students would need to assume explicit roles within a particular imaginative context wherein they would have been faced with a need to listen and respond to the reading of the folktale (e.g., the Library of Congress has heard that the students have been studying French, which is good news because they need someone to listen and record a rare folktale, and they know these students would be great folklorists, etc.). However, in lacking a conceptual framework to (re)orient to a DBI-as-Methodology orientation, Max sees the DBI strategies in this lesson, (role-play and pantomime), simply as useful tools to facilitate L2 comprehension and to support his main learning activity: story-reading.

REFLECTING ON PRACTICE

Reflecting on this particular lesson, Max found himself questioning the effectiveness of his chosen teaching strategies:

> I wonder what more I could have done to convey meaning while using less English. Perhaps doing a more dramatic presentation, but then I don't know that students would have the same opportunity to make vocabulary connections (Weekly Reflection, 10/11/2015).

Max seems to contemplate whether or not pursuing a more dramatic interpretation of the story might have helped facilitate his learners' L2 comprehension while using less English. However, he immediately expresses discomfort with the notion of revoking the opportunity to promote direct translation; an activity he seemed to encourage in his learners and one that he sees as necessary for L2 comprehension to take place.

The workshop on how to use DBI strategies in a way to potentially foster playful/learning ZPD activity occurred three days after this lesson which promoted an approach to L2 teaching/learning that departed from an emphasis on direct translation. Indeed, as Max moved into the seventh week of his elementary field experience, he self-identified using more DBI strategies in his learning activity than at any other point during the elementary field experience. In fact, Max explicitly expressed an interest in further experimenting with a variety of DBI strategies for L2 teaching/learning.

As he concluded his elementary field experience, Max was asked to reflect upon his future goals as he moved forward in his teacher preparation program. He articulated the following:

> In a secondary classroom, you can have a more mature or complex scene/scenario or role-play. I suppose it might be difficult in regards to imagining and being creative, but as a drama geek myself, I think it's important to be a role model in this and show the students that it's A-OK to get into their acting (Weekly Reflection, 11/17/15).

Thus, Max expressed a desire to continue developing DBI for L2 instruction as he moved into other teaching contexts. Interestingly, he seemed to assume the willing use of imagination and creativity amongst students at the elementary school level (grades K–5; ages 5–11) versus the middle and secondary levels (grades 6–12; ages 11–18). Additionally, he seemed to position elementary learners as being incapable of engaging in complex drama scenes/scenarios. Complexity was, unfortunately, left undefined, but it may have had to do with Max's perception of the proficiency level one must attain in order to participate in the DBI activities he envisioned:

> I was just thinking of doing some of the improv[isation] games that I did [in theatre] and doing them in French. It would be a lot harder to do because you'd have to have a certain level of pre-requisite French to partake in it (Interview, 12/10/15).

Max seemed to have reduced DBI to improvisation and role-play scenarios/situations rather than examining the range of strategies to produce playful/learning ZPD situations that were introduced during the DBI workshop in the methods course. This may have been because of his own extensive background in theatre. Throughout his middle and secondary education, he had been heavily involved in his school's theatre program and often volunteered with community theatre organizations. Thus, his conceptual understanding of DBI may have been limited by his own everyday experiences engaging in drama-based exercises that had previously served to strengthen his skills as an actor and were heavily rooted in improvisation.

Certainly, Max seemed reticent to place novice learners in improvisational situations where they might only have been able to produce one or two-word utterances. At this point in his development as a teacher, Max appeared to view DBI as a pedagogical tool that afforded students the opportunity to be language *users* rather than language *learners* in the L2 classroom. He made a distinction between L2 concepts: those that can be taught outside of a "real-life communication scenario" and those that cannot. He seemed to struggle with the notion that students in an L2 classroom might simultaneously be language users *and* language learners; that is to say that through using the language they can learn about its function as a psychological tool to satisfy particular communicative need(s).

His stated rationale for the use of DBI in the L2 classroom reflected his belief that certain L2 concepts (e.g., grammar) that are addressed throughout the process of L2 teaching/learning are divorced from real-life communication scenarios. In these situations, he saw the value of DBI as being significantly diminished. Nevertheless, he anticipated using DBI throughout the remainder of his teacher-preparation program because in his words, "I'm a theatrical person to start with" (Interview, 12/10/15).

CONCLUSION

It is possible that drama may have held the capacity to rupture the conventional script of schooling in the L2 classroom by affording students opportunities to actively negotiate meaning with peers and teachers alike in unpredictable, playful, and highly individualized ways, based on their everyday conceptual understanding of the roles that might exist in the imaginative contexts created by the teachers, and their emerging knowledge in the second language and across content-area disciplines. DBI requires the teachers to put themselves in the position of the learners to anticipate their needs and to understand their points of reference (culturally and linguistically) to successfully engage in the drama scenario. In any instruction, but particularly in DBI, the teachers and students must enter into dialogic relationships wherein students' unique understandings of the rules that determine the behavioral acts of the imaginary roles they assume in the dramas are seen as valuable contributions to the L2 teaching/learning process.

A tension appeared to exist in how teacher candidates came to conceptualize the use of DBI in the language learning classroom. DBI strategies could be considered as another pedagogical tool in a teacher's eclectic collection of instructional tools (i.e., the metaphoric "teacher's toolbox" that contains a variety of teaching methods and strategies) that support an array of teaching methodologies, or as a coherent theoretical view of learning and development that requires a major reorientation to L2 education (i.e., the Vygotskian-informed approach to DBI introduced to the participants in the methods course). As Max and his peers, demonstrated, this tension resulted in complex negotiations between personal beliefs and the potential that play has to disrupt traditional approaches to the second language teaching/learning process. While Max may have struggled to successfully implement Vygotskian-informed DBI into his pedagogical practice, his ability to reflect on his developing practice is encouraging. However, additional research is needed to explore the type and quality of mediation that is required to support teacher-candidates' pedagogical experimentation with play-based learning activities in the language classroom. With ongoing professional development that includes observation, guided, and individual practice in DBI both during and after their teacher-preparation program, it is possible that drama's full potential as a viable teaching methodology can be realized.

REFERENCES

Bodrova, E. & Leong, D.J. (2007). *Tools of the mind: The Vygotskian approach to early childhood education* (2nd ed.). Upper Saddle River, NJ: Pearson Education/Merrill.

Belliveau, G., & Kim, W. (2013). Drama in L2 learning: A research synthesis. *Scenario, 7*(2), 7–27.

Darvin, R. (2015). Representing the margins: Multimodal performance as a tool for critical reflection and pedagogy. *TESOL Quarterly, 49*(3), 590–600.

Di Napoli, R., & Algarra, V. (2001). Role-plays as strategically active scenarios. Paper presented at the annual congress of the Spanish association of applied linguistics (19th, Leon, Spain, May 3–5, 2001).

Di Pietro, R.J. (1987). *Strategic interaction. Learning languages through scenarios.* Cambridge: Cambridge University Press.

Duncan, R. M. & Tarulli, D. (2003). Play as the leading activity of the preschool period: Insights from Vygotsky, Leont'ev, and Bakhtin. *Early Education & Development, 14*, 271–292.

Early, M., & Yeung, C. (2009). Producing multimodal picture books and dramatic performances in a core French classroom: An exploratory case study. *The Canadian Modern Language Review/La Revue Canadienne des Langues Vivantes, 66*(2), 299–322.

Edmiston, B. (2007). Mission to mars: Using drama to make a more inclusive classroom for literacy learning. *Language Arts, 84*(4), 337–346.

Haught, J. R. & McCafferty, S. G. (2008). Embodied language performance: Drama and the ZPD in the second language classroom. In J. P. Lantolf & M. E. Poehner (Eds.), *Sociocultural theory and the teaching of second languages* (pp. 139–162). Equinox.

Holzman, L. (2009). *Vygotsky at work and play.* New York, NY: Routledge.

Holzman, L. (2010). Without creating ZPDs there is no creativity. In M. C. Connery, V. P. John-Steiner, & A. Marjanovic-Shane (Eds.)., *Vygotsky and creativity* (pp. 27–39). New York, New York: Peter Lang.

Karpov, Y. V. (2005). *The neo-Vygotskian approach to child development.* New York, NY: Cambridge University Press.

Lantolf, J. P. & Poehner, M. E. (2014). *Sociocultural theory and the pedagogical imperative in L2 education: Vygotskian praxis and the research/practice divide.* New York, NY: Routledge.

Lightbown, P. M., & Spada, N. (2013). *How languages are learned* (4th ed.). Oxford, UK: Oxford University Press.

Lobman, C., & Lundquist, M. (2007). *Unscripted learning: Using improv activities across the K-8 curriculum.* New York, NY: Teachers College Press.

Matthias, B. (2007). Show, don't tell: Improvisational theatre and the beginning foreign language curriculum, *Scenario, 1*(1), 51–65.

Vetere, T. M. (2018). (Re)writing the script of second language teaching/learning: Exploring teacher-candidates conceptual understanding of drama-based instruction. Retrieved from ProQuest Dissertations and Theses Global. (ProQuest Number: 13804062).

Vygotsky, L. S. (1978). *Mind in society.* Cambridge: Harvard University Press.

Vygotsky, L. S. (1967). Play and its role in the mental development of the child. *Soviet Psychology, 5*, 6–18.

NOTES

1. In the neo-Vygotskian approach to child development (based upon but varied from Vygotsky's theory of how a child cognitively develops) this age span is further divided into infancy (1–12 months), toddlerhood (1–2 years of age), early childhood (3–6 years of age), and middle childhood (7–12) (Bodrova & Leong, 2007; Karpov, 2005).

2. All names in this study have been given pseudonyms.

Chapter Nine

The Element of Play and Dynamics of Interaction in an Adult L2 Classroom With the Communicative Language Teaching Approach

Marine Pepanyan and Sohyun Meacham

COMMUNICATIVE LANGUAGE TEACHING AND PLAY/PLAYFULNESS

Communicative Language Teaching (CLT) is currently considered to be one of the most effective teaching paradigms of second language (L2) teaching (Richards, 2005). This approach to L2 teaching emphasizes communicative competence as a goal of language learning and "seeks to make meaningful communication and language use a focus of all classroom activities" (Richards & Schmidt, 2013, p. 90). Some major principles of CLT are to use authentic and meaningful communication, integrate different language skills in classroom activities, and view language learning as a process involving trial and error. Enjoyable informal pair-work in a playful environment fosters students' discussing topics with new vocabulary, retrieving knowledge, and developing the negotiation skills and interaction tools necessary for sharing their thoughts and experiences (Barcroft, 2007; Richards, 2005; Storch, 2002).

Along with the theoretical principles of CLT, play/playfulness has been considered as an important element among researchers and educators. The instructional strategies most frequently cited by teachers of L2 children are first using games/play, second using talk, discussion, and think-alouds, and third engagement and collaboration (Berne & Blachowicz, 2008). Rich resources for learning are available to adult learners as well, where there is an

145

emphasis on experiential techniques: "group discussion, simulation exercises, problem solving activities, case method, and laboratory methods over transmittal techniques" (Knowles, 1973, p. 57).

There are various definitions of "play" and "playfulness" due to the fact that they have been studied in various disciplines. Regardless of how they are defined, however, the authors refer to their use as beneficial for improving certain aspects of student learning. Play has been implemented in general approaches to teaching, by creating play spaces, and by implementing specific experiences and activities. Characteristics of play that are beneficial for the learning process are reported in the research of Garvey (1977), who listed enjoyment, spontaneity, active player engagement, and intrinsic motivation as necessary components of play. According to Gardner (1993), play is the essential feature in the learning process for productive thought and creativity. A "playful approach" to teaching (especially language teaching) is characterized by task-based activities, the promotion of engagement, collaboration, and fun, and the provision of a relaxed learning environment with meaningful activities (Tuan, 2012). As an example of using playfulness in the adult language-learning classroom, Rice (2009) and Sullivan (2000) described playful exchanges as socially mediated activities where students produce language actively and jointly. To support this claim, Warner (2004) stated that playful language use in education does not arise out of intention, and that play "must be acknowledged as a legitimate and conventional use of language" (p. 81). Moreover, he claimed that playful language instruction is a necessity.

Language Learning in Playful and Authentic Interactions

It is known that learning a word requires at least five to sixteen exposures (Nation, 1990). There is a necessity for vocabulary research on three determinants of vocabulary learning—"input, instruction and involvement. [. . .] most vocabulary studies have investigated how a small number of target words can be learnt during a short period of treatment, a lesson or several lessons" (Laufer, 2017, p. 10). A limited amount of research has been conducted and tested on the retrieval of new words within the long-term process of L2 vocabulary learning (Barcroft, 2007). "Researchers are primarily interested in how the brain processes, stores, and retrieves information, and therefore in such things as memory, attention, automatization, and fossilization" (Foster & Ohta, 2005, p. 402). Meanwhile, Foster and Ohta (2005) acknowledged that knowledge is not obtained in isolation, but in a social setting, because the primary role of language is communication and interaction with other people; and the goal for the learner is to demonstrate increasing independence. Swain's (2011) output hypothesis emphasizes that language learners have to have abundant opportunities to produce comprehensible, significant output. Such opportunities can take place through contact with a more competent partner, a collaborative dialogue, or problem solving. CLT emphasizes the integration of reading, writing, speaking, and listening skills where meaning, authenticity, interaction, and activity are the cornerstones (Lems, Miller, & Soro, 2017; Swain, 2011; Whong 2011). L2 teachers, in turn, incorporate such strategies as explicit instruction, association, rephrasing, elaboration, form-meaning mapping, and use of the L1 in their instruction methods (Niu & Andrews, 2012). Certainly, there is too much teacher-led explanation during vocabulary instruction. This type of teaching leads to a lack of engagement among the learners (Newton, 2001; Sullivan, 2000). Words introduced by the teacher might be memorized on a superficial level but are quickly forgotten.

Cook (2000) suggested language play as particularly important in language teaching, underlining its benefits not only for children's language acquisition, but also for adults'. He demonstrated the advantages of the play element exemplified in such characteristics as the validation of the explicit deductive teaching of rules (through discussion and the elicitation of rules), reinstatement, repetition, recitation of learned material (as an enjoyable experience), and finally, the broadening of the range of communicative patterns in the classroom (permitted interactional activities). Meanwhile, Bushnell's (2008) study with adult Japanese L2 learners who were engaged in language play illustrated that humor, the Ludic model, and engagement in social interactions might be of great benefit for language use and production. Newton (2001) encouraged "learners to leave the security of their bilingual dictionaries and seek help through cooperation with one another" (p. 31). The teacher and learners need to explore new kinds of task-based interactions. Playful cooperation will most probably reduce the language anxiety, a kind of situation-specific anxiety, associated with the fear of learning and using a language (Richards & Schmidt, 2013).

Allowing students to work cooperatively with limited assistance is an opportunity for them to make sense of unfamiliar words in communicative settings and immediately use them for communication. The teacher-facilitator needs to ensure that there is not direct teacher assistance during the cooperative student work. Instead, they are agents who contribute to the language learners' self-reflection and learner-autonomy skills (Whong, 2013). The advocates of playful activities in communicative language teaching classrooms highlight the advantages of pair-work, namely the direct language practice, patterns of contribution, information exchange, student involvement, decision-making, feeling of security, mutual giving of help, and discourse and linguistic features (De la Fuente, 2006; Nation, 1990; Storch, 2001; Sullivan, 2000; Taheri, 2014; Tuan, 2012). Doff (1988) recommended games, role play, and the elicitation of student talk as the motivation and language-production resource. The four stages in vocabulary teaching (presentation, practice, production, and review) contribute to vocabulary retention and retrieval. These steps can be integrated in different task-based and interactive activities in the classroom, including vocabulary games, which have shown the effectiveness of enjoyable vocabulary learning (Tuan, 2012). As learning is socially constructed (Vygotsky, 1978), team learning and collaborative skills motivate and engage learners in a subconscious manner, creating a fun, playful, and interesting learning atmosphere in the classroom (Tuan, 2012; Watanabe, & Swain, 2007). Moreover, in contrast to the teacher being the expert, social intervention comes from peers, and even from less-proficient ones. Students can attain more knowledge and proficiency from helpful classmates than they can from a lecturing teacher. Group experiences engender in most individuals attitudes that are highly conducive to experiential learning (Rogers, 1969).

Empirical Literature

Despite the current interest among educational researchers in play/playfulness most studies are about its use with child learners (Cook, 2000). Some studies of adult play/playfulness in a classroom context have explored the relationship between play and adult learning (Glynn, 1994; Grenier, 2010; Harris & Daley, 2008; Proyer, 2011). Harris & Daley (2008) emphasized such qualities as fostering learning, and enhancing engagement, cooperation, and a sense of connectedness. Glynn (1994) certified that college students performing play tasks in their classroom were highly motivated, paid more attention to the quality of their performance, and gave better responses on their assignments. Although there are some key themes uncovered in research that are relevant to using play for adult learning, it is still uncommon in higher education institutions and contexts (Rice, 2009). With playful approaches to learning, students take initiative and construct new knowledge. Playful learning facilitates students' reflective capacities about their own knowledge. It generates excitement, enjoyment, and interest as part of the process of learning, which helps motivation and engagement, and allows different kinds of learners to approach a subject from different perspectives (Rice, 2009).

However, very little is known about the benefits of the play element in the adult second and/or foreign language-learning classroom. Research on L2 playful learning approaches is more limited for adults than for children; moreover, studies conducted on children's L2 classrooms are mostly about the implementation of language play (Broner & Tarone, 2001; Cekaite & Aronsson, 2005; Mondada & Doehler, 2005). Still, despite limited research perhaps the use of playful instruction in adult L2 classrooms can be an effective form of CLT.

The Current Study

The purpose of the current case study is to address the literature gap in the relationship between adult L2 students' vocabulary learning through pair-work and playful activities using robotics, and to investigate students' perceptions of these novel activities. Based on Knowles' (1973) andragogy theory built on four assumptions about adult learners, motivation to learn emerges as adults experience needs and interests. Learning is life-centered, and adults have a need to be self-directing. It is crucial to keep in mind that unlike young children, individual differences among adults increase with age; therefore, their education must vary in such ways as style, time, and pace of learning.

At the same time, to justify the benefits of playful language instruction for adult L2 learners, it is important to first define the concept. Psychologist Csikszentmihalyi (1997) highlighted the following characteristics of play: stimulating involvement, creativity, exploration, experimentation, flexibility, and quality learning. For the Dutch historian Johan Huizinga (1955), play was different from culture to culture, but always a voluntary activity that had rules and aims. Even though it was a conscious activity, and the rules freely accepted, the rules were binding and accompanied by a feeling of tension. Cook (2000) emphasized the significance of attitude in identifying instances of play: "It is attitude which makes something play rather than anything intrinsic to the behavior per se. People are playing when they say and believe they are playing" (p. 101). Play has also been conceptualized as enjoyable, pleasurable, fun, humorous, non-serious, spontaneous, and voluntary (Csikszentmihalyi, 1997; Huizinga, 1955; Lieberman, 1977). Cook (2000) lamented that the definitions of play reflect its being perceived as primarily a childhood phenomenon. This also speaks to the marginalization of play activities among adult learners. The scholar refers to the difficulty of defining "play" as a term, but also celebrates the comparative ease with which it can be reclassified as something else.

Taking into consideration the distinct characteristics of how play is defined in the literature, and by aligning certain elements from the definitions with the four assumptions of the adult learning theory, the authors of this chapter came up with their own interpretation of playful instruction. "Playful language instruction" is thus the summation of self-directed activity which cultivates a problem-centered orientation, facilitates enjoyable learning, initiates social engagement, guides self-reflection, and expands one's learning experiences. These characteristics are suggested in studies by Chang et al. (2010), Liu, Lin, and Chang (2010), Moundridou and Kalinoglou (2008), Mubin et al. (2013), and Whittier and Robinson (2007). Whittier and Robinson (2007) implemented robotics and artificial intelligence during their study on adult language learning, documenting student satisfaction, self-efficacy, and engagement during enjoyable playful learning.

This chapter addresses the gap in the literature related to the implementation of playfulness in language instruction (PLI) via robotics as a part of CLT in an adult ESL classroom by language instructors. With this end in mind, we explore language learners' experiences in the retrieval of vocabulary in a playful manner, as well as find out students' perceptions of the use of PLI via robotics in their English Language Learning program. The study was guided by the following research questions:

1. What are the observed dynamics of vocabulary retention and retrieval in the adult L2 classroom after using activities with robotics?
2. How do adult language learners perceive the playful classroom environment, and what meaning does the experience have for them?

METHOD

This study explores the link between vocabulary learning in a playful language instruction classroom and the promotion of vocabulary retention and retrieval, self-confidence, and positive attitudes towards an alternative methodology in an ESL context. Due to the exploratory character of this study of PLI with adult L2 learners—its naturalistic and interpretive approach—a qualitative case study was conducted. Limited empirical literature regarding the chosen topic makes the qualitative case study an appropriate paradigm. The currently minimal body of research about PLI in the adult L2 classroom brings uncertainty about subjective experiences with each instructor and student. Further, the qualitative method was chosen because of the importance of a thorough or "thick" description (Geertz, 1973) of the phenomenon of playfulness in language instruction in the adult L2 classroom. Leedy and Ormrod (2016) extended the benefits of a case study method by stating that it "may be especially suitable for learning more about a little known or poorly understood situation" (p. 254).

Selective or purposive sampling was conducted to yield the most illuminating information about the topic under investigation. Four adult male L2 students with low-intermediate proficiency levels in English participated in the study. They were enrolled in an eight-week intensive English program at a comprehensive university in the Midwest. Two students were from Colombia, one from Japan, and one from the Dominican Republic. The participants are referred to as Ken, Jeffrey, George, and Jo (fictitious names to maintain anonymity).

The researchers partially used the participant-observation method (Spradley, 1980), where the first author was the instructor for the participants. The second author was unrelated to the participants in any learning or teaching context. The researchers jointly conducted a member-check (or respondent validation) with the aim of obtaining accurate feedback on depicted experiences, conclusions, and recorded observations. By doing so, the authors sought to increase the trustworthiness of the current study.

Instruments and Procedure

The instruments for data collection included: (a) anxometer for students' level of comfort or anxiety (MacIntyre & Gardner, 1991); (b) students' interactions and vocabulary-retention rates from three activities with robotics (Beebot); and (c) a checklist to measure the evolution of self-confidence before the first and after the final activities (see Appendix A). Additionally, a semi-structured interview with four questions about the students' perceptions of the playful language-learning experience was carried out.

The three interactive activities with robotics were aimed at documenting students' interactions and usage of previously learned and tested vocabulary (two weeks after formal vocabulary testing). The intention in introducing robots (Beebots) was to provide opportunities conducive to the acquisition of vocabulary in an engaging and communicative manner. The low-intermediate adult ESL students were taught the vocabulary of three textbook units during 8 weeks in their level-3 Reading class in the Intensive English Program. They were taught the vocabulary of each unit formally during the first, fourth, and seventh weeks, and were tested during the second, fifth, and eighth weeks (formative quizzes). Among other student learning outcomes of the level-3 Reading class was to correctly spell words from the vocabulary lists in sentences (Culture and Intensive English Program, [n.d.]). During the eight weeks, the students covered three units from the program-assigned textbook, and were taught 111 academic, multiword, and topical vocabulary words in context. For the non-graded activities using robotics, the students were grouped in pairs (dyads). Flash cards with pictures of the topics featured in their textbook were placed on a desk. Beebot is an exciting, colorful, easy-to-operate little robot designed for use by young children. It is a great tool for teaching problem-solving and just having fun while moving it forward, backward, left, and right with directional keys on a controller. After a dyad agreed which topic they were going to discuss, their task was to drive the robot to the preferred flashcard. The students had the opportunity to operate the Beebot three times, each time feeling more confident and excited about an upcoming robot-activity day.

More specifically, on the first day with the Beebot, students followed the directions, smiling awkwardly, unsure if they were doing it right. The picture was dramatically different, however, during the second and final playful operations of the Beebot. The students counted the steps and strategized about directing the robot to the desired destination. They used body language, such as thrusting their elbow downward with their hand in a fist (to show the excitement of "Yes, we did it!"). The playful start of the activity created a relaxed and enjoyable mood. The instructor demonstrated briefly how to operate the Beebot, encouraging the students *to play with it*. The use of the robot ignited enthusiasm for experimentation and learning in students of all ages. The instructor handed out the directions and discussion questions to the groups. The students took notes during their discussions and prepared to share their opinions with the other group. The instructor videotaped the discussions for further observation, coding, and analysis. There was minimal teacher participation or feedback during this time. The students had five minutes to prepare and five minutes for the final discussion. For a more detailed analysis of the frequencies of used vocabulary, the researcher collected the notes taken by the students (as artifacts). The activity was non-graded and took place during the last 10–15 minutes of the level-3 Reading class. It is important to note that the activities took place one week after the formal vocabulary testing with the aim of observing and documenting the effects of the spacing, vocabulary retention, and retrieval rate. Also, each student had the opportunity to work with a different peer during the three different classes.

The self-confidence checklist was used to collect data about the students' confidence level while performing the oral communication tasks (adapted from Sevilla Morales & Méndez Pérez, 2015). It was measured during the first activity and at the end of the last activity (the students checked the statements that applied to them). The instrument included thirteen statements related to anxiety, self-esteem, and other self-confidence-related factors. Examples of statements were as follows: "I prefer not to express my opinion because I feel I do not have enough vocabulary to do it"; "I feel anxious about interacting with my classmates in group discussions"; and "I avoid risk-taking because I fear making mistakes while speaking English."

Finally, the second author used a four question interview administered individually to collect more emotional and perceptual feedback from the students. The questions asked them about their feelings before, during, and after the activity, as well as how useful the pair-work was for them. Their answers were audiotaped for further analysis.

FINDINGS

Individual Participants' Perceptions About Their Learning Experiences

The data collected from the Anxometer, self-confidence checklist, and interview were aimed at documenting the students' learning experiences and perceptions about their (non-graded) vocabulary-learning classroom activity with a robot. We report these data separately for four research participants as follows.

Ken

Using the Anxometer right before and immediately after the three activities Ken, who was from Japan, self-rated his emotions in various ways. Mostly, he had a happy state of feeling at the beginning of the class and was more concerned at the end. Later, in his interview, Ken said, "Robot activity I didn't anxious, I didn't worried. But I cannot speak English very well because I don't have a vocabulary. So my conversation, my . . . I didn't know speak my opinion well." He added, "I am interesting in this activity. Because in Japan I didn't play robot activity." Ken was mostly worried because he couldn't remember the words that he learned. Even though he mentioned that they learned the vocabulary in context during their reading class, he was unable to retrieve well what he had learned two weeks before the activity. He appreciated the pair-work because his friends were scaffolding (helping) him during the discussions. "Yes, my friend (. . .) I (. . .) my friend know I cannot speak English well, so they usually help me, about like translate. Yeah, I say my opinion, but I can't speak English very well, so my partner, changed speaking my opinion." At first Ken rated his self-confidence as "find it hard to express an opinion because I don't have enough information about the topic." Whereas after the final pair-work activity he did not check any statement that applied to himself in the self-confidence checklist, presumably because the activities and lack of vocabulary knowledge were less threatening then.

Jeff

This participant from Colombia rated his emotions as "happy" and "calm" in the beginning of the reading class and "happy" after the three activities with robotics. Jeff explained that he "feel very good, because I can (. . .) I could chat with other people about different cultures. Never anxious because was a good activity. Was funny and I could do things different. I feel good. More happy. hhh. Happier, because, yeah, we can share, and we can explain different things about the things that we were learn in the course." Besides mentioning the joy of having a different activity and sharing the culture of other people Jeff mentioned that the pair-work was helpful, and that they had a chance to work together. Similarly to Ken, Jeff mentioned the difficulty of expressing his opinion because of not having enough information; and also like Ken, he overcame this challenge by the last activity and did not check anything in the self-confidence checklist.

George

This participant from Colombia mentioned "calm" before and after all three activities. George did not feel any extreme feelings of joy or anxiety. Even though in the self-confidence checklist he mentioned that he felt insecure about the ideas that he was trying to express and still found it challenging to express his opinion because he did not have enough information about the topic, by the end of the third activity he did not check anything in the list. This student acknowledged the fun of the activities and appreciated the freedom of choice. Furthermore, he mentioned that they had the opportunity to use all four language-learning skills—retrieve the learned vocabulary, write the words, listen to each other, and answer the questions. "It's interesting because the bees is giving the instruction very easy. Very easy and funny at the same time. But you chose the picture and talk about any topic. I relaxed all the time. While the activity is progressing, after the discussion of the activity we feel very good. Because in this activity we can remember the words and things in other topics. We learned, applied the activity, more or less answer the question. We were writing the sentences. The answer of the question. Is a good idea because discuss the idea with other partner. We can contrast the ideas. And give a better solution of the problem."

Jo

During the first two activities, Jo, a student from the Dominican Republic, was "calm" at the beginning and "happy" at the end. During the third activity with the robotics, Jo circled "happy" at the beginning and added "more happy" at the end. During the interview he mentioned that he forgot many words. "Before I forget a lot of thing. I feel like I don't remember some things about that. I still remember something, but not all. But after that, after we play these games we recorded the things that we studied before. And about different lectures. Different grammars and different (. . .) um (. . .). How do you say? (. . .) Vocabulary. That was really good. We learned about different cities during these games, because we discussed my city, the city of my classmates and that." To the researcher's question about feeling anxious, Jo answered that they (the students) were happy. The Beebot also brought excitement to the activity. "If you see the videos you can see that sometimes we forget that there is a camera. We are enjoying doing some game. We were really happy, discussing about the (. . .) the (. . .) How do you say? (. . .) For example, we discussing about smile, and we was happy talking about that. I remember, we would say bad words, and we will say, not it's not it, it's like this. Like practice the vocabulary. It was nice. We enjoyed a lot this activity. And with the bee (. . .) . Oh my God, I was so happy (. . .) You have to do three steps forward, then to the left! And then you have to do again. I feel prepared. I recalled the things that we studied before. Now I feel better, you know, I know more than before I studied. Before I forget some things. And we practiced again. And we learned more when we practiced. I feel better after each game. I feel good."

Jo highlighted the importance of the pair-work and the scaffolding. "Because I told you it feels so nice act like a team. For example, flamingoes, we were talking about animals, we decided to talk about flamingo, and I said to him [partner] I want to talk about hyena, because I know more about hyenas than flamingos, I didn't know so much about flamingos. We studied that before. I still remember something, you know, and after that we were practicing, he said, 'it's not like that, it's like this.' That was so nice, you know. Every Friday each can (. . .) like different partner. Never was the same. That was so nice. You know, the last was talking about different cities, about your city that traffic, your community, the environment, how your neighbors. That's so nice. We were so happy the last one, too, because that was nice. I was a little bit calm, not worried before we started the game, but when we started talking about my city, Dominican Republic, my country. That was so nice. We enjoyed a lot." Jo was the only participant who didn't check anything from the self-confidence checklist—neither at the beginning nor at the end of the activities. This student felt self-confident throughout the whole Reading class.

Vocabulary Retention

Regarding the activities with robotics (the Beebot), the vocabulary-retention results (academic, multi-word, and topical vocabulary) indicate that, by the end of the three activities the participants retained 28 of 111 words (38.28%). Details are reported below.

The overall findings from the students' group discussions, notes, and final discourse suggest that the students did not fully remember all of the unit's vocabulary words: after two weeks spacing they cooperatively retrieved 36.36% of the learned vocabulary words. The collected data along with the interviews show that the participants acknowledged that they did not remember the unit vocabulary, and that the non-graded activity with robotics gave them a chance to review the previously learned words. Meanwhile, they recognized the joy of playfulness and affirmed the value of pair-work as a contributor to vocabulary retention. The students talked about the fun and exciting learning environment over and over again during their interviews. During his interview, Jo said, "That is so nice. We were so happy the last one, too, because that was nice. I was a little bit calm, not worried before we started the game, but when we started talking about my city, Dominican Republic, my country, that was so nice. We enjoyed a lot." Jeff praised both the learning and fun attributes of the playful element: "I feel good. More happy. Happier, because, yeah, we can share and we can explain different things about the things that we were learn in the course." They also ascertained that a fun learning environment added motivation and promoted their learning skills as a team.

Students' Interaction

It was interesting to observe that the students utilized interactive strategies while taking notes simultaneously, discussing within their dyad and talking with other pairs. It would be arduous for instructors to log all of the language-learning deficits of their students. This study revealed the students using some communication strategies during the activities. Among them, the use of the students' first language (L1) was the one that occurred most frequently (Tarone, 1980; Young & He, 1998). As a general rule, the students would use gestures, confirmation checks with peers, or appeals to the instructor for the right word. Excerpts 1, 2, and 3 provide examples of L1 usage, self-reflection, and attempts to retrieve the covered material, as well as instructor-student interactions. (The special symbols used in the transcripts are explained in Appendix B.)

Excerpt 1

Jo: Teacher, how do you say "alimentar"?

Instructor: Nurture (%act pronounces several times and spells).

Jo: Nurture (%act repeating the word, writing and taking notes in silence).

Often the student would talk to himself and try to come up with the translation of the word, and then negotiate with a partner to know what he thought and how he would translate it. (See Excerpt 2.)

Excerpt 2

Jeff: When people cooperate, so you can begin, the animal behavior. No? Si, si, but (. . .) all behavior animal is similar to (. . .) but (. . .) This is good idea, but it's not important (. . .) but (. . .) eso es escrito bien pero es mal idea (. . .) igual. [*]

Students paired with a peer sharing the same L1 felt more comfortable using that language (Spanish in this case). (See Excerpt 3.)

Excerpt 3

Jo: The light is off, you know. In some cities. For example, in my city we never had light. We do gomas. Gomas (%act looking at his peers for the English word)?

Jeff: Tires.

Jon: We light tires.

They learned from each other as well. One peer called on his partner to recollect the context that they covered during their Reading class. Along with the L1 usage, students were using the technique of approximation, where "learners substitute items that they assume convey semantic meaning related to their intended goal" (Young & He, 1998, p. 210). Excerpts 4 and 5 are examples of recollection and approximation.

Excerpt 4

Jeff: Because bees when in danger they work together. En junto. Ants they are close, for building something. They are learning to pass the plant. Remember, is as to the bridge (%act uses hands to explain).

George: From the bridge?

Excerpt 5

Jo: You can see fire. How do you say goma? Tire! In Dominican Republic before Porto Clara was a tourist area, that was a beautiful, but the crimen is higher now.

[. . .]

Jo: No, but in the capital there are many danger people, like gangsters. They live their life like stinky. Stinky? How do you say?

Instructor: Stealing.

Jon: Yeah, stealing. They don't work, they do not do nothing, they only selling drug and that. And if you walk on the street, somebody can come with you in the motorcycle or something and take your bag (showing his armpit). Your phone or something, and if you try to keep, you know (. . .) they can kill you.

[. . .]

Jeff: Because it easier to show expression eiz (%msp mispronounces the word "eyes").

Jo: Describe?

Jeff: Describe?

Jo: Describe.

Comprehension checks and clarification requests are other strategies where the language learner checks their interlocutor's comprehension (Tarone, 1980; Young & He, 1998). In further analysis of negotiated interactions we encountered episodes where the students tried to see whether their own understanding was correct. Below, Excerpt 6 shows some patterns of interactional discourse.

Excerpt 6

Ken: Body language?

George: Yes, body language (%act uses his hands to explain).

[. . .]

George: Tourist (. . .) (%act taking notes and showing the notes to the peer). Is this highest? This is too high.

Jo: 65. No, 75. And the other percent work, you know, in "zona franca." Business (. . .)

George: Zona franca?

Jo: Yeah, but zona franca is not like (. . .) (%act uses the cell phone to find information to interpret the meaning of the phrase for his peer).

[. . .]

Jo: Mostrar? Cual? Que va a monstrar [%sp] happiness. Different (. . .) (%act reading what they wrote, revising, correcting).

Jeff: (%act reading directions again, interrupting). We can start communication in gestures. Gestures, como (. . .) (%act explaining to each other in Spanish). Con gestos. Gestos (%act looking at the teacher). (hhh.)

Instructor: Yes, the same as in Spanish.

The overall discourse of the students during the three pair-work activities with robotics contained pauses, fillers, turn-taking and self-correction (self or other repairs). Self-corrections are organized repairs in conversations (Tarone, 1980). In Excerpt 7, the L2 learners supplement their speech with the non-linguistic strategies of gestures, facial expressions, laughter, and sounds (Tarone, 1980; Young & He, 1998).

Excerpt 7

Jeff: You could (%act repeating the words while writing down and proof-reading the writing) zmeil (%msp), and there is less stress. Yeah? I could zmeil (%msp), smile (%act self-correction).

[. . .]

Jo: Yeah. Cause they war for livable (%msp) city, to make Dominican Republic livable (self-corrects). Because Haiti people wanted to stay there. They dividir (. . .) how do you say?

Teacher: They divide.

Ken: Um (. . .) people are trying to keep their children. Um (. . .) (%act using hand gesture trying to explain what he wants to say). Like people. Nursery.

These types of modified interactions (e.g., checking for comprehension and clarification, appealing for assistance, repairing) and social-interaction strategies (e.g., elaborating, facilitating the flow of conversation, responding, and seeking information or an opinion) were the main conspicuous strategies exercised by the language learners during their pair-work activity with the robotics (Bejarano, Levine, Olshtain, and Steiner, 1997). The theory of scaffolding, defined by Richards and Schmidt (2013), "emphasizes the role of collaborative discourse in language learning" (p. 466). The instructor proves to be an indirect support to the learners by enabling them to perform activities and build certain communication structures through interaction with each other. Sequential scaffolding is clearly found in games (Richards & Schmidt, 2013).

DISCUSSION

Cook (2000) predicted that the advantages of the play element in language teaching "would validate the explicit deductive teaching of rules and frequent subsequent discussion of them by teachers and students in the light of practice; reinstate [. . .] repetition, and recitation as enjoyable learning strategies; and broaden the range of permitted interactional patterns within the class-room" (p. 194). In this case study of pair-work interactions with robotics in an adult L2 classroom, we found a complex web of communication fea-tures—laughter, fun, attention to spelling, word recalling, grammar chal-lenges, appeals to the instructor for explanation, elicitation, and many more (Bushnell, 2008; Broner & Tarone, 2001, Tuan, 2012).

From the initial moment of operating the robot toward the picture to reveal their choice of topic, the students showed joy and happiness. The robot activity created a safe and relaxing environment that contributed to a joyous learning atmosphere. Indeed, while analyzing the data, the researchers found that the activity, initially planned for 10–15 minutes, extended to 23–34 minutes.

Additionally, a recorded interaction from Activity 2 revealed such lin-guistic features as L1 usage, self-reflection, repetition (clarification), confir-mation checks, and scaffolding.

Jon: (%act nodding, then reading aloud directions of question #2). Eyes?

Jeff: I don't remember [. . .] (%act re-reading the directions, taking notes, erasing).

Jo: Reduce stress (hhh) (%act both posing on the recording camera and laughing).

Jeff: In the eyes, man.

Jo: But [. . .]

Jo: In these countries Japanese and Chinese will focus on eyes [. . .]. Stress [. . .]

Jeff: They are focused on [. . .] um, I don't remember. They can describe. Um [. . .] describir (%act sp).

Jo: Chinese and Japanese always smile and focus on eyes (hhh). They focus on eyes. Because they think the activity, or that facial expression (hhh). (%act writing). Read. Try to read (%act showing his notes to the partner). Japanese tend [. . .] um [. . .] teacher, what is "tend"?

Fun and laughter are the "evidence of the socially inclusive nature of the collaboratively constructed language play frame" (Bushnell, 2008, p. 56). The present study illustrated that adult L2 learners can be engaged in activ-ities where the ESL instructor is able to hybridize between classroom talk and conversation without losing control (Waring, 2014). We reported on and argued for the importance of integrating playful language instruction into the language classroom. The fact that the students read their notes a great deal and tried to help their partners during the playful activity showed how communicative activities give opportunities to language learners to seek strategies to overcome the communication barriers.

The findings of this study contribute to SLA research by accounting for the under-considered functions of playfulness in language instruction, which may be of great benefit in classroom language learning. This study was aimed at helping to fill the research gap by describing how alternative activities may be integrated in the adult L2 classroom (Waring, 2014). The researchers emphasize the importance of allowing the learners to engage in negotiation, as well as of lowering students' anxiety by letting them freely experiment with the L2 (Bushnell, 2008; Richards, 2005). Some important components that contribute to an adult ESL learner's vocabulary retention are: a collaborative learning community, multiple representations of the material, building on prior knowledge, technology-enriched instruction, explicit and implicit vocabulary development, and of course, a challenging curriculum (Lems et al., 2017). Future research should be done to examine the mechanism of adult L2 learners' language internalization, and determine which aspects of playful activities can facilitate it. If negotiated interactions (communicative language teaching) and engagement in alternative activities are important or essential parts of SLA, the restructuring of learners' interlanguage through playful activities is worthy of serious consideration as a contributing factor to adults' second-language development.

In the short term, research is suggested to study how playfulness in language instruction contributes to language development in the adult L2 classroom. The comparison of students' formative vocabulary tests and expressive language productivity during playful activities could also be a subject of future analysis. Interviews with ESL instructors about their experiences and attitudes towards playfulness in language instruction as well could contribute valuable information to supplement the scarce existing literature about playfulness in adult L2 language instruction.

Limitations of the Study

This modest exploratory case study has some limitations that future research and practice could address. This case consisted of three play sessions in an adult ESL language-learning course that had been taught in a traditional way. The other portions of the course remained traditional (e.g., textbook-based). As previously mentioned, the participants reported that the non-graded activity with robotics gave them an opportunity to review the previously learned vocabulary words, regardless of the retention rate (36.36%). However, as this was not an experimental study but a small-scale descriptive study, it does not establish that these play sessions actually caused the students' vocabulary learning. Nevertheless, as the vocabulary retention rate was not compared to other conditions (e.g., traditional course delivery without play sessions, higher frequency of play sessions), it is entirely possible that 36.36% could be higher than results under purely traditional conditions. As three play sessions can be considered a small number, we are unsure if having more play sessions could positively affect the vocabulary retention and retrieval rates. A more systematic research design is required to fully unpack the effectiveness of play sessions in the learning of vocabulary by adult ESL students.

REFERENCES

Barcroft, J. (2007). Effects of opportunities for word retrieval during second language vocabulary learning. *Language Learning*, 57(1), 35–56.

Bejarano, Y., Levine, T., Olshtain, E., & Steiner, J. (1997). The skilled use of interaction strategies: Creating a framework for improved small-group communicative interaction in the language classroom. *System*, 25(2), 203–214.

Berne, J. I., & Blachowicz, C. L. (2008). What reading teachers say about vocabulary instruction: Voices from the classroom. *The Reading Teacher*, 62(4), 314–323.

Broner, M., & E. Tarone. (2001). Is it fun?: Language play in a fifth-grade Spanish immersion classroom. *The Modern Language Journal*, 85(3), 363–379.

Bushnell, C. (2008). "Lego my keego!": An analysis of language play in a beginning Japanese as a foreign language classroom. *Applied Linguistics*, 30(1), 49–69.

Cekaite, A. & Aronsson, K. (2005). Language play, a collaborative resource in children's L2 learning. *Applied Linguistics*, 26(2), 169–191.

Chang, C. W., Lee, J. H., Chao, P. Y., Wang, C. Y., & Chen, G. D. (2010). Exploring the possibility of using humanoid robots as instructional tools for teaching a second language in primary school. *Journal of Educational Technology & Society*, 13(2), 13–24.

Cook, G. (2000). *Language play, language learning*. Oxford University Press.

Culture and Intensive English Program. (n.d.). *CIEP Course Goals, Objectives, & Student Learning Outcomes*. Retrieved fromhttps://uni.edu/ciep/sites/default/files/u6/ciep_course_goals_objectives_slos.pdf

Csikszentmihalyi, M. (1997). *Finding flow: The psychology of engagement with everyday life*. New York: Basic Books.

De la Fuente, M. J. (2006). Classroom L2 vocabulary acquisition: Investigating the role of pedagogical tasks and form-focused instruction. *Language Teaching Research*, 10(3), 263–295.

Doff, A. (1988). *Teach English trainer's handbook: A training course for teachers*. Cambridge University Press.

Foster, P., & Ohta, A. S. (2005). Negotiation for meaning and peer assistance in second language classrooms. *Applied Linguistics*, 26(3), 402–430.

Gardner, H. (1993). *Creating minds: An anatomy as seen through the lives of Freud, Einstein, Picasso, Stravinsky, Eliot, Graham and Gandhi*. Harper Collins Publishers. Garvey, C. (1977). Play. Cambridge, MA: Harvard University Press.

Geertz, C. (1973). *The interpretation of cultures: Selected essays* (Vol. 5019). New Yrok: Basic Books.

Glynn, M. A. (1994). Effects of work task cues and play task cues on information processing, judgment, and motivation. *Journal of Applied Psychology*, 79(1), 34–45.

Grenier, R. S. (2010). All work and no play makes for a dull museum visitor. *New Directions for Adult and Continuing Education*, 127(1), 77–85.

Harris, P., & Daley, J. (2008). Exploring the contribution of play to social capital in institutional adult learning settings. *Australian Journal of Adult Learning,* 48(1), 50–70.

Huizinga, J. (1955). Homo ludens: A study of the play-element in culture. Boston: Beacon Press.

Knowles, M. (1973). The adult learner: A neglected species (3rd Ed.). Houston, TX: Gulf Pub. Co.

Laufer, B. (2017). From word parts to full texts: Searching for effective methods of vocabulary learning. *Language Teaching Research,* 21(1), 5–11.

Leedy, P. D. & Ormrod, J. E. (2016). Practical research: Planning and design (11th Ed.). Boston: Pearson.

Lems, K., Miller, L. D., & Soro, T. M. (2017). *Building literacy with English language learners: Insights from linguistics.* New York: Guilford Publications Press.

Lieberman, J. N. (1977). *Its relationship to imagination and creativity.* New York: Academic Press.

Liu, E. Z. F., Lin, C. H., & Chang, C. S. (2010). Student satisfaction and self-efficacy in a cooperative robotics course. *Social Behavior and Personality: An International Journal,* 38(8), 1135–1146.

MacIntyre, P. D., & Gardner, R. C. (1991). Investigating language class anxiety using the focused essay technique. *The Modern Language Journal,* 75(3), 296–304.

Mondada, L., & Doehler, S. (2005). Second language acquisition as situated practice: Task accomplishment in the French second language classroom. *Canadian Modern Language Review,* 61(4), 461–490.

Moundridou, M. & Kalinoglou, A. (2008): Using LEGO Mindstorms as an Instructional Aid in Technical and Vocational Secondary Education: Experiences from an Empirical Case Study. In Dillenbourg, P. & Specht, M. (Eds.): *Times of Convergence: Technologies across learning contexts (Proceedings of the 3rd European Conference on Technology Enhanced Learning –EC-TEL 08),* Lecture Notes in Computer Science, Vol. 5192, Springer-Verlag, Berlin Heidelberg, 312–321.

Mubin, O., Stevens, C. J., Shahid, S., Al Mahmud, A., & Dong, J. J. (2013). A review of the applicability of robots in education. *Journal of Technology in Education and Learning,* 1(209–0015), 1–7.

Nation, I. S. P. (1990). *Teaching & learning vocabulary.* Boston: Heinle Cengage Learning.

Newton, J. (2001). Options for vocabulary learning through communication tasks. *ELT journal,* 55(1), 30–37.

Niu, R. & Andrews, S. (2012). Commonalities and discrepancies in L2 teachers' beliefs and practices about vocabulary pedagogy: A small culture perspective. *TESOL Journal,* 6(1), 134–154. Retrieved from https://www.tesol-international-journal.com/

Proyer, R. T. (2011). Being playful and smart? The relations of adult playfulness with psychometric and self-estimated intelligence and academic performance. *Learning and Individual Differences,* 21(4), 463–467.

Rice, L. (2009) Playful learning. *The Journal for Education in the Built Environment,* 4(2), 94–108.

Richards, J. C. (2005). *Communicative language teaching today.* Southeast Asian Ministers of Education Organization (SEAMEO) Regional Language Centre.

Richards, J. C., & Schmidt, R. W. (2013). *Longman dictionary of language teaching and applied linguistics.* Routledge.

Rogers, C. R. (1969). *Freedom to learn: A view of what education might become.* Columbus Merrill.

Sevilla Morales, H., & Méndez Pérez, G. (2015). Towards an understanding of the benefits of short stories in oral communication courses. *Actualidades Investigativas en Educación,* 15(1), 75–97.

Spradley, J. P. (1980). Participant observation. *New York: Wadsworth Thomson Learning.*

Storch, N. (2001). How collaborative is pair work? ESL tertiary students composing in pairs. *Language Teaching Research,* 5(1), 29–53.

Storch, N. (2002). Patterns of interaction in ESL pair work. *Language learning,* 52(1), 119–158.

Sullivan, P. (2000). Playfulness as mediation in communicative language teaching in a Vietnamese classroom. *Sociocultural theory and second language learning,* In Lantolf, J. P. (Ed.), *Sociocultural Theory and Second Language Learning* (115–131). Oxford: Oxford University Press.

Swain, M. (2011). The output hypothesis: Theory and research. In Hinkel, E. (Ed.), *Handbook of Research in Second Language Teaching and Learning* (495–508). Oxfordshire: Routledge.

Taheri, M. (2014). The effect of using language games on vocabulary retention of Iranian elementary EFL learners. *Journal of Language Teaching & Research,* 5(3), 544–549.

Tarone, E. (1980). Communication strategies, foreigner talk, and repair in interlanguage 1. *Language learning,* 30(2), 417–428.

Tuan, L. T. (2012). Vocabulary recollection through games. *Theory and Practice in Language Studies,* 2(2), 257–264.

Vygotsky, L. S. (1978). *Mind in society.* Cambridge, MA: Harvard University Press.

Waring, H. Z. (2014). Managing control and connection in an adult ESL classroom. *Research in the Teaching of English,* 49(1), 52–74.

Warner, C. N. (2004). It's just a game, right? Types of play in foreign language CMC. *Language Learning & Technology,* 8(2), 69–87.

Watanabe, Y., & Swain, M. (2007). Effects of proficiency differences and patterns of pair interaction on second language learning: Collaborative dialogue between adult ESL learners. *Language Teaching Research,* 11(2), 121–142.

Whittier, L. E., & Robinson, M. (2007). Teaching evolution to non-English proficient students by using Lego robotics. *American Secondary Education,* 35(3), 19–28.

Whong, M. (2011). *Language teaching: Linguistic theory in practice.* Edinburgh University Press.

Whong, M. (2013). A linguistic perspective on communicative language teaching. *The Language Learning Journal,* 41(1), 115–128.

Young, R., & He, A. W. (Eds.). (1998). *Talking and testing: Discourse approaches to the assessment of oral proficiency* (Vol. 14). Amsterdam: John Benjamins Publishing.

Index

Messer, D., 35

metaplay, xx, 79–80

mixed-age groupings, 99–100; benefits of, 109–110; frequency of types of scaffolding by ST in, 105; outcomes of scaffolding types in, 106; same-age groupings compared to, 92–93, 95–96; in social contexts, 97; ST in, 97–98

mixed-method approach, 118

mobile apps, 43–46

modeling, 92; definition of, 102; example of, 99, 102, 103; through participation in play, 16; by teachers, 23

Mudkin (Gammell), 57

Munsch, Robert, 75, 76

music, 51, 59

narrative comprehension, 21–22, 23–24

National Council for the Social Studies (NCSS), 54, 56

NCLB. *See* No Child Left Behind

NCSS. *See* National Council for the Social Studies

negotiating, 101, 102; definition of, 102; example of, 104; meaning, 137

New Critics, 67–68

Next Generation Science Standards for Engineering and Design, 57

Next Generation Science Standards for Forces and Interactions, 54

No Child Left Behind (NCLB), 10

Notable Trade Books for Young People, 54

novice role, 8

object transformations, 94, 97–98, 99–100, 101, 107

oral language, xx, 35; development of, 124; recordings of, 36; skills, 114

oral reading, 4, 46

pantomime, 133–134, 135, 136, 138–140

The Paper Bag Princess (Munsch), 75, 76

parallel social context, 96, 97

Peabody Picture Vocabulary Test (PPVT), 120, 121, 122

Peckover, R., 6

peer scaffolding, xx

peer sharing, 156

Pellegrini, A. D., 9, 18

persistence, 16

phonemic awareness, 72

photographs, 36, 37

physical abilities, 49

physical play: *A Dark, Dark Cave* exemplifying, 58; definition of, 55

Piaget, Jean, 11, 114

play: affordances of, 71; birth of literacy and, 4–7; children's literature, school and, 51–54; children's literature depicting types of, 61; CLT, playfulness and, 145–146; as content of writing and drawing, 39–41; creativity and, xix, 47, 146; digital, 25–26; discovery and, 34; drama, ZPD and, 131–133; drawing as, on page, 41–43; eliminating, 49; evidence of three approaches to, 36; exploration, expression and, 47; as fundamental cognitive activity, 7; guided, 20; history of, xviii; imagination, literacy and, 53; joy from, 63; literacy, behavior and, 34; literacy, language and, 67, 68–69; materials for promoting literacy during, 7; modeling through participation in, 16; narrative comprehension, word learning and, 23–24; quality of, 18; as reader response, 70–71; relearning, 133–135; role of, in early childhood education, 4; schools inclusion of, 52; scripts for, 20; spaces for, in classrooms, 34; as standard, 50; superhero, 34; traditional, 43–44; as type of literacy, 53; types of, xix, 45, 50–51, 54, 55–60; value of, 123; as vital, 49; writing and, 34; writing as, on page, 41–43. *See also specific topics*

play advocates, xvii, 67

Play and Early Childhood Development (Christie, Johnson, and Yawkey), 6

Play and Early Literacy Development (Christie), 7–8, 34

Play and Literacy in Early Childhood: Research from Multiple Perspectives (Christie), 9

play and literacy research, xvii–xviii; achievements of, 10; history of, 3; meta-analysis on, 11; strategies for, 10

play and literacy researchers, 6, 46

About the Contributors

M. Angel Bestwick is a faculty member in the Elementary Education Department at Kutztown University. She has also worked in higher education as faculty at Manhattan College, and adjunct faculty at Wilkes University. She has been a national Clinical Practice Fellow since 2018. She was formerly an elementary teacher and elementary science coordinator at the Dallas School District in Dallas, PA. During her tenure at Dallas School District, she received national and regional teaching awards. Most notably, she was awarded a Toyota TAPESTRY Grant Award for an interdisciplinary project to study the local watershed during which fifth grade students utilized mobile technology. Her research interests are focused on innovation in education, inquiry-based learning, and children's literature.

Renée Casbergue is the Vira Franklin and James R. Eagles endowed professor at Louisiana State University where she works with the early childhood and literacy undergraduate and graduate programs. Her work focuses on early literacy, with a particular emphasis on preschool children's writing. She coauthored *Writing in Preschool: Orchestrating Meaning and Marks* with Judith Schickedanz, and *Reading and Writing in Preschool: Teaching the Essentials* with Dorothy Strickland. Her current research focuses on young children's use of digital media for both reading and writing. She is a licensed provider of the Classroom Assessment Scoring System observation training, and has recently developed training modules for the Louisiana State Department of Education that help teachers address aspect of the CLASS through developmentally appropriate literacy instruction for toddlers and preschoolers.

174 *About the Contributors*

Tori K. Flint, PhD, is an Assistant Professor of Literacy Education/Early Childhood Education at the University of Louisiana at Lafayette. Dr. Flint's research focuses on young children's emergent and early language and literacy practices-in and out of the classroom and on the culture of childhood, broadly. Her research explores the intersections of children's languages, literacies, play, and meaning-making and highlights the ways that young children use play to respond to literature. She also works with incarcerated parents and their families and children in order to learn from and support them as they engage in meaningful family literacy practices. Dr. Flint suggests that we must value the bountiful knowledge of children and listen to and amplify their voices.

Myae Han is a professor in the Department of Human Development and Family Sciences at the University of Delaware. Her areas of research include literacy and play, early intervention and implementation. She is a Chair of Early Education/Child Development (EECD) SIG at the American Educational Research Association. She is a past president of The Association for the Study of Play (TASP) and Literacy Development in Young Children (LDYC) SIG at the International Literacy Association. She has codirected various federal and state funded grant projects including three *Early Reading First* grants funded by US Department of Education, *Early Head Start University Partnership* grant, *Child Care Research Partnership* grant funded by US Department of Health and Human Services. She is a coeditor of *Play and Curriculum: Play & Culture Studies, Volume 15* for The Association for the Study of Play.

James E. Johnson is a Professor of Early Childhood Education in the College of Education at The Pennsylvania State University. His research interests center on play, curriculum, parent beliefs and culture. He is co-facilitator of the Play, Policy, and Practices Interest Forum of the National Association for the Education of Young Children, and Series Editor of *Play & Culture Studies* for The Association for the Study of Play. His recent publications include (with Sevimli-Celik, Al-Mansour, Arda-Tuncdemir, and Dong) play in early childhood education in *Saracho, O.: Handbook of Research on the Education of Young Children*, 4th edition, and (with PoolIp Dong) methods of studying play in P. Smith & J. Roopnarine (Eds.) *The Cambridge handbook of play.*

Sohyun Meacham, PhD, is an Associate Professor of Literacy Education at the University of Northern Iowa. Soh's research centers on young children's language and literacy development in various early childhood classroom contexts. She is specifically interested in how children's playful and dialogic interactions in classrooms are associated with their literacy practices.

Julie Parrish has over 25 years of public education experience in Texas. She began her teaching career working with infants and toddlers with special needs in 1988 after graduating from the University of Texas at Austin. Her journey as a teacher has taken her through classrooms that served prekindergarten students with special needs, kindergarten students, 5th-grade students, 3rd-grade students, and 1st-grade students. In 2008 she received her Master of Education Degree in Reading and then worked as a reading intervention teacher, Education Service Center consultant, and Elementary English Language Arts Coordinator. She recently defended her dissertation, *Text-Influenced Expressions of Understanding: Differences in Kindergartners' Discourse and Written Retellings of Traditional and Digital Texts During Buddy Reading.* Her research interests include the impact of digital devices on emergent reading and writing and the home/school connection and emergent literacy.

Marine A. Pepanyan is a doctoral candidate at the University of Northern Iowa in the Department of Curriculum & Instruction. She received her MA in TESOL/Spanish from the University of Northern Iowa and her BA in Linguistics—English and Spanish languages from Yerevan State Linguistic University, Armenia. Marine currently teaches as a temporary faculty at the Curriculum & Instruction Department of the University of Northern Iowa. She has previously taught linguistic and language development, English language, and ESL courses at various national and international universities and programs. Marine's broad research interests are in the field of linguistics with focus on improvement and facilitation of language instruction. In particular, she has experience in playful vocabulary instruction for adult additional language learners. Marine is specifically interested in applying alternative and non-traditional approaches to studying language teaching for the purpose of curriculum development and instructional interventions.

Matthew E. Poehner is Professor of World Languages Education and Applied Linguistics at the Pennsylvania State University. His research focuses on Vygotskian Sociocultural Theory and its application to questions of second language teaching, learning, and assessment. Professor Poehner has published numerous research articles and book chapters. He is Associate Editor of the journal *Language and Sociocultural Theory* and is most recently co-editor (with J. P. Lantolf) of the *Routledge Handbook of Sociocultural Theory and Second Language Development*.

Kathleen A. Roskos is Professor Emerita at John Carroll University in Cleveland, Ohio. Her research includes the relationship between play and early literacy. Recent studies examine the design and use of digital books as instructional resources. Formerly a classroom teacher, Dr. Roskos has served as director of federal programs in the public schools, department chair and Director of the Ohio Literacy Initiative at the Ohio Department of Education. She has secured numerous educational grants, including Early Reading; developed one of the first public preschools in Ohio; and coordinated statewide online professional development. Dr. Roskos has authored numerous articles on links between play and literacy, co-authored textbooks on early literacy, and co-edited three volumes on play and early literacy development.

Brian A. Stone is a Senior Lecturer at Northern Arizona University. He teaches undergraduate and graduate methods courses in elementary science and social studies. He also directs the Professional Development School program and Museum of Northern Arizona partnership program at NAU. He is the STEAM editor for the International Journal of the Whole Child, and he has published numerous articles and book chapters in the areas of science education, play, and authentic teaching and learning practices. Dr. Stone's research interests include science education, play, inquiry-based learning, child-centered practice, authentic assessment, integrated curriculum, and multiage education. Dr. Stone leads university study tours all over the world to study integrated curriculum, place-based education, and multiage education.

Sandra J. Stone is Professor Emeritus at Northern Arizona University. She founded the *National Multiage Institute*, an international leader in providing professional development for educators from all over the world. At the university, Dr. Stone has taught graduate and undergraduate courses on literacy, play, and multiage education. Dr. Stone is the author of the books *Playing: A Kid's Curriculum, Creating the Multiage Classroom*, and *Understanding Multiage Education*. Based on her research, she has written multiple articles on play, symbolic play, and literacy and play. Dr. Stone is past editor for the *Journal of Research in Childhood Education*. She serves on editorial boards for international research journals.

Timothy M. Vetere is an Assistant Clinical Professor of ESOL/Bilingual Education in the College of Education at the University of Florida. To date, much of his research has focused on the role of creativity, play, imagination, and drama in PK–12 language learning contexts as understood through the lens of Vygotskian Socio-Cultural Theory. In addition to preparing teacher-candidates, he has conducted research that critically examines the dialogic voices of multilingual/multicultural classrooms, including the lived experiences, expectations, and practices of language learners, their teachers, and teacher-educators.